German Public Policy and Federalism

POLICIES AND INSTITUTIONS
Germany, Europe, and Transatlantic Relations

Published in association with the American Institute for Contemporary German Studies (AICGS), Washington, D.C.
General Editor: **Jackson Janes**, Executive Director of the AICGS

Volume 1
GERMAN UNIVERSITIES PAST AND FUTURE: CRISIS OR RENEWAL?
Edited by Mitchell G. Ash

Volume 2
TRANSFORMATION OF THE GERMAN POLITICAL PARTY SYSTEM:
INSTITUTIONAL CRISIS OR DEMOCRATIC RENEWAL?
Edited by Christopher S. Allen

Volume 3
THE GERMAN SKILLS MACHINE: SUSTAINING COMPARATIVE ADVANTAGE
IN A GLOBAL ECONOMY
Edited by Pepper D. Culpepper and David Finegold

Volume 4
BREAKDOWN, BREAKUP, BREAKTHROUGH: GERMANY'S DIFFICULT
PASSAGE TO MODERNITY
Edited by Carl Lankowski

Volume 5
GERMAN PUBLIC POLICY AND FEDERALISM: CURRENT DEBATES ON
POLITICAL, LEGAL, AND SOCIAL ISSUES
Edited by Arthur B. Gunlicks

GERMAN PUBLIC POLICY AND FEDERALISM

Current Debates on Political, Legal,
and Social Issues

Edited by

Arthur B. Gunlicks

Berghahn Books
NEW YORK · OXFORD

First published in 2003 by

Berghahn Books

www.berghahnbooks.com

First paperback edition published in 2004
Reprinted in 2006

© 2003, 2004 Arthur B. Gunlicks

Library of Congress Cataloging-in-Publication Data

German public policy and federalism : current debates on political, legal,
and social issues / [edited by] Arthur B. Gunlicks.
    p. cm. — (Policies and institutions ; v. 5)
    Includes bibliographical references and index.
    ISBN 1-57181-393-4 (alk. paper) — ISBN 1-57181-394-2 (pbk.: alk. paper)
    1. Germany—Politics and government—1990– 2. Germany. Laws,
statutes, etc. I. Gunlicks, Arthur B., 1936– II. Series.

JN3971.A58G466 2003
320'.6'0943—dc21
                                                            2002043659

British Library Cataloguing in Publication Data

A catalogue record for this book is available from
the British Library.

CONTENTS

ILLUSTRATIONS

FOREWORD

The impact of unification on Germany's politics, economy, and society continues to reverberate more than a decade after October 1990. The challenge of achieving a level of fiscal equalization among the Länder remains a daunting task well after more than a trillion deutsche marks (2 marks=1 euro) in support have been transferred from West to East. Political parties and political behavior in the East and West remain marked by differences, as can be seen in the continuing and even growing support (at least until the fall of 2002) for the former communists in the East and the virtual absence of support for the Greens or the Free Democrats in the new Länder. And as the European Union begins to include new Central and Eastern European members, the strains on the political, legal and social fabric of German society are reflected in the debates over unemployment, immigration policies, and the future of social security.

Germany remains a fascinating laboratory for those interested in examining the development of a larger Federal Republic challenged by both old and new problems after unification. The American Institute for Contemporary German Studies (AICGS) has been closely following the transformation of the political and constitutional environment in Germany since 1990. Along the way, we worked with many of the scholars who are represented in this book. In February 2001 we asked them to join us for a look back and a look forward in evaluating the issues and challenges that Germany has been confronting in its efforts to take advantage of one of the most exciting opportunities in its history. The analyses found in this book provide the reader with helpful tools not only to review the last ten years but also to anticipate the second decade of a unified Germany.

I wish to express my appreciation to the scholars who contributed to this book, and in particular to Professor Arthur Gunlicks, who organized the conference held in Washington, D.C., on 16 and 17 February 2001, and also took on the demanding task of editing this volume. We are grateful for his tenacity and dedication and for his own insightful contributions in this collection. AICGS would also like to express its special thanks to the main sponsor of the conference and the publication, *Die Zeit Stiftung Ebelin und Gerd Bucerius*. We are also grateful for additional support for the conference from Lufthansa and the German Marshall Fund of the United States.

JACKSON JANES, EXECUTIVE DIRECTOR

The American Institute for Contemporary German Studies
The Johns Hopkins University

CONTRIBUTORS

Elisabeth Dette-Koch is responsible for the coordination of activities regarding European institutions in the Office of the Prime Minister of Baden-Württemberg. From 1997 to 2001 she was responsible for the Office of European Affairs in the mission of Baden-Württemberg in Bonn and later Berlin. She was also the Observer for the Länder at the EU in Brussels in 1996–97. She is an adjunct professor at the Professional College of Public Administration in Kehl.

Udo Diedrichs is research fellow at the Department of Political Science of the University of Cologne. His main research areas are institutional issues of European integration, EU external policy, and transatlantic relations.

Gisela Färber is Professor of Public Finance at the German Postgraduate School of Administrative Sciences in Speyer and director of the section Multilevel Government Systems of the Research Institute for Public Administration (FÖV) at the same institution. She has published widely in the field of German and comparative public finance.

Franz Greß, retired, taught comparative politics at the Johann-Wolfgang-Goethe Universität, Frankfurt am Main, and is a member of the board of directors of the university's Center for North American Studies. He has published extensively in the field of federalism with a special focus on Germany, the United States, and the European Union.

Wolf D. Gruner holds the Chair of Modern and Contemporary European History and Jean Monnet Professor of European Integration

History and European Studies at the University of Rostock. His research interests include international relations; federalism; European, German, regional, and constitutional history; European and international institutions; and the German question in European history.

Arthur B. Gunlicks is Professor of Political Science and Chair of the Department of Political Science at the University of Richmond, Virginia. He has published widely on German politics, especially German federalism and party and campaign finance. His most recent book is *The Länder and German Federalism* (Manchester University Press, 2003).

Hermann K. Heußner is a professor of law and administration at the Catholic Professional College of North Germany in Osnabrück. He has been a visiting scholar at the Notre Dame School of Law and the University of California, Berkeley, School of Law. His publications have focused on direct democracy in Germany and the United States.

Charlie Jeffery is Professor of German Politics and Deputy Director of the Institute for German Studies at the University of Birmingham. He also directs a U.K.-wide research program on devolution and constitutional change for the British Economic and Social Research Council. He is the editor of *Recasting German Federalism: The Legacies of Unification* (London: Pinter, 1999), and has published widely on various aspects of German politics.

Uwe Leonardy was a high-level civil servant who worked in the legislative staff of Schleswig-Holstein, in the federal chancellor's office, and in the Mission of Lower Saxony to the Federation in Bonn, a position from which he retired in 1999. He has published widely in German and English on a variety of topics concerning German federalism, European integration, and parliamentary issues. He is currently a senior fellow at the Centre for European Integration Studies at the University of Bonn.

Peter Lösche is Professor of Political Science at the University of Göttingen. He has been a visiting professor in the United States and Italy. His research interests include the history of the working-class movement in Germany, politics and society in the United States, and political parties and interest groups in cross-national comparison.

Werner J. Patzelt is Professor for Comparative Government at the Dresden University of Technology. He is the author of numerous books on German members of parliament, three textbooks on political science and research methodology, and many articles in German and English on deputies, parliamentarianism, and political institutions. In addition, he has edited volumes on parliamentary symbols and on the former GDR's *Volkskammer*.

Introduction

GERMAN UNIFICATION, PUBLIC POLICY, AND FEDERALISM

Arthur B. Gunlicks

That every country is confronted by "current debates" is a given. But these debates are not the same even in neighboring countries, and they are not the same at any one time in a particular country. Some debates are more transient or permanent, some are very different from one another in their impact on the general society as opposed to a segment of society, some are more or less threatening to the stability of a government or even a political system, some are purely domestic, and a growing number have foreign policy implications due to globalization.

The "current debates" featured in this book deal with selected aspects of domestic and European policy, political parties, the challenge of direct democracy, and federalism in unified Germany. They are all issues that for many years and even decades have been the subject of much discussion, political posturing, legislation, and, to some extent, constitutional amendments and court decisions. They seem to be perennial issues in large part, in spite of reform efforts of various kinds over the years, and, as a result, they have been sources of frustration for those who think there should be more or different kinds of changes. Because they are not transient and seem always to be somewhere on someone's political agenda, they can be seen as among the defining issues of contemporary German politics. The purpose of this book, then, is to present an assessment of a number of important current issues by experts on German public policy and institutions and to contribute to an understanding of contemporary German politics.

We begin with a chapter by Wolf Gruner, who provides an overview of German history as it relates to federalism and fundamental issues affecting the nature of the political system. Unification in 1990 raised a series of questions about the role of Germany in Europe and the implications for Europe of a larger, unified Germany. These questions were not new; in fact, they had been asked before on several occasions during the nineteenth century, especially in 1871. They were also asked during much of the twentieth century, when the country was engaged in two devastating world wars, the aftermath of which led to significant reductions in German territory. Indeed, having failed in 1945 to achieve the goals set by a despotic leader, Germany was deprived of one-fourth of its pre-war territory and divided in the three-fourths that remained. In addition, a massive ethnic cleansing of Germans from territories in the East and South involved up to twelve million people. That there was some concern about the implications of unification among Germany's nine neighbors and others in Europe, given this tumultuous background, was historically understandable.

On the other hand, Wolf Gruner notes that West Germany had been founded in 1949 as a democratic, federal, social welfare state that had firm anchors set in the West. East Germany, of course, was also founded in 1949. Each state reflected different political and ideological traditions in German history, and each state raised in some manner constitutional issues that had divided the country during the past century. In 1849, 1871, 1919, and 1949 there were serious questions concerning the basic territorial division of the country into some kind of confederation, federation, or unitary state. Furthermore, there were questions about the number and size of the constituent states, called Länder after 1919, with the dominance of Prussia playing a major role in this discussion. Finally, there were issues in 1849 about monarchical versus liberal government and in 1919 about monarchical, liberal, social democratic, and radical socialist government.

With the dissolution of Prussia, a federal system of eight "territorial" states and three city-states (including West Berlin) emerged in

West Germany, with only one of the former and two of the latter having any direct historical tradition. As indicated in chapter 3, written by Uwe Leonardy, plans for additional changes in the number and size of the Länder did not materialize, except in the case of Baden-Württemberg. West Germany became a liberal-social democratic political system like its Western European neighbors, while East Germany finally emerged as a highly centralized, unitary, radical socialist state.

The Bonn republic that emerged after 1990, therefore, had a firm foundation based on the Basic Law of 1949. The result was that while a number of important changes have taken place in the Berlin republic, most obviously the accession of the former East Germany and five new Länder, Germany today does not represent a break with the past as its predecessors did in 1949 and 1919. We see in the following chapters, however, that there are serious issues with roots in the past that have not been addressed adequately in the minds of many Germans, including boundary reform of the sixteen Länder and fiscal federalism.

Starting in the late 1940s and early 1950s, a process of European integration began in which the new Federal Republic of Germany was an active and enthusiastic participant. This process presented Germany with many challenges, not the least of which was the role the Länder could and should play. This question has finally been answered to a considerable extent as a result of developments in European integration since the mid-1980s and especially since the addition of the new Article 23 into the Basic Law. Today Germans are actively involved in the debate on a revised constitutional order for the European Union (EU). Thus, Gruner suggests that "more than a decade after the fall of the Berlin Wall, Germany presents herself as a sensitive and creative player in the European debate on the final stage of the EU."

The financing of the German federal system has been a focus of controversy and reform efforts since German unification in 1871. It was a major issue in 1919 and after, and it became a major issue in 1949. Today it still arouses not only a great deal of political controversy but it has also occupied the Federal Constitutional Court on numerous occasions. It has been a constitutional issue, because public finance is the subject of Section X of the Basic Law. The provisions of this section were last changed in the late 1960s, but a number of statutory changes have occurred since then.

At the time of unification, it was apparent that reforms were required. Some changes directed at the new Länder in eastern Germany were made, but they were soon seen as inadequate. In 1993 a "solidarity pact" was arranged and has been in effect since 1995. Unfortunately, it did not solve a number of problems, and by the late 1990s dissatisfaction among several old Länder had grown to the point that they challenged the constitutionality of the system before the Federal Constitutional Court. The Court decided that changes had to be made, and in June 2001 the federal government broke the impasse in the negotiations between the richer and poorer Länder by agreeing to provide more federal funds to the poorest Länder so that the richer Länder could reduce somewhat the proportion of the revenues they have had to transfer to the poorer Länder. This change does not, however, represent a fundamental reform.

In her description and analysis of fiscal relations in Germany today, Gisela Färber points out that the financial system is highly centralized through the federal regulation of almost all taxes. It is true that the most important taxes are shared between the federal and Land (state) governments, with the local governments even involved in some of the sharing mechanisms. It is also true that the Länder could exert more influence for change through their position of strength in the Bundesrat, but they seem to be unable or unwilling to agree on the necessary measures.

Under the current provisions, fiscal equalization procedures in Germany involve multilevel sharing and transfers of funds by both vertical and horizontal means. The most important taxes are distributed on the basis of residence, place of production, and population. Second, there is a distribution of 25 percent of the value-added tax (VAT) to poorer Länder to bring them up to 92 percent of the average revenue of the Länder. Third, a horizontal transfer occurs from richer to poorer Länder based on fiscal capacity. Finally, there is a vertical transfer from the Federation to the poorest Länder to bring them up to 99.5 percent of the Länder average. The horizontal transfers from the richer to the poorer Länder especially aroused the opposition of Bavaria, Baden-Württemberg, and Hesse until the agreement of June 2001. This agreement between the Federation and the Länder reduces somewhat the maximum payment by the rich Länder to the poorer ones, but at the expense of the Federation.

Färber sees the centralization of the taxing powers as a major cause of the persistent controversy over fiscal relations in Germany.

She notes that there is too little connection between the Land parliaments, which are basically revenue-spending rather than revenue-raising bodies, and the voters and taxpayers, relatively few of whom understand that it is federal law that determines the taxes that pay for the programs administered by the Länder.

An issue closely related to fiscal federalism that Professor Färber does not address is the perennial and controversial question of whether and to what extent there should be boundary reform and consolidation of the Länder. Uwe Leonardy is a strong advocate of territorial reform, because he sees the number and size of many of the current Länder as a major cause of the financial "misery" that is the focus of Professor Färber's chapter. Leonardy notes that even the Allies urged the Germans to think about the size of the Länder in their new federal system and that the Basic Law contained a provision in Article 29 according to which "the federal territory shall be restructured by a federal law." As it turned out, only one new Land, Baden-Württemberg, was created in 1952, and Article 29 has been revised to make territorial reform more difficult and less of a requirement than before.

Following a detailed description of constitutional developments from 1949 to the present, Leonardy analyzes the reasons for the lack of territorial reform. These have to do with partisan reasons as well as bureaucratic resistance to changes that would affect electoral outcomes, careers, and entrenched rights and privileges. Leonardy believes that territorial reform is still necessary for a variety of legal, "factual," and financial reasons. He discusses the decision of the Federal Constitutional Court in 2000 that requires changes in the financial arrangements in Germany and notes the relevance of territorial changes to that decision. He believes that territorial reform is possible, and he outlines how this might be accomplished. He recognizes that the political cost would be high, but he argues that the cost of doing nothing will be even higher.

Another issue in Germany that has aroused considerable discussion and controversy and is related to the issue of public finance is the question of the powers or competences of the Land parliaments. We have seen that they have virtually no legislative authority in the area of taxation, and Leonardy would argue that they have been unwilling or unable to exercise any initiatives in territorial reforms. The one exception was the attempted merger of Berlin and Brandenburg, which failed in a referendum in 1996. Especially because of the current controversy over "competitive federalism," which suggests that the Land parliaments should have more competences in public finance as well as in other areas, the debate has focused on the transfer of certain powers from the Federation (Bund) to the Land parliaments. The reasons for the imbalance of legislative powers lies in the expansion of federal competences in the German system of cooperative federalism as well as the growth in authority of the European Community, now the European Union. In the meantime the Land governments have been compensated to a considerable extent for the loss of Land powers by being given participation rights in the Bundesrat, described by Udo Diedrichs and Elisabeth Dette-Koch in chapters 8 and 9.

Franz Greß is somewhat skeptical of the argument that Land parliamentary activity has declined in certain core areas, such as educational policy, and he points to the continued importance of the Länder in the area of party politics and their function as testing grounds for the public reaction to a number of political issues. On the other hand, he notes that German federalism is one based more on participation than on "substance" (e.g., autonomy). There is a close, interlocking relationship between the federal government and the Land governments, but the Land parliaments do not instruct their governments in the Bundesrat. This conforms with the functional logic of parliamentary systems, but the result is still a shrinking of Land legislative powers.

The important role of the Land governments in the Bundesrat in the EU decision-making process is also not shared by the Land parliaments. The flow of information to the Land parliaments concerning EU matters has increased, and the Land parliaments have created committees on European affairs, but there are limits to how much information these committees can handle and how much is relevant to other committees such as local government, transportation, or even education. There have also been a number of reforms in the form of privatization of administrative functions, but these raise the question of the extent to which the functions affected are then removed from the routine oversight and participation of the Land parliaments. Finally, the much larger issue of transferring powers from the Federation back to the Länder is now a hot topic, but it is not at all clear how much of the rhetoric about increased responsibility and autonomy of the Länder the responsible politicians actually want to see put into effect.

Perhaps an even more serious challenge not only to the Land parliaments but also to the parliamentary system in Germany is the apparent lack of understanding or support on the part of many Germans for their parliamentary system. It is clear that there are fundamental differences between the parliamentary and presidential systems, but it appears that there is a good deal of misunderstanding in Germany about this difference and what the political consequences are. Werner Patzelt has studied the attitudes of German parliamentarians and citizens and discovered that a significant proportion of Germans believe that "true democracy" is undermined by a strong party system, party group discipline, a lack of separation of powers, and the influence of interest groups, all of which are characteristics of German politics and the parliamentary system. Needless to say, there are also significant differences between the pattern of attitudes found in the general public and those of the elected politicians. The disjunction between public attitudes and the reality of German politics contributes to the alienation that many Germans feel toward the parties and their political system in general. In other words, even if the system works well according to its own internal logic, there will be considerable public dissatisfaction because it does not seem to conform to expectations. Astonishingly, even some German politicians seem to misunderstand some of the fundamental principles of the parliamentary system.

This "latent constitutional conflict" can, of course, be ignored in the hope that the damage will not be too great and the problem might go away some day. Or the political system could be changed from a parliamentary to a presidential system at the federal and Land levels, in which case all of the uncertainties and unintended consequences would have to be faced and dealt with. Or there could be a greater focus on a process of political education that does a better job of explaining the "real existing political system" within the context of a parliamentary structure rather than a misunderstood presidential theory of government. Finally, Patzelt proposes that some direct democracy might be introduced at the national level in order to answer those critics who see the parliamentary system as too elitist.

Students of German politics have long described the German political system as a "party state," where the parties dominate the executive and legislative branches of government and a number of other nongovernmental institutions to a far greater extent than in the United States. As in other industrialized democracies, however, political and party alienation (*Politik- und Parteienverdrossenheit*) appears to have become widespread even as political participation remains high, as measured by a wide variety of citizens' groups and ad hoc organizations outside of the parties.

Some of the more obvious changes in the German party system since unification are the separation of the country into two different party systems, namely the Christian Democrats (CDU/CSU), Social Democrats (SPD), the Liberals (FDP), and Greens in the former West Germany and CDU, SPD, and Party of Democratic Socialism (PDS) in what was East Germany. This separation includes the two large German parties, CDU and SPD, which are not the same in the West and East. In the East, for example, party membership is significantly lower, the party activists make up a much higher proportion of the members, and party discipline is lower. Overall, a new type of party appears to be emerging, one that combines the characteristics of media party, professionalized party, and party in public office.[1]

Party membership is declining, and the traditional sociocultural milieus of the CDU and SPD are eroding. The floating voters form an increasing focus of party appeals, which means that traditional party principles must be compromised. This, in turn, annoys many of the older members and activists. A certain "ossification," "pensionization," and "patronagization" seem to be leading to a decline of the parties.

Peter Lösche asks whether certain features of direct democracy might help to rectify some of these problems, and he looks at closed primaries/caucuses and open primaries as possibilities. He also considers inner-party plebiscites, or membership referenda, on certain policy issues.

With respect to direct democracy and the broader political system, Lösche looks at the popular election of mayors and local and Land referenda. He notes that the election of mayors is now common throughout Germany, but, like Franz Greß, he is critical of

---

1. The "party in public office" as described by Peter Lösche is hardly confined to Germany. An entire section of four chapters, "Parties in Government," can be found in *Parties without Partisans: Political Change in Advanced Industrial Democracies*, ed. Russell J. Dalton and Martin P. Wattenberg (Oxford: Oxford University Press, 2000).

those who argue in favor of the direct election of Land prime minis-ters. He points out that this proposal is not compatible with a parlia-mentary system, in which (as Werner Patzelt points out in chapter 5) there is no separation of powers in the sense of the American presi-dential/gubernatorial system. Lösche is also skeptical of referenda, especially at higher levels. In conclusion, he suggests that the Federal Republic has a "mixed constitution" that features representative democracy but has certain direct democratic elements at the local and Land levels. This is true not only of the political system but also of the party system.

Peter Lösche's general skepticism about direct democracy is not, of course, shared by everyone in Germany. Since the "roundtable" dis-cussions that were held in East Germany between the time the Berlin Wall fell and unification, a good deal of attention has been devoted to the subject of direct democracy at all levels. At the local level this attention resulted in the adoption of the direct election of mayors in those parts of West Germany, for example, North Rhine-Westphalia and Lower Saxony, that had a council-appointed mayor similar to the American council-mayor system or the British town clerk system. With the adoption of direct election of mayors in the East as well, direct election of mayors is now common throughout Germany. The new Länder included provisions for direct democracy in their consti-tutions, and three Länder in the West added or revised provisions in their constitutions so that today all of the Länder offer their citizens the option of resorting to the initiative and referendum. Efforts to introduce direct democracy into the Basic Law failed, however, and the only provisions that allow for such procedures are still in Article 29, which deals with territorial reform of the Land boundaries.

Hermann Heußner, an advocate of more direct democracy in Ger-many, describes these developments that took place during the 1990s; however, his chapter focuses more on the citizens' initiative in the Länder than the referendum. He points out that while ten initiative petitions qualified, and five succeeded in becoming referenda, another sixteen petitions failed to secure sufficient signatures. He notes that there is a wide range among the Länder in signature requirements, and, while he is critical of thresholds that are too high (e.g., 20 percent), he is also wary about requirements that are as low as in California. He notes that procedures for collecting signatures differ, with only six Länder permitting collection on the street or house to house. In six Länder there are also narrow time periods of two weeks for collecting signatures. He also points to several other important differences between the German and American procedures for initiatives and referenda. In Germany there are subject matter restrictions; for example, no initiatives may deal with budgets or taxes. There is also a preelection review process to ensure that the initiative does not violate the law (e.g., civil liberties); negative decisions can be challenged in court. Another important difference is that no direct initiatives in Germany bypass the parliament: successful petitions for initiatives go to the parliament for its consideration, and only if the parliament fails to act within a fixed period of time does the procedure for placing the issue on the ballot go into effect. Even then, the parliament can propose an alternative to the initiative.

As in the case of general elections, political commercials on radio and television are not permitted, which reduces sharply the influence of interest groups. In five Länder there is some public funding. But there is no disclosure of campaign expenditures, and there are no informational pamphlets in Germany. Initiative elections are not held on the same day as general elections, and the calculation of majorities is different. In the United States and Switzerland, only a majority of those voting is required for approval, regardless of the voter turnout. In Germany constitutional initiatives require an affirmative vote of 50 percent of all eligible voters except in Bavaria, which has a 25 percent threshold; in five Länder a two-thirds vote is also required. For statutory initiatives affirmative vote thresholds range from 25 to 33 percent, and in only three Länder is a simple majority sufficient.

With the introduction in January 2002 of the euro as a common currency in twelve EU member states, even more attention than in the past is being directed toward the process of European integration. One result of this process is the strong interest of students of European affairs in the roles of the individual member states in the EU and the decision-making processes within these states regarding EU policy as well as decision-making at the EU level in Brussels, Luxemburg, and Strasbourg.

Udo Diedrichs provides a detailed description and analysis of the German decision-making process regarding the EU. He notes that this process has often been described as highly fragmented, complex, and multilayered. At the federal level, various ministries are involved in

EU matters, and ministerial autonomy sometimes leads to conflict. The chancellor is, of course, a key player, which became clear especially with Helmut Kohl. But the chancellor is not involved in routine or technical matters. The ministries have special staffs for EU affairs, and coordination is the responsibility of a special interministerial committee. Decisions are made by consensus, but the ministers themselves, the federal cabinet, or the chancellor may be called upon to resolve conflicts.

Not only the government but also the Bundestag is involved in EU decision-making, especially since the Treaty of Maastricht (TEU). A Committee on European Union Affairs has been created, composed of members of the Bundestag as well as nonvoting members of the European Parliament. It serves as an "integration committee," a "horizontal committee," and a specialized committee for European affairs. The new Article 23 of the Basic Law requires the federal government to keep the Bundestag and Bundesrat informed about EU matters. The federal government is also obliged to take into account the position of the Bundestag. If it does not accept that position, it must provide the reasons why. There is a constant process of consultation and flow of information between the government and the parliament, with ministers and even the chancellor sometimes appearing before the Committee.

What distinguishes German decision-making from that of most other member states, however, is the role of the German regions, that is, the Länder. Since the mid-1980s they have been increasingly involved in the decision-making process. After unification their role was strengthened by the new Article 23 of the Basic Law. Udo Diedrichs describes this role in some detail, and he also notes their influence in the German negotiations at the EU intergovernmental conferences (IGC), which are the settings for treaty revisions. The Länder even had two representatives at these conferences in the 1990s, and they have achieved considerable satisfaction in the results of the IGC in Amsterdam in 1996 and Nice in 2000.

Diedrichs concludes by suggesting that while German policy making is fragmented, it has also been quite successful, especially in achieving strategic goals. The multilevel decision-making process at the EU level has not been as great a barrier for the Germans as it might have been, in part because it resembles the national decision-making process in Germany.

Elisabeth Dette-Koch also notes the fragmentation of the decision-making process regarding the EU, and, like Udo Diedrichs, suggests that it is not so bad as it may at first appear. She points to the
new Article 23 of the Basic Law and its provisions concerning the
participation by the Bundestag and Bundesrat in EU decision-making. Her focus is on the process in the Bundesrat and the role of the
Länder. As a representative of Baden-Württemberg on the Bundesrat's Committee on European Affairs, she is well placed to comment on the work of the various committees of the Bundesrat and
the representatives from the missions of the Länder.

She notes that whether the Bundesrat's opinion is decisive or
merely taken into consideration by the federal government depends
on the distribution of powers between the federal executive and Länder chamber as well as whether the Bundesrat can gather a two-
thirds majority for its position. She describes the circumstances when
representatives of the Länder are sent to EU committees and working groups, of which there are hundreds of examples in Brussels. She
also notes the presence of Land missions in Brussels and the
Observer of the Länder.

She concludes that the system of cooperation between the federal government and the Länder generally works well in practice. It
is indeed a complicated system, but it does serve some purposes,
such as providing the federal government with regional views on
many issues. She sees regionalism as increasing in importance in
Europe, and she notes with satisfaction that some member states
have even looked at federal-Land cooperation in Germany for ideas
to apply at home.

In chapter 10 Charlie Jeffery focuses on constitutional change in
both Germany and Great Britain over the past decade. Change is
perceived by many in Germany as badly needed, for example, in the
areas of public finance, territorial reform, Land autonomy, or direct
democracy, but with little happening. On the other hand, there is a
perception of radical change in the United Kingdom since Prime
Minister Tony Blair took office in 1997. Jeffery suggests that these
two perceptions are misleading and too one-dimensional. Formal
constitutional change may not be the only indicator of important
political changes in a society.

The British and German constitutions could hardly be more different. The British have a "'curious compound of custom and precedent,

law and convention, rigidity and malleability concealed beneath layers of opacity and mystery,'" whereas the German Basic Law is a
"'long, detailed, highly specific and explicit'" "constitutional code."
The question is whether the Germans have gone too far in their "love
of legalism," that is, whether the "reform gridlock" in Germany may
not be a result in part of the effort to focus too much on the constitution. The danger, as Jeffery sees it, is that the Germans may be
undermining the constitutional order by an overreliance on constitutional regulation.

In the United Kingdom he sees the opposite problem. Pressures
for constitutional changes have emerged because of too little constitutional regulation. Parliament has absolute sovereignty. The constitution does not represent a higher order of values. The lack of limits
on parliamentary power has provoked constitutional debate, especially because of the dramatic and controversial changes introduced
by Prime Minister Margaret Thatcher.

The perceptions that constitutional change occurred in Great
Britain but not in Germany are based on an oversimplification.
There have been some important underlying changes in Germany,
and, in spite of the Blair reforms, it is not clear what the results are.
Informal constitutional "praxis" can change, as can the relationship
between the people and the constitution, for example, between the
Scottish people and the British constitution.

The focus of attention in many European countries has been on
territory, that is, on regional powers and influence. In the United
Kingdom this has led to constitutional changes concerning "devolution," whereas in Germany discussion has centered on "competitive
federalism." In Britain the changes were secured through referendum, which distinguishes constitutional change from ordinary laws
and qualifies the notion of parliamentary sovereignty. But it is not
clear to what extent the Blair government really accepts the consequences of these changes. One sees that the formal dimension of
constitutional change is only a first step.

In Germany the issue of federalism seems to be stuck in the formal dimension. The beneficiaries of the status quo block attempts to
reform the system, which leads to pessimism about the very possibilities of reform. But Jeffery argues that this is too formal a view. While
formal change is unlikely, informal developments are another matter.
He believes that change is in fact under way.

Chapter 1

HISTORICAL DIMENSIONS OF GERMAN STATEHOOD

From the Old Reich to the New Germany

Wolf D. Gruner

Preliminary Considerations

More than ten years after the fall of the Berlin Wall and German unification, visible and less visible transformations have taken place in the political, constitutional, social, intellectual, economic, and historical environment of the new Federal Republic of Germany. The following considerations will attempt to approach these complex transformations from the historian's point of view. Long-term phenomena and features of the history of the Germanys will have to be taken into account as well as more recent developments. We will have to ask questions such as: What are the German and European implications of this process of transformation in Germany and Europe? What does a "greater Germany" mean for her European neighbors and for the process of European integration and reform? Will the German debate on the legal codification of the role of the German federal states (Länder) concerning their rights and obligations in the process of EU integration, constitution making, and institutional reform—a long-lasting debate ever since the foundation of the European Coal and Steel Community (Gruner 2001: 35ff.)—have a positive influence on considerations to establish a functioning third level in the institutional system of the EU between Maastricht, Amsterdam, Nice and beyond?

Many of the phenomena, aspects, and developments that interest the historian of German, European, and European integration history have been dealt with from different angles and perspectives by other experts in this book. Thus, the following considerations will focus on the historical dimensions and traditions of German statehood since the late eighteenth century. Because of the given format, my remarks will have to concentrate on some basic phenomena that, from my point of view, still prevail. It will not be possible, however, to elaborate on all historical and constitutional traditions that would be necessary for understanding modern Germany (see Gruner 1999a: 277ff.). Many interesting features and structures and also some historical phenomena that play an important role for German history in a European environment, such as the impact of historical landscapes on German identity and what this means for European unity in diversity, can only be touched on briefly.

For discussing constitutional questions at a European and at a nation state level, it is quite fruitful to look into Germany's divergent constitutional traditions which often differ from a Western approach (see Limbach et al. 1999: 44ff.; Gruner 1999a: 285ff.; Vorländer 1999: 39ff.). This naturally provokes the question of whether the Federal Republic and the new Germany have arrived in "the West," that is, if the model of the German Federation (Deutscher Bundesstaat) guarantees unity and freedom at the same time, combining national unity and a liberal political system. Daniel Webster's phrase of 1830, "Liberty and Union, now and forever, one and Inseparable," can be applied to today's Germany. The Federal Republic has arrived "in the West," integrating "Western traditions" and German constitutional and historical traditions. In this process the United States has played a pivotal role, long before the period of the occupation of Germany after World War II. Therefore, I shall take into account the understanding of federalism in the United States and compare it to the perceptions of federalism in German constitutional and political thinking.

For an understanding and analysis of Germany's institutional, legal, intellectual, and political problems from a historian's point of view, there are certain aspects and historical facts to consider:

- The GDR (East Germany) ceased to exist after 3 October 1990. Nevertheless, the separate developments of the FRG (West Germany) and the GDR in their respective political, military, economic, and ideological camps since 1948–49 and the historical background of their foundation have to be considered.
- Certain traditions of human and civil rights in German constitutional life have existed since the early nineteenth century and must be dealt with—at least briefly.
- We have to deal with the unfinished business of certain clauses of the German constitution of 1949, such as Article 29 (2). In its original version it demanded a new structure and new boundaries for the German Länder in order to establish a functioning federal system for the Federal Republic and a future united Germany (see Leonardy, chapter 3, this volume). The Luther Commission and the Ernst Commission proposed options and solutions without a final decision of the institutional bodies of the Federal Republic on this issue (see, e.g., BHStAM StK: 10095–11169). The present phrasing of Article 29 (2) is the result of changes in 1969, 1976, and 1994 (*Bundesgesetzblatt* 1969: 1231, 1976: 2381, 1994: 3146) and offers a watered-down version of the original mandate (document II) of the Frankfurt Documents of 1 July 1948 (Feldkamp 1999: 55f.).
- From the perspective of transformation and reform, we should take into account the present debate on cooperative and competitive federalism and its impact on considerations and debates for establishing a "third level" within the institutional system of the EU, which would assign to the Committee of the Regions (CoR) of the EU legislative rights and an equal institutional status similar to the European Parliament, the European Commission, the EU Council, the European Court of Justice, and the European Court of Auditors.
- We must ask whether the federal system of the Federal Republic of Germany, as German contributions to the debate by Joschka Fischer, Johannes Rau, Roman Herzog, and others on the reform of the institutions of the EU have suggested, serves as a model for federalization of the EU. Could a nineteenth-century model of German constitutional history, which was discussed in connection with the task force for the Intergovernmental Conference of the EU in 1996, possibly be useful and productive in

dealing successfully with the issue of EU enlargement by adopting the idea of a closer and wider federation under a common
community framework?

The Historical Setting: Old and New Traditions in Nineteenth- and Twentieth-Century German History

In May 1989 the Federal Republic of Germany was celebrating the
fortieth anniversary of its foundation. A few weeks before, the controversial and disputed local elections in the GDR had taken place.
A few weeks later General Secretary Gorbachev visited Bonn. At
this moment, nobody could imagine that a month after the festivities
for the fortieth anniversary of the GDR, which Gorbachev also
attended, the Wall would come down; only twelve months later the
German unification train would be speeding toward monetary and
social union, the Unity Treaty, the EU Treaty, the Two-Plus-Four
Treaty, and German unity on 3 October 1990, according to Article
23 of the Basic Law. In the meantime the GDR would cease to exist.

West Germany was founded in 1949 as a federal state and as a
social and parliamentary democracy. Like the Federal Republic, the
German Democratic Republic was also founded in 1949. Its first constitution, however, was already drafted by 18 March 1948, to com-
memorate the one-hundred-year anniversary of the beginning of the
March Revolution in Berlin when Prussian troops killed a number of
revolutionaries. They were remembered as the Victims of March
(*Märzgefallenen*). The centenary of the failed revolutions of 1848–49
was celebrated in all zones of occupation in postwar Germany. Intellectuals, politicians, and writers met in conferences and congresses;
books and pamphlets were published, speeches were delivered, and an
impressive meeting was convened in Frankfurt's Paul's Church to
remember the first session of an all-German parliament. The revolutions of 1848–49 were considered to be an important German heritage
and the basis for building up a new and democratic Germany. The
events of 1848–49 were perceived as one of the major roots of German democracy, as one of the positive traditions in German history,
and as a motive to establish a non Prussian "other Germany." The
memory of the failure of the bourgeois liberal revolution to establish a
German national state in 1848–49 was also used for ideological aims.

The political and ideological discussions between the two camps in Germany from 1945 to 1948–49 in the period of constitution making for the German single states reflect and underline an ongoing historical debate in Germany about the character of the best political and constitutional system for Germany and the Germans. Should the new postwar Germany be a *unitary and centralized state* or a *federal state*? The staunch anti-federalists, advocates of a unitary state for Germany after the war, blamed the reactionary and particularist governments of the German states for the miscarried foundation of a German Empire (Reich) in 1849 and for the failure of the Weimar Republic. The federalists, on the other hand, argued that the centralist and unitary character of the German constitution of 28 March 1849 was responsible for the failure to establish a German national state and that the provisional German government and the German National Assembly at the time were not recognized by the European powers. It was also argued by many constitutional experts and former Weimar politicians after World War II that the unitary and centralized character of the Weimar constitution of 1919 has to be considered one of the major reasons why the first German democracy was doomed to failure.

Thus, from a German nation-state perspective, there seems to be an immediate connection between 1849, 1919, 1949, and 1989. The question remains, however, whether these are the only traditions and real landmarks for German constitutional history. Can we reduce modern German history to a prehistory of the German Empire of 1870–71 and Prussia's German mission to achieve this goal? Definitely not. German history in the eighteenth and nineteenth centuries and beyond does not equal Prussian history. James Sheehan has reminded us in a wonderful article entitled "What Is German History?" that the German *Reichsgründung* (foundation of the German Empire) can no longer be understood as the main event of German history in the nineteenth century. Rather, we have "to acknowledge that the present period has a legitimacy of its own, a legitimacy which comes not from its relationship to the old Reich, but from its place within a broader and deeper historical tradition. The German present is not a postscript to the imperial past; it is a new chapter in a much older history" (Sheehan 1981: 23). Today's Germany has to be considered as a "new chapter in a much older history" that reaches far beyond the foundation of a German national state in 1870–71. In order to better understand the forces of transition, the initiatives for reform, and the powers of preservation in Germany, we need to discuss in more detail the "broader and deeper traditions" of German history.

Critical Elements of German History

I would like to discuss some features of German history, which still have an impact on the present debate, from a broader angle. These aspects, which influence German political and constitutional thinking, shall hopefully lead to a better understanding of Germany in its European environment, the nature of the German question, and some "genuine German" features that can be perceived as a result of its history (see in more detail Gruner 1993: 22ff.).

- The *nature of German statehood* differs from that of other European states. For example, whereas in France, Britain, and Spain the dynastic nation state served as the basis for the formation and development of the modern state and modern statehood, modern statehood in Germany (i.e., during the period of the Holy Roman Empire of the German Nation) emerged and developed within the framework of the "territory." A common feature of Germany's historical landscape, therefore, is its federal structure (cf. Langewiesche and Schmidt 2000: 19ff.; Gruner 1993: 40ff.).
- *In German history there is no "one and indivisible" nation* compared to France and the United States. German historical identity has many layers. Thus, it is appropriate to talk about German historical landscapes that constitute a common German historical landscape (*Geschichtslandschaft*) as an integral part of a European historical landscape. Because of its history, unity in diversity is a characteristic feature of our part of Europe.
- There is *a different perception of the idea of the nation in Germany.* The modern concept of the political nation was one of the effects of the French Revolution of 1789 which replaced the idea of the dynastic nation of ancien régime Europe. The political concept of the "one and indivisible nation" as the building block for statehood stood in sharp contrast to the federal idea of statehood binding different parts of the nation together.

Thus, in the German case it is more appropriate to talk about a "federative nation" (*föderative Nation*), as Dieter Langewiesche has recently suggested. The concept of the political nation demanded a nation-state that would be strong enough to defend the interests of the nation and to provide its liberty and security. In order to fulfill its functions, the national government must have the power to act. The national movements all over Europe were in favor of a strong unitary state and against a seemingly weak federation. In the German case this is important insofar as the historic roots of all the major political parties in Germany—liberals, conservatives, socialists/social democrats, and communists—date back to a period when the idea of a strong national state was seen as the best means for achieving the togetherness demanded.

- It may be appropriate to make a few comments about the perception of the terms "federal" and "federalism" in Germany and in the United States. As Arnold Brecht stated, "American federalism from its inception was an integral part of the country's democratic institutions." The Americans wanted to be independent from foreign rule; they wished to be free in their local and personal affairs from interference by some central government. They were ready, however, to handle their "common affairs in common." Matters of national concern were handled by the federal government, others were retained for the states, and "some were withdrawn from the reach of any government.... In giving federal power and state power each its due, 'Dual Federalism' was regarded as a great democratic innovation" (Brecht 1945: 3). Federalism was considered, as James Madison said, to be "the best guardian ... of the liberty, safety and the happiness of man" (Madison 1910: vol. 9, 136).
- German federalism had different historical and political origins. In the beginning it did not originate from democracy but from the historical landscape and the political traditions of the Holy Roman Empire of the German Nation and European thought. The origins of modern German federalism, however, can be dated back to 1806, as Karl Otmar Freiherr von Aretin has pointed out, when the Old Empire ceased to exist and was replaced among others by sovereign reformist middle states such as Bavaria, Baden, and Württemberg (Aretin 1985: 15).

In drawing up their 1808 and 1819 constitutions that provided the transformation from a "society of subjects" (*Untertanengesellschaft*) to a "society of citizens" (*Staatsbürgergesellschaft*), the authors of these constitutions were influenced in part by the American constitutional model. Whereas the American term "federalist" was applied to advocates who wished a strong federal government, the German equivalent, "Föderalist," was used in a negative sense to characterize conservative, monarchical advocates for states' rights and a weak central government. Thus, from this incorrect perception of German federalism and what it stood for, Thomas Nipperdey could state that federalism was the "unity of the reaction" against the "unity of the nation" (Nipperdey 1983: 355f.). A closer look from the perspective of constitutional law will prove that the assessment of German federalism in the early nineteenth century was biased and unjustified. It was the product of political and ideological overtones as well as a result of the perception of the role and historical legitimacy of the German nation state. The "Second" German Empire had to be historically legitimized.

Thus, the so-called "historiography of the Empire," established by historians and spokesmen of "Political Prussianism," such as Heinrich von Treitschke and others, tried to prove that Prussia since the late seventeenth century started its "historic mission" of bringing about the unification of the German nation and the foundation of the German Empire. They "mutated"—as Stamm-Kuhlmann put it—into "historiographers of the Prussian state: so to speak Purveyors to the Royal Household for history" (Stamm-Kuhlmann 2001: 11). Since Prussia was perceived as the "core state" for German national unification, historical writing had to show superior Prussian achievements in German history since the times of the Great Elector and Frederick the Great. Heinrich von Treitschke was one of the prominent "drummers for the Empire." His "History of Germany in the Nineteenth Century" was designed to influence German public consciousness in favor of Prussia.

Thus, Prussian history between the seventeenth and nineteenth centuries became a "pre-history" of the German Empire. This approach denied the role of other German territories and states and the role of the "federal nation" in the process of modernization and in German history as such (Langewiesche and Schmidt 2000; Gruner 2003: 24–38). This view is no longer dominant in German historiography and international research on German history.

- In the German case, more than in other nations, the perception of statehood by major parties runs counter to the historic regional and national memory. There was no German nationality before 1913. Someone who was born in Munich was a Bavarian national, while a person born in Cologne was considered a Prussian national. The birth certificates indicate: *Nationalität Bayern, Nationalität Preußen.*
- Against this historical background, the concepts of German statehood oscillate between unitary unity and union in diversity, between cohesion and fragmentation, between unitary and federal forms of government. Because of the geographic position of Germany in the heartland of Europe, the constitutional order of Germany was and is of major importance for a functioning European state system, that is, a German balance is necessary for a functioning European balance. Thus, the constitutional bond for the German nation agreed on was and still is of vital interest for Germany's neighbors, that is, there is always a German and a European-international dimension to German statehood as well as to German history. Ever since the time when the idea of the classic European nation-state became predominant, there has been a polarization between the protagonists for a unitary state and those for federal statehood. Thus, we can emphasize certain continuous constitutional questions and issues in German constitutional thinking in the nineteenth and twentieth centuries that originated in the eighteenth century and are still kept alive in the present.

Constitutional Issues before Weimar

An example of a constitutional question and issue is the debate over the best political and social system as a common bond for the German nation. Should all power be concentrated in the hands of a central government, downgrading the states to the status of mere provinces, or should power be distributed equally between the central government and the state members? This debate is equally characteristic of

1848–49, 1919–30, and 1945–49, as well as the more recently revived debate on the shift from the *Leitbild* of cooperative federalism
to competitive federalism (*Wettbewerbsföderalismus*) at a German and
European level (Große Hüttmann and Knodt 2000: 37f.) (see Jeffery,
chapter 10, this volume).

The belief in the concept of the unitary state or the federal state
resulted in scholarly and political debates on reforms of the existing
federal system: for example, the German Confederation between
1815 and 1866, or the political, emotional and learned discussions
on a reform of the Empire in Wilhelminian and Weimar Germany
and on a new territorial reorganization within the Empire (Reich).
This was true for the period 1848–49, for Weimar Germany, for the
Federal Republic of Germany, and today for the "Berlin Republic."

One issue that brought about repeated conflicts between the central government and the states was the financial constitution of the
respective German state. The distribution of financial resources
stimulated the debates during the first attempt to establish a national
state in 1848–49. It was a key issue in the discussions on *Reichsreform*
in Weimar Germany, and it was one of the major reasons why the
Bavarian parliament voted against the Basic Law for the Federal
Republic of Germany in May 1949. Indeed, it is still on the agenda,
as can be seen in chapter 2 by Gisela Färber in this volume.

The discussion about the financial constitution of Germany is a
never-ending story of conflict and compromise. Only recently this
issue came to the foreground again when Bavaria, Baden-Württemberg, and Hesse brought a complaint to the Federal Constitutional
Court at Karlsruhe connecting the question of the financial compensation between the German Länder (*Länderfinanzausgleich*), the competences of the Länder, and the problem of a more precise definition
of the principle of subsidiarity according to Article 3b of the European
Treaty of Maastricht and the annex to the Treaty of Amsterdam.

There was one element of continuity that would become a determining factor for German constitutional history: the size and overall
potential of Prussia within a German state without Austria. The decision of the Frankfurt Parliament in 1849 to create a German nation-
state without Austria became a serious problem for all future attempts
to find a functioning federal solution for Germany. The political system of Prussia blocked the process toward parliamentary government
in the German Empire between 1871 and 1918. In Weimar Germany

three-fifths of the territory of the German state belonged to Prussia. The discussions concerning a dismemberment of Prussia between 1919 and 1932 did not bring about a solution. The breakup of Prussia into its successor states to provide a solid basis for the establishment of a functioning federal system in Germany was also discussed by the allies of the anti-Hitler coalition during World War II. Since 1945–49 the problem of Prussia no longer exists as a constitutional issue. In discussing German statehood we always have to use a three-tier model, which also applied to German unification in 1990, namely the *regional level* of the member states ("Staaten" or "Länder"), the *German national level*, and the *European level*.

In 1849, after long deliberations, the German National Assembly voted to found a German national federal state. There were among the members of the Frankfurt Parliament different ideas as to the constitutional structure of a federal state. Besides the protagonists of a unitary state, there were three different concepts of a federation (Bundesstaat):

- the federal state with strong unitary features (*unitarischer Bundesstaat*), that is, the distribution of powers is in favor of the central institutions;
- the federal state of the federal type (*Bundesstaat des föderativen Typs*), that is, there is an equal distribution of power between the institutions of the federation and the federal states. The federal parliament *and* the federal council constitute the legislature; and
- the federal state with strong confederate features (*Staatenbund, Staatenverein*), that is, the distribution of powers favors the federal states.

The Committee for Constitutional Affairs had proposed in October 1848 that the future form of government should be between unitary government and a confederate system, but it stressed that the interests of the nation at large should be given priority in a federal state. This statement brought up the basic domestic problem in the process of any German constitution making, namely, the relationship between central power and single state, between central government and state government. Fields of conflict were the distribution of power, the types of revenue, and the financial constitution.

The constitution for a "small" German Empire (i.e., Germany without Austria) adopted by the National Assembly on 28 March 1849 was a federal state with strong unitary features, that is, a federation of the unitary type. An example can be found in Part I, dealing with the Empire: "The individual German states keep their independence unless it is restricted by the constitution. They retain all sovereign rights unless these were transferred to the executive of the Empire." Thus, whereas the first part of the clause stresses state independence, the second restricts it or moderates it.

The Empire claimed the sole right to make war and to negotiate and conclude peace, to represent Germany internationally, to conclude treaties, and to have the army and navy of the Reich at its sole disposal. In addition, the Empire claimed the sole legislative rights concerning all sectors of private and public law as far as it was deemed necessary for German unity. It took on responsibility for patents, customs, trade, and postal services and claimed the right to supervise railroads, waterways, and telegraphs.

The unitary thrust for the constitution of 1849 provoked the resistance of the individual states, especially the larger states in Germany such as Austria, Prussia, Saxony, Hanover, and Bavaria. Despite the fact that 29 out of 39 states endorsed the constitution, it did not become the constitution for all of Germany. The larger single states argued that the National Assembly did not have the power to adopt a constitution without the consent of the member states. In a note (28 April 1849) the Bavarian government also reminded the National Assembly that the unitary constitution agreed on posed a threat to the security, politics, and culture of Germany. It referred to the negative impact of unitary government on all walks of life and argued that Germany as a nation-state would assert itself without such a centralized government. The outbreak of revolution in Baden to save the constitution, the leftist radicalization of the process to force the adoption of the constitution by civil war, and the crackdown on the revolution by Prussian troops brought about the end of the attempt to establish a liberal German nation-state.

Why did the constitution of 1849 fail? Besides the fact that the provisional government was not recognized by the European powers, the resistance of the individual states was of major importance. Most likely, a more balanced federal constitution that would have conceded more powers and rights to the states would have been more successful in the complicated German, regional, and European situation of 1848–49.

As in the case of the revolutions of 1848–49, the historical framework for the foundation of the Weimar Republic and its history was of major importance. The German Empire of 1871 was founded from above. The spirit of the Constitution of the German Empire, published on 16 April 1871 as an "Act concerning the Constitution of the German Empire," which did not include human and civil rights, can be perceived from the first lines of the Imperial Constitution: "We, William, by the Grace of God German Emperor, King of Prussia … decree in the Name of the German Empire after the Consent of the Federal Council and the Diet" (*Deutsche Verfassungen* 1999: 132). All attempts to introduce parliamentary government at the level of the Empire and to federalize the German Empire failed before 1914. Between 1871 and 1918 the powers derived from legal custom (*Gewohnheitsrecht*) shifted, without changes in the constitution of the Empire, from the sovereign of the Empire, the Federal Council (Bundesrat), to the Federal Chancellery and the Prime Minister of Prussia, both offices being in one hand. Paul Laband, in his analysis of the history of the German constitution of 1871, pointed out that the Empire increasingly interfered with the rights and jurisdiction of the federal states (Laband 1907: 1–46). Because of the role and status of Prussia, the German Empire, which formally was a federation, degenerated into a mock federal system. Thus, René Brunet, an outstanding expert on German constitutional law in the first decades of the twentieth century, published a study on "The New German Constitution," which looked back on the "constitutional problem of Prussia" and its impact on federalism. In this study, he stated that in "contrast to the other federated states whose Constitutions were based on the principle of equality of the component states, Germany's was based on the notion of the inequality of the states federated in it. Prussia exercised a true hegemony in Germany" (Brunet 1922: 5).

In order to solve the "Prussian problem" in the German federal system, the American ambassador to Berlin, George Bancroft, proposed two options for reducing Prussia's influence in the Empire and furthering the unity of the German Reich. First, all legal jurisdiction of the Prussian state should be transferred to the Empire. Since the Bundesrat was the sovereign of the Empire, this option could not be realized. It was used, however, as a model in the discussion of reform of the territorial structure of the Weimar Republic. The second option proposed the transfer of the legal jurisdiction from the Prussian state to the provinces. In 1918 Hugo Preuss took up this idea in his plan for the territorial reorganization of the German Commonwealth. He wanted to redraft the political map of Germany by eliminating the minor German states—with the exception of the Hanseatic city-states of Bremen, Hamburg and Lübeck—and eliminating oversized states such as Prussia. The Prussian provinces were to be elevated to the status of states. The Preuss plan would have established fairly equal political units. The average population would have been, with the exception of a few states such as Bavaria and the new Rhenish state, about four million inhabitants. Thus, there was a chance for establishing a fair equalization as a prerequisite for a functioning federal state. The idea of the decentralization of Prussia was again picked up in British and American plans during World War II for the political structure of postwar Germany (see PRO F.O. 371/39080 1944; Brecht 1945: 132ff.; Gruner 1993: 209ff.).

Constitutional Issues and Weimar

Arnold Brecht, who wrote his study on *Federalism and Regionalism in Germany* as background for officers and civil servants participating in training programs to prepare them to serve in Germany after the fall of Hitler, pleaded for the restoration of "some kind of federal structure" in postwar Germany, now that the single political unit of Prussia and the totalitarian structures introduced in Germany during the Nazi period had been eliminated. As a political actor in Weimar Germany who had to leave his fatherland, Brecht was highly influenced by his work and experiences in Germany during the 1920s. In his options for a territorial reform of the German Commonwealth, he favored a middle way between a highly centralized Reich and a "Federation of German Länder" (*Bund deutscher Länder*). His proposals in *Federalism and Regionalism in Germany* therefore place certain fundamental rights of all the states, both new and old, beyond the reach of simple national legislation, namely, their right to elect their own governments, and the right of these governments to be represented in the Federal Council. The basis of the German federal system should be sought in the states' constitutional share in the federal government rather than in any unalterable distribution of jurisdictions between federal and state governments (Brecht 1945: 136).

The constitutional scheme elaborated by Professor Hugo Preuss—at the time German secretary of state for the interior—which sought the partition of Prussia, the rearrangement of German state boundaries and the formation of a German Republican Confederation, was "firmly opposed" and turned down by the Prussian government. This sealed the fate of the proposal. Preuss's contention that Prussia wanted to continue to exercise a preponderant influence in the new German Commonwealth was confirmed. In his scheme he had stated: "A single state which contains four-sevenths of the population of the whole Empire is only possible as a hegemonic state" (cit. in: PRO Cabinet 24/75 1919). Preuss showed convincingly in his scheme that the Prussian state never formed an "organic whole." There was a lack of homogeneity. From his point of view Prussia was an "artificial unity." Thus, in order to achieve a "perfect unity" of the new federal German Commonwealth, it was necessary to split up Prussia into eight successor states.

Preuss also complained about the fact that the German federated states had elected their parliaments before the election of a German Constituent National Assembly. In his view this was incompatible with the necessity to reach a successful constitutional settlement for the new republican and democratic German Commonwealth. This was especially true in the case of the Prussian Constituent Assembly, representing the majority of the German people, which was determined not to accept any future political formation of Prussia wrenching away portions of the modern Prussian state as it had existed since 1815. Thus, Preuss, looking back to the failed attempt to establish a German national state in 1848–49, disappointedly stated that "little appears to have been learned in Germany from this experience" (PRO Cabinet 24/75 1919).

The signal event of the 1871 Empire was, of course, World War I, which Germany lost in 1918. Starting with a mutiny of the navy, revolution broke out in Germany. First the Kaiser and then the German princes abdicated. The news broke on 9 November 1918 at 2:00 P.M. At that time the socialist Philipp Scheidemann proclaimed the German Republic from the balcony of the Reichstag, "in order to steal a march on radicals like Ledebour and Liebknecht." At 4:00 P.M. the communist Karl Liebknecht proclaimed the free socialist German

Republic from the balcony of the Berlin palace. The government was handed over to the leader of the majority socialists, Friedrich Ebert. In the time span between the resignation of the last imperial government and the adoption of the new Weimar constitution in August 1919, there was an interregnum in which the administrative institutions of the November Revolution filled the power vacuum and dominated the political landscape. During that period the social foundations of Germany were transformed and democratized. In order to stabilize the situation and avoid a system of worker's and soldier's councils on communist lines, the German Social Democratic Party (SPD) concluded an alliance with the army and the bureaucracy to ensure order.

On 9 November 1918 the German Republic was proclaimed twice, but this was no coincidence. The proclamations by Philipp Scheidemann and Karl Liebknecht stood for two different concepts of the state in Germany that returned after World War II and found their expression in the foundation in 1948–49 of the Federal Republic of Germany and the German Democratic Republic. Which one would prevail after World War I and the November Revolution? There were at least "four distinct lines," as Frederic August Ogg observed (1924: 715–16), "along which political development in the [German] empire might run":

1. a "moderate reconstruction of the governmental system, with a revival of monarchy";
2. "[c]ontinued control by the moderate socialists which would mean a republic, fortified with the instrumentalities of advanced democracy, and a gradual and cautious nationalization of the means of production and distribution";
3. "[c]ontrol by the more radical socialists which would probably mean an immediate attempt to install the socialist type of state outright"; and
4. "[f]inally, Spartacist dominance which would lead, like the Bolshevist regime in Russia, to the summary annihilation of all existing political forms, the introduction of the soviet, the turning of society upside down by the establishment of the dictatorship of the proletariat."

The socialist variant had good chances to succeed. The question was, however, which line within the socialist camp would prevail, the

moderate or the radical position, social democracy or a soviet republic? Would "social revolution" or "political revolution" get priority?
The provisional government headed by Friedrich Ebert decided in
favor of completing the "political revolution" through making a new
constitution for the Germans and carrying out an administrative
reform. It was no coincidence that the Constituent National Assembly was meeting at Weimar to draft a constitution for the German
Commonwealth. Weimar stood for the "other Germany," for the Germany of Goethe and Schiller, of Kant and Wilhelm von Humboldt.
The new German Republic should, in the words of Friedrich Ebert,
breathe "the spirit of Weimar, the spirit of true humanity." The fathers
and mothers of the Weimar Constitution of 1919 also wished to com-
bine the ideas and traditions of 1789 and 1848–49 with Bismarck's
Germany. The politicians of the so-called Weimar coalition—formed
by the SPD, the liberal parties, and the Center Party—who represented the majority in the National Assembly, were the protagonists
of democratic principles and of the unitary national state. Thus, as in
1848–49 and later on in 1948–49, the Weimar National Assembly
was confronted with the question of whether the new German Commonwealth should remain a "federated state," whether Germany
should become a "unitary state" like France, or whether the Assembly should decide on an intermediate solution. There were strong supporters, however, of becoming a unitary state. They argued that
before the war the de facto constitution of the Empire had already
shown strong unitary tendencies. These tendencies were strengthened during the war, and the state of Germany after defeat and revolution demanded a unitary state in order to counter separatist
movements, which had shown themselves in several parts of Germany, and to deal with the financial burdens Germany was facing as
a result of the war. Therefore, they were convinced that the best
means "to save Germany" was to build up a unitary state that would
concentrate all powers in the hands of the central government and
thus "diminish to the greatest possible measure the powers of the
member states" (Brunet 1922: 42). They underscored the advantages
of this type of state which "possesses an undivided and exclusive sovereignty. There is unity of law, of power and of will with one Constitution, one administration and one authority" (Brunet 1922: 40).

In the wake of the first meeting of the Constituent National Assembly, President Ebert expressed his views on establishing a constitution

with a strong role for the central government, against German traditions and sentiments, in an interview for the *Frankfurter Zeitung*. He
admitted that drawing up a new German constitution "will be a difficult piece of work":

> For the remaking of the Empire will involve the demolition of a great
> deal which is entwined with the heart of the individual German on
> grounds of history and sentiment. We, more than any nation, are
> attached to what is traditional. Centuries of the system of small states
> have demonstrated this fact, as we know to our cost. But the revolution
> would forfeit its most precious and most necessary results, if it did not
> clear away in the domain of the State things that have only served dynas-
> tic interests and which were, so to speak, preserved in the interests of the
> separate power of some sovereign House. In the new German Republic,
> the only things peculiar to the different branches of the German people
> that ought to be preserved are those things which are of real value, but
> not any harmful particularism that would be perpetuated at the expense
> of the whole body politic. By "particularism" I mean in this sense both
> the selfish interests of a small Federal State and lust of domination and
> of hegemony on the part of a Great State. "Neither anarchy nor hege-
> mony"—that must be the watchword of the new Germany. (cit. PRO
> Cabinet 24/75 1919)

In his interview, Ebert touched on all the prejudices and emotional antipathies of the supporters of the unitary state, who after
World War II would blame the federalists for having furthered the
advent of Hitler in 1933. Yet it was quite clear from the beginning
that it was impossible to establish a unitary German republic. Most
of the former states of the Empire were transformed in the period of
revolution into democratic free states with democratically elected
parliaments and governments. Despite the tendencies, even in the
Commission of Representatives from the States meeting in late January 1919 to merge all German states into a single great republic,
there were still strong state feelings and regional identities—in the
sense of historical landscapes—that made it necessary to find a compromise in the constitution of the German Commonwealth between
the wish for a strong and effective central government and the sovereign rights of the German States. It was true that the sovereign
rights of the dynastic houses had been demolished by the November
Revolution at the end of the monarchical system, but the States continued to live on despite German defeat and revolution. They never

surrendered their sovereignty to the new Commonwealth. It was argued that sovereignty in the free states as well as in the Common-wealth emanated directly from the people. The states were also masters of their state territory. Thus, any new German constitution agreed on had to implement some kind of federal structure.

In the process of constitution making, the National Assembly had to discuss its proposals with the Commission of the States. It had to accept the "principle of Land representation" (Dorondo 1992: 6). The outcome of the deliberations of the Constituent National Assembly "bears throughout the stamp of *compromises*" (Brunet 1922). Never-theless, the Weimar Constitution which was passed on 31 July 1919, established a Commonwealth "as unitary as possible without sup-pressing every trace of the federal regime" (Brunet 1922: 201).

Thus, the Weimar Constitution was more unitary than the Con-stitution of Paul's Cathedral in 1849. As in 1849 it was impossible to eliminate all federal elements, but despite the fact that the Preuss plan did not succeed in splitting up Prussia and dissolving the smaller states, the Commonwealth had constitutional means to force changes or exchanges of territory, fusions of states, or parceling of states. The Weimar Constitution departed from the constitutional organization of the German Confederation and the German Empire of 1871 which guaranteed the historic composition of its state mem-bers. It put forward the "principle of the mobility of frontiers." Article 18 of the Constitution acknowledged the right of the Common-wealth (Reich) to force territorial changes for the common welfare of the German nation.

Many of the States—Länder, as they were now called—were dis-satisfied with the provisions of the Constitution for the new German Commonwealth concerning the relationship between the German "Länder" and the Commonwealth. From the "Länder" point of view they also derived their "Political authority … from the People," and Article 2 of the Constitution ruled that the "territory of the Com-monwealth consists of the territories of the German States." Com-pared to German political federal traditions and their status in the Federal Council of the German Empire, the rights assigned to the Ger-man Länder in the Council of the Commonwealth ("Reichsrat" Sec-tion IV, Articles 60–67) were dramatically reduced, especially as far as state legislation, the financial constitution of the Commonwealth, and the participation in law making were concerned. Conflicts were

programmed between both levels if necessary changes were not realized, for, as Brunet remarked, "in this edifice [i.e., the Weimar Consti-
tution] all parts are mutually interdependent, and the whole will not
endure unless the parts are solid. The downfall of any of them will
drag down the others" (Brunet 1922: 291). Because of the strong unitary elements in the political, social, and economic system of Weimar
Germany, a debate started early on regarding a territorial reconstruction of the German Commonwealth that would utilize to the maximum the productive energy and resources of Germany. The battle
between centralists and federalists was renewed. Should the outcome
of the reform of the Commonwealth (*Reichsreform*) be a unitary republic that would take away all powers from the member states and transfer them to the status of provinces that solely had to execute the laws
of the central government? Or should the Commonwealth become a
federation of German states (*Bund deutscher Länder*) with an equal
distribution of powers of jurisdiction between the institutions of the
Commonwealth and the institutions of the federal states? Germany
would change from a unitary state with a few "traces of a federal
regime" into a federation of the federal type (*Bundesstaat des föderativen Typs*). The lifetime of Weimar Germany was too short to deal successfully with serious reform (cf. Brecht 1945: 73ff.; Gruner 1999a:
309ff.). The traumatic experiences of World War I and the political
developments of the republic in the 1920s and early 1930s as well as
the impact of international politics confirmed Brunet's caveats that a
"legal document" is "worth little unless it accommodates itself to the
realities for which it is created, unless, too, it is strong enough to resist
the thrusts directed against it and to master them" (Brunet 1922:
290). A successful federal polity for Weimar Germany was thwarted.

Constitutional Issues after 1945

Soon after the beginning of World War II, the experience of a highly
centralized regime during the Nazi period led to the question concerning the best political and constitutional organization for Germany. Weimar politicians, academics and intellectuals in exile,
members of the German resistance, and committees set up by the
governments of the coalition against Hitler were discussing possible
options for postwar Germany (see Gruner 1995: 1419ff.). Besides a
"dismemberment of Germany" that was discussed among the Allied

powers at Teheran and Yalta, there was the option of a unitary Germany under a central government as well as a federal or confederal Germany with varying degrees of decentralized administration. There certainly were plans for splitting up Germany into a number of separate states, such as the Morgenthau plan, the Churchill plan, and the Stalin plan. The post-hostilities committees, however, especially in Britain, favored as early as 1943 German unity as the lesser evil and supported a "dismemberment of Prussia" instead. For historical and European reasons, Great Britain and the United States opted for some kind of federal political system for postwar Germany, because federalism was seen as the "natural political constitution for Germany" and because after the experience of a centralized state during the Nazi period, the Germans would be in favor of a federal system. The view prevailed, however, "that any internal reorganization of Germany can be carried out only by the German people themselves" (PRO F.O. 371/34460 1943).

It was quite clear that the German people had to accept the new political and constitutional organization. Because of effective Nazi propaganda, the Weimar system had been discredited. Perhaps it was true that the Western-style Weimar Constitution was too modern for the Germans and that there was a lack of experience of "political democracy" at the national level. From this perspective it would make sense to build up a new democratic system in Germany from the roots, that is, to further German traditions of self-government, which were strong in those regions of Germany that had long-standing constitutional traditions and which in the early nineteenth century had experienced the transition from a society of subjects to a society of citizens. Influenced by German experts in exile working in Allied "think tanks" and the plans of the German resistance, a strong tendency developed to build the foundations for a strong German democracy organized on federal principles (cf. Brecht 1945: 132ff.; Gruner 1999a: 318ff.; Gruner 1998: 60ff.).

This is not the place to discuss in detail Allied ideas for the future constitutional framework for Germany, but we can state that the Western Allies for various reasons were more in favor of a federal structure for postwar Germany, whereas the Soviet Union supported the concept of "democratic centralism." When the Allied cooperation in the Control Council for Germany was suspended, every occupying power tried to establish its concept of the state in its zone of occupation.

After the statement of the London conference of the foreign secretaries of the four Allied powers in December 1947 in which they agreed not to agree on their German policy, the pace for setting up a German state in the East and a German state in the West accelerated. In the Soviet zone of occupation the constitutional committee of the People's Congress for Unity and Just Peace (Volkskongress für Freiheit und gerechten Frieden) drafted an all-German constitution that was published on 18 March 1948, as the constitution of the German Democratic Republic (cf. Müller 1999: 235ff.; Gruner 1999a: 326ff.).

In the West after the breakup of the conferences of the Allied foreign secretaries, there was a reform of the bi-zonal institutions. The London Six-Powers-Conference, consisting of the United States, Britain, France, and the Benelux countries, agreed in June 1948 on the so-called London Recommendations to create a West German state. These recommendations were handed over to the German prime ministers on 1 July 1948, as the so-called Frankfurt Documents. These asked the German Länder to set up a Constituent National Assembly to draft a constitution, to redraw the state boundaries in Germany, and to establish a functioning federal system for postwar Germany. The outcome was the Basic Law (*Grundgesetz*) for the Federal Republic of Germany enacted on 24 May 1949.

Like the constitution of the German Democratic Republic, it was conceived as an all-German constitution. It claimed to speak for those parts of Germany that were not allowed to participate in the process of drafting a democratic and federal constitution. Thus, it provided in Article 23 that other parts of Germany could join the Federal Republic. This first occurred when the Saarland joined the Federal Republic in 1957 and again when the Länder of the GDR joined the Federal Republic on 3 October 1990. The preamble of the Basic Law also asked the Germans to work for the unification of the German nation *and* for European unity.

The Basic Law was the result of the intentions of the Western Allies that there should be a democratic and federal German republic, because they believed "that the idea of the return to federalism would appear to the German people as emanating from themselves and not imposed by the foreign conqueror" (PRO F.O. 371/34460 1943:2). In the process of constitution making, however, it was a difficult task to find the right way between Allied intervention in favor of federalism and accepting the will of the Germans to find a new internal reorganization for postwar Germany (see Feldkamp 1999: 26ff.; Grabbe 1978: 396ff.).

At the end of World War II, there was a totally different situation for Germany compared to 1815, 1848–49, 1871, and 1919. There was almost no room for the Germans and Europeans to maneuver. Nevertheless, between 1945 and 1949 there was a public exchange on the future constitution of Germany and of a United Europe. Would the German, European, or American federal traditions prevail in reconstructing Germany and Europe? In the German case, old battles from the Weimar period were fought again. Ever since the end of World War II, there were discussions among the German constitutional experts and postwar German politicians, who had their political roots in Weimar Germany, as to the best constitutional framework for a new and democratic Germany and how a new Germany could be best integrated in a united Europe. The federalists were pleading for a reformed and democratic "German Confederation" that would become part of a "Federation of European States" (see IfZGM Hoegner 1945; Gruner 1995: 1420ff.). The protagonists of the unitary state such as Otto Grotewohl (Grotewohl 1947: 85ff.) and Wolfram von Hanstein (Hanstein 1947: 5ff.) argued that the German constitutional question could be decided only in favor of a "unitary German state" (Gruner 1995: 1449ff.). The majority of the SPD was also in favor of some kind of unitary state. By 1947, however, the SPD had generally come around to supporting a constitution that established a decentralized government (SPD Parteitag 1947: 225). The CDU generally supported a unitary state, but Christian Democrats in the South favored a federal republic.

In August 1949 the Bavarian government invited experts and politicians to the Herrenchiemseer Verfassungskonvent. The convention started its discussions with a Bavarian proposal for a Basic Law (BHStAM StK 10010—Bayerische Leitgedanken) and prepared a draft proposal for the Parliamentary Council (BHStAM StK 10012—Entwurf Grundgesetz). The exchange of views and the majority and minority votes on many sections showed the wide spectrum of positions between federal and unitary solutions to the constitutional question. The distribution of votes in the Parliamentary Council was in favor of a more unitary constitution for West Germany. The Basic Law created a German federation with strong unitary features concerning the distribution of powers between the federation and the member states, that is, a unitary federation (*unitarischer Bundesstaat*). This was especially true of the financial constitution, the competences of the federation and the Länder, the right of the Länder to conclude treaties, and the role of the Bundesrat in the constitutional system of the Federal Republic. Despite its deficits which would become apparent within a few years after its enactment, the Basic Law was passed by an impressive majority because of the international situation in the spring of 1949 and because of the wish of the members of the Parliamentary Council to find a broad consensus for the future constitution.

Germany and Europe

After 1948–49 we can see the beginning of an integration process in Eastern and Western Europe, in which each German state became a part of a divided continent. For the neighbors of the Germanys, the German problem was not solved by the foundation of two states. Since the partition of Germany along a military frontier was unnatural and, moreover, unhistoric, the possibility of an eventual unification was an option that played an important role in German policy. In the case of France, for example, German policy after 1945 became European policy and security policy in the process of the integration of the Western democracies and the integration of the Eastern European states into the hegemonic system of the Soviet Union. Given their historic experience with Germany's quest for European hegemony, it had been in the interests of other European states to agree on checks and balances to contain Germany, divided or reunited, within a European framework. From this point of view it was also important that West Germany was a federal state and that a future united Germany would have a federal political system.

It was also quite clear that a reconstruction and revival of Europe without Germany was impossible. Thus, within a decade the Federal Republic of Germany became a member of the Council of Europe and played an important role in the foundation of the European Coal and Steel Community (ECSC 1951) and the establishment of the European Economic Community (EEC) and the European Atomic Community (Euratom) through the Treaties of Rome (1957). Together with France, the Federal Republic played an active role in the process of European integration beyond the sphere of economics by establishing the European Communities (EC) and widening the political and security responsibilities of the members of the EC through the Single European Act, European Political Cooperation (EPC), and support for EC Commission President Jacques Delors's vision of "Europe 92." On the other hand, the attempts to form a European Defense Community (EDC) and a European Political Community between 1952 and 1954 failed—to some extent because of the problem of Germany.

Since the early 1950s, West Germany has been one of the major protagonists for (western) European integration. This was a result of its economic and political interests. Sitting at the table as an equal partner in negotiations was important for the German federal government in order to regain as much sovereignty as possible. Because of the unsolved national question, the Bonn government in all its European activities and negotiations had to safeguard German interests in any transnational European organization. Thus, Walter Hallstein, then undersecretary of state for foreign affairs, in reading the declaration of the Federal Government to the Bundestag, referred to the "deplorable fact that Germany is integrated into the new European community burdened with the political mortgage of forced division. But it is also true that no German federal government, irrespective of its composition, will ever approve of a deepening of German division" (*Bulletin* 1957: 475).

Early in the European integration process one problem came to the fore that is still a topic in German domestic politics, namely the role, the rights, and the responsibilities of the German Länder in the process of European integration (see Udo Diedrichs and Elisabeth Dette-Koch, chapters 8 and 9, this volume). When the Basic Law was proclaimed, those who were engaged in the drawing up of the constitution, as well as the Western occupying powers, did not realize the long-term consequences of the "constitutional compromise" for the rights, jurisdiction and competences of the Länder and the Federation on European issues and the process of integrating the member states of the ECSC, EEC, Euratom, EC, and EU into a community. The Federal Republic was the only federal state involved when the European process of integrating the European democracies started in the early 1950s. The Basic Law gave to the Federation the right to conclude international treaties, which was a minor problem for the Länder when West Germany joined the Council of Europe.

But already at this point the Länder were asking for the same right as the Bundestag to be equally represented in the Consultative Assembly of the Council of Europe (see Gruner 1999b: 203ff.).

This changed, however, when the federal government negotiated the treaty for the European Coal and Steel Community. From the point of view of the Länder, this was a treaty that had a direct impact on the rights and jurisdiction of the German Länder (see Gruner 2001: 38ff.). In 1951–52 the Länder did not succeed in their efforts to be informed in advance and to participate directly in negotiations at the European level. Ever since the battle for the ratification of the ECSC treaty, the Länder improved their position in the triangle composed of European institutions, federal government, and Länder.

The new Article 23 of the Basic Law is vital from this perspective. It would not have come about in the way it did if the Länder had not been able to put pressure on the federal government to improve their constitutional position in European Union affairs. The Bundesrat had to ratify the Treaty of Maastricht by a two-thirds majority. Thus, the Länder could negotiate a better position in European affairs. In the process the Federal Republic of Germany shifted to some extent from the status of a "unitary" federation toward a more "federal" federation. Nevertheless, the future of the German Länder in an EU setting is not guaranteed as long as the question of the levels of governance is not solved, for example, according to the principle of subsidiarity.

In any case, it seems from the European viewpoint of German politics that the Länder could improve their position vis-à-vis the federation, a position that had declined since the late 1950s. The Federation in the course of the 1960s took over responsibilities from the German Länder in the areas of social legislation, higher education, and university planning and financing, for example, and strengthened its position by passing emergency legislation (*Notstandsgesetzgebung*). These measures had reduced the jurisdiction of the Länder and affected the financial constitution of the Federal Republic. This had been made possible, however, by the readiness of the German Länder governments to vote in favor of constitutional changes that strengthened the position of the federal institutions (Scharpf 1994: 47ff.). This process was accompanied by a public debate on the role of federalism and the necessity to move toward cooperative federalism (Gruner 1992: 309ff.; Hesse 1962: 10–41).

Today the German Länder are searching for their appropriate role in the process of further deepening of the EU. How can the principle of subsidiarity at the European level be best applied? In the proposals and discussions leading to the 1996–97 Intergovernmental Conference, it was argued by the Committee of the Regions that Article 3b of the Maastricht treaty could be implemented only if the Committee of the Regions would receive a status equal to the Commission, the Council, the Parliament, the European Court, and the Court of Auditors. This demand is still on the European agenda for institutional reform.

From my point of view, the improved constitutional position of the Länder in European affairs has contributed since 1994 to the debate regarding the "finality" of the European integration process. What will be the German contribution to a reformed EU that would be able to live up to its European and global responsibilities for the peoples of Europe? There was a lively German debate on Europe at the federal level and among the major parties (Große Hüttmann and Knodt 2000: 33ff.) that was started by the so-called Lamers-Schäuble Strategy Paper of the CDU/CSU Parliamentary Group of the German Bundestag (*Bulletin Quotidien Europe* 1994: 7.9; *Debatte* 1955: 11ff.) in September 1994, which dealt with German interests and the best means to make progress in the process of European integration. This paper could be seen as an answer to French Prime Minister Baladur's ideas of a "Europe of different speeds" (*Bulletin Quotidien Europe* 1994: 3.9), of "widening" and "deepening" the EU and how to reform its institutions. The SPD contributed ideas on "differentiating" while "integrating" (Friedrich-Ebert-Stiftung 1995; Gruner 2003: 49–50).

When the Treaty of Amsterdam in 1997 did not bring about the expected progress in reforming the EU, the debate was renewed in the spring of 2000 and is still under way. The major contribution came from German and French politicians. In his private speech to students at Berlin's Humboldt University, Foreign Minister Joschka Fischer presented his ideas on the final stage of European integration. He argued that enlargement was in Germany's interest, since it was a "unique opportunity to unite our continent ... in peace, security, democracy and prosperity" (Fischer 2000: 8). In order to be able to act, however, the EU would have to reform its institutions that were created for six member states and were not suitable for an enlarged EU of thirty members. He spoke up against "the existing concept of a federal European state replacing the old nation-states," which from his point of view would be "an artificial construct which ignores the established realities in Europe." It would be "an irreparable mistake in the construction of Europe" to try to "complete political integration against the existing national institutions and traditions rather than by involving them." He envisaged a "division of sovereignty between Europe and the nation-state" and therefore proposed a two-chamber European Parliament. The "Chamber of States" could be established according to the model of the German Bundesrat or along the lines of the U.S. Senate. Fischer also provided two options for the "European executive." This position could be created through a reform of the European Council or the European Commission. The last step in the completion of the integration process would be a "European Federation."[1] To achieve this the EU will need a 'constituent treaty' as a precondition of 'full integration.' This, however, will require a deliberate political act to reestablish Europe."

In his speech to the German Bundestag, French President Jacques Chirac set other priorities and rejected the idea of a European superstate. The future Europe should be a union of the European nation-states that would distribute jurisdiction at the different European levels and would develop a "Power Europe," making Europe fit to act effectively at an international level. In the process of the construction of this kind of Europe, France and Germany should take on the role as an "avant-garde" (Chirac 2000). In the wake of the Nice summit, the question of an obligatory Charter of Fundamental Rights for the European Union, which should become part of a European Constitution, was discussed.

German Federal President Johannes Rau, in his speech to the European Parliament on 4 April 2001, made a "plea for a European constitution." It will be the task of the European Parliament and all of the other European institutions to make the process of integration more transparent and to answer the questions of the citizens, such as:

- How can we organize the European Union in such a way that citizens can find their way around it better?

---

1. There is no precise definition for "federation" in Fischer's speech. The German text refers to "*Föderation.*"

- What must we do to ensure that decisions made by the European Union have a broader legitimacy at the European level?
- What, finally, should the organizational framework look like (Rau 2001: 4)?

Despite the fact that President Rau spoke in favor of a federal system for the EU, he talked about a "European Federation of nation-states." To some extent this was because he wished to avoid the impression that he was pleading in favor of a "Europe 'à la Federal Republic of Germany.'" For him, the transformation of Europe "into a federation of nation-states ... will enhance the democratic legitimacy for joint action while, at the same time, safeguarding the competences of the nation-states which they want to and indeed should maintain" (Rau 2001: 5). He demanded a "Charter of Fundamental Rights" that should have binding power. A European constitution

> must divide competences between the member states on the one hand and the European Union on the other with the necessity of clarity. It would thus largely determine the relationship between the member states and the Federation. We should endeavor to anchor the principle of subsidiarity on a broader basis: only those matters should be decided at European level which the member states cannot better deal with themselves. That must be the guiding principle! (Rau 2001: 6)

President Rau also proposed a "genuine bicameral parliament"— the Chamber of States. The former Council of Ministers would be responsible for preserving the nation-states' sovereignty, and a directly elected European Parliament would serve as the "Citizens' Chamber." For the election of the president of the EU Commission, he had two models in mind:

- the election of the president of the Commission directly by the people, or
- the election of the president of the Commission by the two chambers of parliament (Rau 2001: 7).

President Rau's approach toward a future constitution of the EU member states is based on German constitutional and federal traditions. Federal chancellor Gerhard Schröder, in his proposal for the SPD Party rally in Nürnberg in November 2001 (Schröder 2001a) and in his speech to the German Bundestag, "Do we need less Europe or more Europe?" (Schröder 2001b) also argued along these lines. There should be a two-chamber system for the EU and a strengthening of the national parliaments that should play a prominent role in the network as well. The European Parliament should get more power and the Commission should become a strong executive (Schröder 2001b).

The reactions to the German initiatives and contributions to the debate about the institutional framework of the EU were positive in some quarters, but were rejected by Great Britain (Blair 2001) and France (Jospin 2001). Nevertheless, in spite of an occasional relapse toward a national position, Germany is and has been, since Walter Hallstein's plea for a European Federation in the 1950s, a strong protagonist of a federal solution for the final stage of European integration. The former federal president and constitutional lawyer, Roman Herzog, in his speech to the European Parliament on 10 October 1995, reminded the members of the diversity of the European regions and the fact that ever since Greek and Roman times Europe has seen itself "as a single entity beyond the mere geographical definition" (Herzog 1998: 42). From his perspective as a scholar trained in constitutional law, he was highly supportive of

a political system that begins with the letter "F" but which of late has become taboo in European debate.... Nonetheless, I still consider that system—the one which begins with "F"—to be the best history has ever had to offer.... Federalism ... is, after all, the opposite of centralism. Indeed, as exemplified in Germany's postwar history, it can almost be said to be a method of decentralization. For this reason our Anglo-Saxon Europeans need not be put off. The fact that the arch centralist Alexander Hamilton ... founded a party in 1791 that he called the "Federalist Party" can be blamed only on Hamilton, but not on federalism. On the other hand, federal decision-making procedures ensure the rationality and effectiveness that have always been at the heart of the great French political tradition. There is nothing to stop nation-states from forming a federation and still remaining nation-states. Europe as a "motherland of motherlands" has always rung true in the ears of federalists, too. For it was not the advocates of German particularism who first spoke of a "United States of Europe" ... but such great Frenchmen as Saint Simon and Victor Hugo.... [N]othing compels the members of the European Union to opt for, say, the Swiss, the American or the German federal system. And there is undoubtedly the reassuring alternative of coming up with a totally different model. (Herzog 1998: 44f.)

German policy aiming at the completion of European integration has become more active since the broadening of the participation in German European policy by including the German Länder in the process. Thus, German unification and the debate on the rights and jurisdiction of the federation and the Länder in European affairs, as well as the discussion on "competitive federalism," has initiated a process of transformation and innovation as well as self-assertiveness that contributed much to thinking about an effective and federal reform of the institutions of the EU. The German debate on adopting federalism to the needs of the present and preparing it for a European future may have a fruitful impact on the debate on how to construct a functioning and effective future European Union.

More than a decade after the fall of the Berlin Wall, Germany presents herself as a sensitive and creative player in the European debate on the final stage of the EU. German views range from a European confederation to a European federation of nation-states. These debates today are similar to those in nineteenth- and twentieth-century Germany. We do not know yet what the outcome of the debates will be on European institutional reform, the drafting of a European constitution, and the future institutional shape of an enlarged Europe. There has been a deep process of transformation and change taking place not only in Germany, but also all over Europe since the end of the Cold War. The new Germany is still facing the dual challenge and task of working for the integration of the new Federal Republic of Germany and strongly engaging in promoting the process of European integration and the establishment of a European Union that will live up to its European and global responsibilities. Because of Germany's historic federal traditions—which form a part of European and American traditions—and the fact that "living federalism" is never static, Germany will be able to make a major contribution in convincing her partners in the EU that a political system, based on the "F" word, will be the right path for the European Union to take even if many member states of the EU and future members of an enlarged European Union are not yet prepared to give up the nation-state. German history proves that there can be a nation-state without giving up a federal political system.

Thus, we may see a Europe in the years to come that will appreciate the advantages of a federal form of government which would allow for the adoption of a multilevel system that would assign, according to the principle of subsidiarity, the tasks that the responsible European institutions at the respective European levels of governance will have to fulfill. The German Länder have successfully worked for a precise definition of the principle of subsidiarity, which was realized by the Annex 21 (protocol) to the Treaty of Amsterdam. The German historical experience from the old Reich to the emerging new Germany may serve as a stimulating example for reflection, implementation, improvement, and innovation at a European level and for establishing a multilevel system of governance for Europe.

Chapter 2

ON THE MISERY OF THE GERMAN FINANCIAL CONSTITUTION

~

Gisela Färber

Introduction

The German financial constitution was reformed for the last time more than thirty years ago in 1969–70. It remained almost unchanged after the unification of the two German states in 1990, although at that time there was an intense debate about the further need for reform. A fundamental reform was required, particularly with concern for the consolidation process necessary to save public money in order to restructure the economy of the new eastern Länder and to get a better position in the globalized economic competition. The problems of the interconnected political decision-making processes as well as diverging financial interests of federal and state governments caused a failure of all reforms in 1993. At that time the governments had negotiated and agreed to integrate the new Länder into the fiscal equalization scheme. However, except for marginal changes, for example, concerning the formula of horizontal transfer payments, the whole system remained unchanged. On the other hand, since 1995, the date when the "new" fiscal equalization scheme began, the horizontal and vertical payments, particularly those in favor of the extremely poor new Länder have multiplied.

In 1998 Baden-Württemberg and Bavaria along with Hesse 1999, started a proceeding before the Federal Constitutional Court. They wanted the Court to determine whether the fiscal equalization regime was constitutional. The Court decision in November 1999 required a separation of the general rules of fiscal equalization and the details of execution until the end of 2002. The difficulties of the political negotiations that had just begun again prevented a far-reaching reform of the financial constitution. In June 2001 federal and state governments succeeded in agreeing, as usual, to a marginally changed fiscal equalization scheme. Important politicians in the governing parties of the federal government, however, promised that after the next elections in 2002 they would attend to the difficult task of reforming the whole fiscal constitution.

For foreigners—even if they come from other federal states—it is very difficult to understand the particular arrangements of German federalism (for detailed descriptions in English, see Gunlicks 2000; Larsen 1999). It follows a special type of federalism that is called administrative federalism and otherwise exists only in Austria. Some features are also recognizable in the "constitution" of the European Union, where the "second chamber" is formed by the Council of Ministers which represents the governments of the member states rather than elected parliaments or senates. In Germany as well as in Austria, the second chamber, or Bundesrat, consists of members of the state governments. Furthermore, the federal government has only a small administration of its own. In general, federal laws are executed by the Länder. These particularities provide special arrangements also in the financial constitution, which will be presented in the following sections. In the conclusion, a short summary of the specific actual problems of financial policies in Germany is outlined (for recent discussions of German fiscal federalism, see Färber 1999, 2001).

The Rules and Details of the German Financial Constitution

The rules of intergovernmental financial relations are fixed in a special chapter of the German Basic Law. This can be interpreted as a confirmation of the importance given to that subject. This standpoint is also a traditional one, because even in 1919, after World War I when the Weimar Republic was in its early stages, Max Weber emphasized: "The financial relations in a federal state are the most decisive factors determining its real structures" (Weber 1919: 37).

Section X of the Basic Law contains, in addition to the rules of intergovernmental relations, regulations for the federal budget, the Federal Accounting Court, and the limits of public debt, which are in a similar way also contained in the state constitutions. The articles concerning intergovernmental relations follow the logic of academic public finance: Article 104a starts with regulations for spending competences, Articles 105–106 deal with taxation competences, Article 107 with vertical and horizontal fiscal equalization, and Article 108 with tax administration. In general, public finance includes the division of financial responsibilities among the federal tiers. These rules are given in Sections VII and VIII, which deal with federal legislation and the execution of federal laws. In 1969–70 a new section, VIIIa, was introduced into the Basic Law establishing the rules of "joint tasks," which have special arrangements also concerning financial aspects. Following the logic of fiscal federalism, the German financial constitution will be explained now in four steps. Each step establishes particular features that lead to needs of special construction with the next steps: (1) the distribution of legal responsibilities; (2) the distributions of spending competences; (3) the distribution of taxation competences; and (4) the vertical and horizontal fiscal equalization scheme.

It has to be mentioned that local governments in Germany, like their American counterparts, do not have the legal status of states. Therefore, they do not represent a federal tier from the legal point of view. But they do from a functional perspective, and the Basic Law provides in Article 28 a special protection for the rights and autonomy of local governments as well as their financial autonomy. In the constitutional regulation of intergovernmental financial relations, local governments are only mentioned on the periphery. They are treated as parts of their Länder.

Division of Responsibilities among the Federal Tiers in the German Constitution

In the area of legislative competences, or powers, the German federal system also provides special constructions that are not usual in other federal states. Based on historical reasons, the Allies after World War II did not want the federal government to be the dominating federal tier. They required the Parliamentary Council, which wrote the Basic Law, to establish the Länder as the central elements of the German state. Thus, Article 70 of the Basic Law gives the legislative competence in general to the Länder governments. The Federation has only an exceptional legislative competence, which is divided into:

- an exclusive legislative competence concerning a certain number of explicitly enumerated subjects (e.g., foreign affairs, German citizenship, regulation of passports, immigration, emigration, currency issues, domestic money, weights and measures, etc.) in Article 73 of the Basic Law, and
- a concurrent legislative competence again for a certain number of functionally determined and explicitly enumerated subjects in Article 74 BL; Article 74a BL adds the regulation of salaries and the special civil servants' pension scheme to the subjects of the concurrent legislation.

The federal government can only assume the concurrent legislative competence in these fields if there is a need for federal regulation because state governments are not able to provide an effective regulation, or because the regulation of a state could interfere with the interests of other Länder or of the nation as a whole, or because the protection of the legal or economic unity or the equivalence of living conditions would require the federal regulation (Article 72 [2] BL).

A third and particular legislative competence is regulated in Article 75 BL, which gives the federal government the right to establish general frameworks for certain subjects that limit the legislative powers of the Länder. The subjects concern the public service employees of state and local governments; university administration; press and film affairs; hunting, nature, and land conservation; and the distribution of land, land use planning, and water resource management.

With regard to the execution of federal laws, the Basic Law gives the general competence to the Länder. They are responsible for executing federal laws (Article 83 BL). Although the federal government has the competence to pass general rules for administration, the approval of the Bundesrat is then needed. State governments pass their own laws with all regulatory details for the establishment of authorities and administrative procedures for the execution of federal laws (Article 84 BL). The government is not allowed to intervene directly in the state administrative process. It only has the right to appeal to the Bundesrat when there are doubts about the conformity of a state's administration of a federal law. A direct intervention is only possible concerning a very few subjects that are under a special type of state administration on behalf of the Federation (Article 85 BL).

Therefore, the Federation only has a small administrative capacity. The largest number of public employees work in the administration of the armed forces. The larger administrative agencies are established at the state level, and the most important field of public employment concerns the states' own responsibilities, that is, school teachers, police, tax administration, and universities. Local governments play the most important role in the field of local public infrastructure institutions. They also execute federal and state laws, partly under very strict regulations. They have a large responsibility for social administration, because they have to administer the federal law on social assistance.

Finally, a special type of joint responsibility should be mentioned: Articles 91a and b BL. These two amendments were introduced into the Basic Law in 1969–70 to establish a joint responsibility of both tiers for the subjects of enlargement and new construction of universities (including university hospitals), the improvement of the regional economic structure, the improvement of the agricultural structure, and coast preservation. Joint responsibilities are also determined for the field of educational planning and the promotion of research institutions. Here special institutions are established, of which half of the board members are nominated by the federal government and the other half by state governments. They take all important decisions under special majority rules, which secure that no tier can outvote the other.

Spending Competences

In federal states in general it is assumed that those jurisdictions that are responsible for a certain task and pass the necessary regulations would be responsible for the costs of execution. The special case of administrative federalism works differently from that model. Article 104a (1) BL says that federal and state governments have to cover the costs of carrying out their responsibilities; however, the spending competence is not linked with the legislative competence but with the executive competence. Therefore, state governments have to finance the expenditures resulting from the execution of federal laws. Not so strictly, but in a similar way, local governments have to cover the costs of administering federal and state laws.

The Basic Law also indicated the exception from that general rule in Article 104a (2–4) BL.

- The costs resulting from state administration on behalf of the federal government are covered by the federal budget.
- Federal laws providing financial transfers that are executed by state administrations can provide that the federal government carry the costs totally or partly. In those cases where the federal government bears 50 percent or more of the expenditures, state administration is on behalf of the federal government.
- The federal government can financially support state governments in favor of particularly important investment projects that are necessary to counter an economic imbalance, or to provide compensation for a decline in economic capacity, or to promote economic growth.

The types of local responsibilities differ slightly among the Länder, as do the rules about how to cover the costs which result from a delegation of state responsibilities to local administration. Some state governments pay direct compensation, whereas others cover the burdens in the context of local financial equalization schemes. Costs resulting from original local administration competences, such as the general social assistance expenditures, are not repaid. Recently, some state constitutional courts have established stronger requirements that local expenditures resulting from state legislation have to be covered by true compensation rules.

Division of Taxation Competences

The patterns of interconnected legislative and administrative competences are continued in the field of taxation competences. These can be divided into legislative, revenue, and administrative competences.

The division of *legislative competences* is regulated in the following way (Article 105 BL).

- The federal tier has the exclusive legislative competence for customs and financial monopolies.

- It also has the concurrent competence for which it receives the revenues and with which the conditions of Article 72 (3) BL comply. These conditions apply to the field of taxation on the legal and economic unity in Germany, which was valued more highly by the members of the Parliamentary Council than an autonomous taxation right of state governments.
- The approval of the Bundesrat is required in those cases where state or local governments receive the tax revenues.
- State governments have the legislative competence for some minor local consumption and expenditure taxes (such as the dog tax and tax on second homes).

Actually, the Federation has centralized all legislative competences. Even the tax bases and rates of local taxes on real estate types A and B (see below) and the trade tax on gross enterprise gains are regulated by federal laws. The payroll tax and the enterprise capital tax, that formerly were part of the trade tax, were abolished by federal law. Local governments, however, have the constitutionally secured right to determine multipliers that are applied to the "raw" tax amount of the taxes mentioned above, which offers the local governments some flexibility in covering the costs of different financial needs among municipalities.

The *revenue competences* are divided in the following way.

- The Federation receives the revenues of:
  - customs and other charges that are revenues of the European Community;
  - the tax on insurance;
  - the solidarity surcharge tax;
  - all excise taxes (on liquors, sparkling wine, coffee, natural gas and mineral oil products, and tobacco) *except the beer tax*; and
  - 50 percent of the trade tax apportionment.
- State governments receive the revenues of:
  - the inheritance tax;
  - the land acquisition tax;
  - the motor vehicle tax;
  - the beer tax;
  - the tax on horse racing and lotteries;

- the fire protection tax;
- the casino tax; and
- the state share of the trade tax apportionment.
- Local governments receive the revenues of:
  - the trade tax (minus the trade tax apportionment);
  - the taxes on real estate (type A on agricultural properties, type B on all other real estate); and
  - the local consumption and expenditure taxes.
  - Furthermore, local governments have the constitutionally fixed right to receive a certain share of the state tax revenues.
- For the most important tax revenues, joint revenue competences are established, that is, the revenues are shared among the levels according to the following rules:
  - personal income tax (42.5 percent federal, 42.5 state, 15 percent local governments);
  - capital income tax (50 percent federal, 50 percent state government);
  - tax on interest revenues at the source (50 percent federal, 50 percent state government);
  - corporate income tax (50 percent federal, 50 percent state government); and
  - goods and services tax in the form of a value-added tax (VAT), which has a flexible key, namely:
    ~ a preshare 1 percent of the 16 percent general VAT rate in favor of the public pension scheme;
    ~ 2.2 percent of the remaining revenue in favor of local governments (as compensation for the losses of revenues from the abolishment of the enterprise capital tax); and
    ~ remaining revenues: 50.5 percent in favor of federal government, 49.5 percent in favor of state governments.

The tax administrative competence generally follows the revenue competence, with a few exceptions.

- The federal tax administration levies the VAT on imports and the beer tax.
- State governments administer—on behalf of the Federation— the tax on insurance, the solidarity surcharge tax, and all joint revenue tax (except VAT on imports).

Table 2.1 Tax Revenues of the Government Tiers in 1999

1999—billions DM	Federal Government	State Government	Local Government	European Union
Own tax revenues	141.28	38.26	60.74	6.23
Shared tax revenues	272.82	283.91	49.44	33.44
Among them:				
personal income tax	120.28	120.28	43.87	
corporate income tax	32.92	32.92	0.00	
VAT	129.40	117.38	5.57	15.91
Trade tax apportionment	2.55	8.13	−10.68	
Share of tax on gasoline	−11.98	11.98	0.00	
Total = 886.12 bil DM	402.12	334.15	110.18	39.67
Share of total	45.4%	37.7%	12.4%	4.5%

Source: Federal Ministry of Finance; author's calculations.

Table 2.1 gives the empirical results of tax revenues of the four federal tiers in 1999.

Fiscal Equalization

Fiscal equalization in Germany is a multilevel procedure. On the one hand, there are fiscal equalization schemes between the federal and the state tiers as well as between the state governments and their respective local governments. On the other hand, each equalization scheme contains vertical and horizontal elements. The vertical elements aim for a financial balance between the two directly involved tiers, whereas the horizontal elements are designed to equalize certain differences among the per capita tax revenues of the jurisdictions of the same tier. It is by itself a multistep procedure that in the end provides a structure for the involved jurisdictions.

More famous and spectacular is the so-called state fiscal equalization scheme, which also contains the vertical and the horizontal equalization elements. It consists of four steps.

1. State and local tax revenues are first divided according to the principles of residence for the personal income tax and the place of production for the corporate income tax. The other taxes are not divided, which means that the revenues remain in the jurisdiction where the tax was levied. The important

exception is the distribution of the Länder share of the VAT revenue, of which 75 percent is distributed according to the number of inhabitants. Regional revenues of the VAT vary widely due to the taxation procedures according to which enterprises are reimbursed for the VAT they have paid for pre-deliveries, as well as the exclusion of exports from the VAT. As the intention of the tax is to apply it to the final purchaser, it was decided in 1969 that the best available indicator for this final stage would be to use per capita data. Therefore, 75 percent of the state VAT revenues are distributed according to the number of inhabitants.

2. The next step is called VAT preequalization. Here the remaining 25 percent of the state share of VAT is used to supplement low state tax capacity to 92 percent of the average for all of the states. If the complete sum of that VAT share is not needed to raise all states to a 92 percent fiscal capacity, the remainder is again distributed according to the number of inhabitants.

3. The third step is the proper horizontal fiscal equalization among the Länder. Here the equalization is undertaken based on the "fiscal capacities" and the "fiscal needs" of the states. Fifty percent of local governments' fiscal capacity is added to the state fiscal capacities. Both indicators—fiscal capacity and fiscal needs—are calculated as follows:

   • the fiscal capacities of the states are their tax revenues (because of the lack of tax autonomy, the revenues indicate the capacity);
   • the local fiscal capacity is calculated under the assumption of average local multipliers for the respective taxes and the exact revenues for the local shares of the personal income tax and of the VAT—only 50 percent of the values are added to the fiscal needs indications of the states;
   • flat sums are subtracted for the harbor costs of Lower Saxony, Hamburg, Schleswig-Holstein, and Mecklenburg-Vorpommern;[1]

1. From a systematic point of view it is not correct to reduce fiscal capacity indicators by special cost factors, but the measure was introduced into the fiscal equalization scheme in the Weimar Republic in the 1920s and has survived until now. After 2005, however, it will be removed by the reforms of 2001 and the harbors will be given 75 million DM, or half of their current subsidy.

- the fiscal needs indicator is derived from the average fiscal capacity per inhabitant and shows deviations of the needs of certain jurisdictions from the average; in general it is 100 percent for each inhabitant in the so-called territorial states and 135 percent for each inhabitant of a city-state (Berlin, Hamburg, Bremen);
- the average local fiscal capacity is transformed into fiscal needs by placing a value on local inhabitants from 100 percent to 130 percent according to the size of the municipality and the density of population; again, only 50 percent of the values are added to the fiscal needs indicators of the states.

Onto these pairs of fiscal indicators the equalization rates are applied. If the fiscal needs indicator is higher than fiscal capacity, a state receives transfers from the other states; in the opposite case, a state has to pay transfers to the poorer states according to the following formulas:

- if the fiscal capacity is less than 92 percent of the fiscal needs, the difference is made up;
- if the fiscal capacity lies between 92 percent and 100 percent of the fiscal needs, 37.5 percent of the amount under 100 percent is made up;
- if the fiscal capacity lies between 100 percent and 101 percent of the fiscal needs, 15 percent of the 1 percent "surplus" has to be paid to the poorer states;
- if the fiscal capacity lies between 101 percent and 110 percent, the "surplus" is "taxed" by a rate of 66 percent; and
- if the fiscal capacity exceeds the fiscal needs by more than 110 percent, 80 percent of the surplus must be given to the poorer states.

The equalization formula is supplemented by a complicated guarantee formula designed to ensure that no state should have a fiscal ranking after fiscal equalization that is different from its previous position.

Figure 2.1 shows the equalization rates and the effects of equalization for fiscal capacities between 85 percent and 115 percent of the fiscal needs indicator. After the horizontal equalization, fiscally weak Länder reach a level of financial capacity of at least 95 percent of the average. A rich state of

Figure 2.1 Marginal Rates of Fiscal Equalization among the States

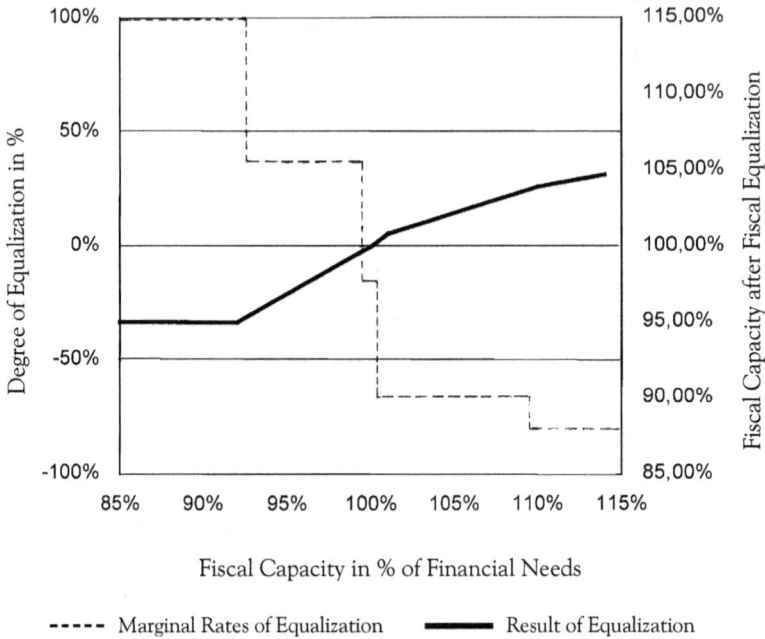

Fiscal Capacity in % of Financial Needs

- - - - - Marginal Rates of Equalization　━━━ Result of Equalization

formerly 115 percent fiscal capacity relative to its fiscal needs still has 105 percent.

Table 2.2 shows the amounts of transfer payments made from 1995 to 1999. There are only a few large Länder making sizeable transfers to the poorer states. The total amount of transfers has increased, although in the meantime important tax reforms were undertaken that—together with weak economic growth—brought about revenue losses. Compared with 1994, when the new Länder had not been included in the fiscal equalization scheme (they had a separate system and Saxony was the most important paying Land among the poor new Länder), the amount of the transfers has exploded while the revenue transfers for the poor western states have decreased. Although the huge differences among the fiscal capacities are based on the fact that the new Länder are subsidized by

Table 2.2 Horizontal Fiscal Equalization, 1995–99, Compared with the Transfers in 1994

In million DM	1995	1996	1997	1998	1999	1994
States obliged to pay:						
North Rhine-Westphalia	3,449	3,125	3,059	3,096	2,578	–156
Bavaria	2,532	2,862	3,102	2,907	3,188	669
Baden-Württemberg	2,803	2,521	2,410	3,477	3,426	410
Hesse	2,153	3,240	3,148	3,439	4,744	1,827
Hamburg	117	482	273	615	665	–61
Schleswig-Holstein	141		5	0.1		–72
States receiving transfers:						
Lower Saxony	452	553	672	788	1,037	958
Rhineland-Palatinate	229	231	296	429	379	657
Schleswig-Holstein		16			174	72
Saarland	180	234	204	228	294	434
Bremen	562	635	350	912	665	568
Berlin	4,222	4,336	4,432	4,891	5,316	
Saxony	1,773	1,965	1,918	1,994	2,149	
Saxony-Anhalt	1,123	1,241	1,175	1,207	1,300	
Thuringia	1,019	1,127	1,123	1,164	1,218	
Brandenburg	864	1,035	986	1,044	1,147	
Mecklenburg-Vorpommern	771	856	843	877	921	
Total	**11,195**	**12,229**	**11,998**	**13,534**	**14,602**	**2,906**

Source: Federal Ministry of Finance, *Finanzbericht 2001* (Berlin, 2000).

significant tax exemptions (degressive deductions and investment subsidies, which are subtracted from the tax liability even up to a negative amount), it can easily be understood that the changes in transfer payments after 1995 put the system under political pressure.

4. The fourth step of German fiscal equalization is based on a vertical financial relationship. The Federation distributes from its tax revenues so-called federal supplementary grants (FSG) according to the following rules:

- deficiency compensating FSG are provided up to 90 percent of the remaining deficient fiscal capacity after horizontal fiscal equalization;
- FSG compensate for above average costs of political leadership, that is, flat sums are given to the small states except Hamburg with a declining amount per inhabitant;

- interim FSG are given to the old fiscally weak Länder (these are decreasing flat sums until 2004 to compensate for the above average losses of this group of states from the last reform in 1995);
- FSG for the special needs of the new Länder are provided in flat sums until 2004;
- FSG are designed for budget consolidation in Bremen and Saarland (flat sums until 2003, mainly for repayment of state debt).

Table 2.3 contains data on the FSG paid in 1999. They amount to almost 26 billion DM, almost twice the sum of the horizontal payments. Although the FSG decrease slightly from year to year because of the decreasing interim and budget consolidation FSG, the financial burden on the federation is tremendous. It is obvious that the most important part of the FSG goes to the new Länder; they are therefore part of the integration process which, however, will take much more time and money than the German governments negotiating the inclusion of the new Länder into the fiscal equalization scheme had expected in spring 1993.

Table 2.3 Federal Supplementary Grants, 1999

FSG in 1999, in mil. DM	Deficiency compensating FSG	FSG for costs of political leadership	Interim FSG for the old poor Länder	Special needs FSG for the new Länder	FSG for budget consolidation
Lower Saxony	1,556		304		
Rhineland-Palatinate	568	219	271		
Schleswig-Holstein	261	164	136		
Saarland	218	153	48		1,200
Bremen	139	126	48		1,800
Berlin	919	219		2,662	
Saxony	910			3,658	
Saxony-Anhalt	540	164		2,208	
Thuringia	498	164		2,008	
Brandenburg	525	164		1,985	
Mecklenburg-Vorpommern	364	164		1,479	
Total	6,497	1,537	807	14,000	3,000

Source: Federal Ministry of Finance, Finanzbericht 2001 (Berlin, 2000).

It is not surprising that a political conflict finally emerged after the change of federal government in autumn 1998 to spring 1999, because the majority of the paying Länder (Baden-Württemberg, Bavaria, Hesse) were then governed by conservative governments, and most of the poor old Länder were governed by the social democrats. Therefore, the conflict was not directed against the "expensive" new Länder but against the "lazy," poor, old Länder that were willing to accept funds rather than attempt to implement a successful economic policy that would generate higher tax revenues. A serious debate about the reasons for the differences in tax capacities has not taken place until now.

This debate would raise important questions: How much of the difference comes from federal tax policies, for example, an uneven distribution of children allowances which are tax reductions since 1998? How much in transfers do the economically strong Länder "save" in case of a higher demand for tax exemptions? What are the regional revenue outcomes of the progressive tax rates of the personal income tax? Does the system of dividing taxes reflect correctly the use of public infrastructure among the production places, or are there justified doubts that, for example, transport industries and banking services including interest payments are not taxed according to the regional origin of the economic values? As long as the fiscal equalization scheme described above continues in operation, the potential conflicts over the distribution of tax revenues in a totally uniform German tax system will remain subdued because of the high equalization effect. This could change after 2005.

Current Problems of German Intergovernmental Financial Relations

Under the still valid financial constitution, many problems have logically emerged long before the final step of fiscal equalization. It can be assumed that the problems have put additional pressure on the fiscal equalization scheme, but they are the true reasons for the misery of the German financial constitution.

- The distribution of competences among the federal tiers can be criticized for being overcentralized. Too many subjects are regulated uniformly by federal laws. There are very few areas of competences belonging solely to state and local governments. These areas are now also threatened by European regulation. From the point of view of public choice theory, the reasons for this development are clear: the Federation not only has the competences to shift the responsibilities from the state level to the federal tier in cases of concurrent legislative competence, it also has a strong motivation to do so because it generally does not have to pay for the additional regulations, since the expenditure competence lies with the executing state governments. Only a majority of state governments could try to bring competences back to the state level. But this majority appears to be politically impossible. No state government can take back former state competences by its own political will. Therefore, the construction of the division of competences in the German constitution is like a noncontestable monopoly market. Economists know how expensive the welfare losses from those constructions are.

- The overcentralization is also connected to an inefficient over-regulation of the provision of state and local public goods. There are too many details regulated by federal laws and decrees intervening in the proper competence of the states in an administrative federalism to decide about the ways and procedures of administration according to the regional and local preferences and institutional habits. This is, therefore, an additional source of inefficiency and related welfare losses.
- The centralization of taxation competences has led to a strain on tax laws with intervention functions. The typical, and in truth, more important revenue function of the taxes is pushed into the background. State and local governments pay for a federal tax policy with which they cannot attract voters. And state governments have no right of autonomous taxation. Most of them are even afraid of the idea that they could decide their own tax rates in the future. There is also some reason to believe that the centralized tax policy, which supposedly does not meet the preferences of the voters of the different jurisdictions, is an important reason for the strongly increasing shadow economy in Germany.
- The problems concerning the above mentioned three steps of the financial constitution have also led to a strain on the fiscal equalization scheme and the recent loss of consensus about the

system of revenue sharing. It is astonishing that the critical state governments of Bavaria, Baden-Württemberg and Hesse do not complain about the other fundamental deficiencies with the same political energy as they do against the poor old Länder which have to carry the burdens of above-average compulsory social expenditures because of their problems of structural economic change.

- The asymmetries of the financially relevant competences among the federal tiers have also led to a lack of political power of state parliaments. Because they have no right to determine the volume of the state budget by deciding about the necessary tax rates, they only decide about expenditures. In Austria the state parliaments have been described as "expenditure parliaments" which would apply to Germany, too. The logic of these expenditure budgets is that all revenues must be expended to the last DM and even more to compete for voters. State governing parties cannot choose between additional expenditures or a cutback of state taxes; they can only spend. And they do so even if they have to take on more and more public debt. Voters of state jurisdictions are scarcely aware that all the public goods they require are financed by the taxes based on federal tax laws. State budgets seem to come from heaven.

The other side of the coin of lack of tax authority by state political institutions is the lack of power and control of the voters and taxpayers. With regard to the complexity of intergovernmental relations in Germany, it becomes clear why the politicians love to focus their efforts on the "reform" of fiscal equalization only. For many of them even this is at the intellectual limit. The fiscal equalization scheme today can be brought up on a computer and all changes accurately calculated. This offers a seeming transparency and security against unexpected results of the reforms. Therefore, the governments prefer negotiating distributional issues in spite of proposals dealing with more autonomy.

Unfortunately, the politically realistic idea of agreeing to sufficient, far-reaching, and at least partly autonomous taxation competences for state and local governments has not emerged. Such a reform would be crucial for a better functioning of the financial constitution, a more intense political control, and an increase in political participation of the German voters. Sometimes, when one considers the political immobility of the financial framework of the public sector, the idea emerges that nothing should be changed. More responsibility would disturb all the arrangements that have made those who dominate the public sector cartels comfortable. Then it seems that many of the members of the political and administrative system would fight for the maintenance of the German "system of organized irresponsibility," as Hans-Peter Schneider called it more than 15 years ago in a public address.

Chapter 3

TERRITORIAL REFORM OF THE LÄNDER

A Demand of the Basic Law

Uwe Leonardy

Introduction

Three introductory remarks would seem to be appropriate in writing about this subject in English for Americans.[1] First, the title of this chapter in German, "Neugliederung des Bundesgebiets," has been translated as "territorial reform of the Länder" rather than the literal translation, "restructuring of the federal territory." Although the latter version reflects the exact wording of the relevant constitutional provision in Article 29 of the Basic Law (BL), the impression that it would create in English would be misleading. It would sound as if the federal territory were subdivided into administrative units like those of a centralized state, while in fact it is the Länder that constitute the Federation (Bund). Thus, it is the Länder structure rather

---

1. This chapter represents a slightly modified but, with regard to fiscal equalization (as of 15 July 2001), updated English version of the author's essay entitled "Die Neugliederung des Bundesgebietes: Auftrag des Grundgesetzes" in *Föderalismus in Deutschland*, edited by K. Eckart and H. Jenkis (Berlin: Duncker & Humblot, 2001). The author is obliged to the editors and the publishers for their permission to reproduce that essay here for English-speaking readers.

than the federal territory to which the reform project of Article 29 is addressed—hence the deliberate deviation from a literal translation here. (The terminology of Article 29 was "inherited" from Article 18 of the much more centralized Weimar Constitution of 1919, which referred to the "structuring of the Reich in Länder" [*Gliederung des Reichs in Länder*].) Given that a territorial reform of the structure of the American states would hardly be feasible, it might be difficult for American readers to understand why a foreign federal constitution should provide for such a reform at all. The reasons for the underlying differences in the philosophies of federalism will be dealt with and explained at the end of this chapter.

Second, in order to prevent misunderstandings among lawyers (of whom the author is one), there is no doubt or dispute that since the second revision of Article 29 BL in 1976, there is no longer a *legal* demand on the Constitution for a territorial reform of the Länder. Instead, there is now only an empowerment of the federal legislature to proceed with such reform. However, in spite of this option, territorial reform of the federal system continues to be on the agenda as an unfulfilled *political* demand. It is the purpose of this chapter to illustrate just exactly why.

Third, since many seem to think that territorial reform of the Länder is close to the popular "sport of map drawing," many feel called to this subject simply for the fun of that "sport." Too often the results are poorly substantiated products of fancy. Endeavors of this kind are not the aim of this chapter. Instead, it restricts itself to the task of outlining the necessity of territorial reform in the German federal system, and for this purpose it is written with a background of broad professional experience with the subject. From 1970 to 1972 the author was the responsible liaison of the Federal Chancellor's Office to the Expert Commission for Territorial Reform of the Länder at the Federal Ministry of the Interior (Sachverständigenkommission für die Neugliederung des Bundesgebiets beim Bundesminister des Innern), and from 1971 to 1974 he had to coordinate the federal government's position on the Bundestag Commission of Inquiry on Constitutional Reform (Enquête-Kommission des Bundestages zur Verfassungsreform) from the Chancellor's Office. From 1975 to 1994 he was involved with the topic on several occasions in the Mission (*Landesvertretung*) of Lower Saxony to the Federation. First he was an adviser to the then minister-president of Lower Saxony, Alfred Kubel, in the negotiations between the Federation and the Länder, which preceded the revision of Article 29 in 1976. Then (after German reunification) he served again as part of the Constitutional Reform Commission of the Bundesrat (from 1991 to 1992) and the Joint Constitutional Commission of the Bundestag and Bundesrat, as well as took part in the ensuing legislative procedures on the revision of the Basic Law (between 1992 and 1994). These activities were also the basis of several German and foreign publications by the author (see the bibliography) that either wholly or partly dealt with the subject matter to be discussed here.

Development and Changes of Article 29 BL

It would seem to be a remarkable historical fact that already prior to the start of the deliberations in the Parliamentary Council that drafted the Basic Law, the military governors of the three Western occupation powers admonished the heads of the then Länder governments in their occupation zones "to avoid if possible the creation of Länder which in comparison with the other Länder would be too large or too small" (Document II of 1 July 1948, in von Mangoldt 1953: 4–5). Already at that time, however, it was clear that addressing such a request to the holders of territorial power themselves would hardly be an appropriate means to achieve changes in the territorial structure (even though that power was still a rather restricted one under the occupational regime). In any case the structure of the Länder remained unchanged, and under the time pressure of the political aim of creating the Federal Republic, the military governors felt obliged to accept the status quo.

Nevertheless, a clear legal demand made its way into the constitutional text with Section 1 of Article 29 under the impact of the military governors' request (*Bundesgesetzblatt* [BGBl] 1949: 1). That section read as follows: "The federal territory shall be restructured by a federal law with due regard to regional unity, historical and cultural connections, economic expediency, and social structure. The restructuring shall create Länder which by their size and by their potentials for performance [*Leistungsfähigkeit*] are able to fulfill efficiently the functions incumbent upon them."

For the implementation of this demand, this original version required also that (partial) referenda (*Volksentscheide*) should take place in the areas affected by the federal law on territorial reform; and in those areas the principle of simple majorities should apply to the referenda to be held. In case of a rejection in at least one such area, the federal law concerned should be subject of a referendum in the entire federal territory after it had been introduced again in the Bundestag and passed by it. In addition, the population in those territories that had been shifted from one Land into another by measures of the occupation powers was given a right to petition (*Volksbegehren*) regarding the Land in which they wanted to live. For all of these changes, and in particular for the implementation of the general demand for restructuring, there was a time limit of three years. However, for the time being this limit remained inoperative, together with the entire Article 29. The occupation powers suspended the implementation of territorial reform at the moment when the Basic Law came into power, because they considered the proper time for this measure to have passed (von Mangoldt 1953: Note 1 on Article 29: 188 and Appendix No. 2). There was only one exception to that suspension (in Article 118 BL) concerning a special provision for the territory of what is today the Land of Baden-Württemberg. The borders between the American and the French zones of occupation had originally led to the creation of three Länder. The suspension for the implementation of general territorial reform by Article 29 was not lifted until May 1955. But no steps for reform were taken after that date, either.

Irrespective of this, however, there are three main elements in the original version of the constitutional provision demanding reform that remain worth keeping in mind:

1. a clearly obliging demand for reform;
2. the application of the principle of simple majorities, which should be sufficient for consent in referenda in areas to be restructured; and
3. the finalization of the reform procedure by a referendum in the entire territory of the Federal Republic.

The first revision of Article 29 came in 1969 (BGBI. I: 1241). The revision became necessary because until then the referenda still had not taken place in those territories in which popular petitions for the alteration of territorial measures of the occupation powers had been successful. There were four such areas in Rhineland-Palatinate[2] and two in Lower Saxony.[3] It was now decided that these referenda should take place no later than 31 March 1975. However, the original version was not changed by the revision of 1969 regarding:

- the preservation of the demand for reform itself, although the time limit for its implementation was deleted;
- the preservation of the principle of simple and therefore sufficient majorities in areas affected by restructuring; and
- the final referendum in the entire federal territory, which should also be superior to partial referenda deviating from the full project of reform.

The fundamental and critical revision of Article 29 followed, however, in 1976 (BGBl.I: 2381). The reasons were manifold, and they had partially political and partially legal origins.

An expert commission, which had been convened by the Adenauer government under the chairmanship of the former chancellor of the Reich, Dr. Hans Luther,[4] when the original version of Article 29 was still in force, had already experienced a failure in October 1955, mainly because of the multitude of alternative proposals (Bundesminister des Innern 1955) that it had produced (a failure that had in no way displeased the Adenauer government). In early 1973 new and much more substantive proposals of a second expert commission under the chairmanship of former Undersecretary of State Dr. Werner Ernst (Bundesminister des Innern 1973) were presented to the federal chancellor. These had been worked out between 1970 and 1972 and had avoided the mistake of producing too many alternatives. However, these new proposals were immediately and literally "praised to death" by the decision-makers after it had become clear that there was no political will for their implementation. This fact and the reasons for it will be discussed in more detail below.

2. The Administrative Districts of Koblenz and Trier for restructuring into North Rhine-Westphalia and the administrative districts of Montabaur and Rhine-Hessen for restructuring into Hesse.

3. The restoration of the historic Länder of Oldenburg and Schaumburg-Lippe.

4. According to a Bundestag resolution to that effect of 13 June 1951.

A legal obligation to pass a federal law had resulted from the referenda on 19 January 1975, which had become necessary in the territory of Lower Saxony following the successful popular petitions there for the restitution of the old Länder of Oldenburg and Schaumburg-Lippe. To everybody's surprise, the necessary quorum of these referenda had come out in favor of the restitution of these previous Länder.

With these results the further existence of Lower Saxony as such was in question, and the federal legislature had to find a solution to this question. With the so-called Lower Saxony Act (also called the Oldenburg Act—Act on the Land Affiliation of the Administrative District of Oldenburg and the County of Schaumburg-Lippe under Article 29 Sec. 3, 2nd Sentence of 9 January 1976; BGBl. I: 45) it decided to reject those two referenda in favor of Lower Saxony's preservation.

Regarding full territorial reform in the Federal Republic, however, it was much more important that with these events politics had discovered the constitutional opportunity to delete what was then called the "inconsistency of the Basic Law." That inconsistency was rightly seen in the fact that the constitutional demand for territorial reform had still not been implemented even twenty-six years after the Basic Law went into effect (and twenty years after the removal of the original suspension by the Allied Powers; see Kubel 1981: 54.)

For these reasons the revision of Article 29 drafted in 1975 and put into effect in 1976 brought about several serious changes of its contents. The first change was that the legal demand for territorial reform was deleted and watered down in Section 1 to say that territorial reform *can* now be brought about by the federal parliament.

Second, a completely new Section 3 was inserted for a potential (and in reality no longer desired) implementation of territorial reform, for which now an interlocked system was introduced, requiring double majorities in referenda both in the affected Länder as well as in the partial areas concerned. In effect, this system turned the originally reform-*demanding* provision of the Basic Law into an article for the *prevention* of such reform, because those corresponding double majorities in referenda of the new kind will clearly never be achievable.

As a consequence of this reform-preventing change, the requirement of a referendum in the entire territory of the Federal Republic was also abolished. The original purpose had been to assume the role of a finalizing referee vis-à-vis negative referenda in parts of the territory. This was and is now no longer possible.

Nonetheless, two supporters of territorial reform were successful in keeping alive at least one potential future impetus for such reform. In the drafting group, which had been convened by the then federal minister of the interior (Prof. Werner Maihofer) and which consisted of representatives of the federal government, the Bundestag factions, and some Länder, the Lower Saxon minister-president, Alfred Kubel, and the former deputy minister-president of Baden-Württemberg, Walter Krause, prevailed in securing at least a chance for reform in urbanized and densely populated areas divided by Länder boundaries. That chance came to be inserted with the following provisions in a new Section 4 of the currently valid version of Article 29:[5]

> If in any clearly defined and contiguous residential and economic area located in two or more Länder and having at least one million inhabitants, one-tenth of those entitled to vote in Bundestag elections petition for the inclusion of that area in a single Land, a federal law shall specify within two years whether the change shall be made in accordance with Section 2 of this Article [by a federal law requiring confirmation by referendum] or that an advisory referendum [*Volksbefragung*] shall be held in the affected Länder.

The potential of this new provision will be discussed later. After German unification a new Section 8 was finally added to Article 29 in this revised version by the Constitutional Reform Act of 1994 (BGB1. I: 3146), which was one of the results of the Joint Constitutional Commission of Bundestag and Bundesrat (Part 23 of the report of the Joint Constitutional Commission of Bundestag and Bundesrat, Deutscher Bundestag, *Zur Sache* 5/93). Measures of reform, which were only possible on the basis of a federal law, can now also be implemented by state treaties of neighboring Länder for all or parts of their territories; and these treaties require confirmation by referenda in each of the Länder concerned. The referenda can alternatively also be restricted to certain areas, if the state treaty only affects part of the territories of the treaty-making Länder.

---

5. The author of this chapter drafted the original text for Minister-President Kubel of Lower Saxony.

A special provision for the territories of the Länder Berlin and Brandenburg in a new Article 118a of the Basic Law was also introduced by the Constitutional Reform Act of 1994, an innovation that was directly caused by the achievement of German unity. It implemented Article 5 of the Unification Treaty (Part 2.4 of the Joint Constitutional Commission's Report), and as an exception to the procedural provisions of Article 29 it created a basis for a merger of these two Länder "by an agreement of the two Länder and with participation of those entitled to vote in them." The historical model for this (not in its details but in the fundamental idea) had been in the already quoted Article 118 BL, which in 1951 had led to the creation of Baden-Württemberg by a merger of the previous Länder Baden, Württemberg-Baden and Württemberg-Hohenzollern.

Reasons for the Nonimplementation of General Territorial Reform

When the reasons for the watering down of Article 29 into a provision for prevention of reform were described above, it was pointed out that in 1976 the opportunity had been seen to "correct the inconsistency of the Constitution" by changing the demand for reform into a mere empowerment. The political background of this change is illustrated in three phases that show clearly the lack of will for territorial reform.

The inconsistencies and self-contradictions of the proposal, which emanated from the Luther Commission, were in fact welcomed by the Adenauer government as an alibi for not pursuing the issue. The Adenauer government realized that from a partisan perspective any measure of reform would have necessarily resulted in the dissolution of the Land of Rhineland-Palatinate, which was then considered to be a safe stronghold of the Christian Democrats (CDU). The dangers for the CDU were connected with the strong resistance of the Social Democratic-governed city-states of Hamburg and Bremen to consolidation with a territorial Land. This was all the more valid as the status of these city-states could also be defended by the argument that their dissolution would further emphasize the special position of the island-city of (West) Berlin in the Soviet sphere, which would then have remained as the only city-state.

Similar "unholy alliances" of party-political constellations occurred during and after the deliberations of the Ernst Commission. Hamburg and Bremen, for example, had a very powerful defender for the preservation of their position as Länder in the Brandt government in the person of Helmut Schmidt, who came from Hamburg and was an important federal minister. Willy Brandt's Liberal (FDP) coalition partner, federal Minister of Interior Hans-Dietrich Genscher, had political reasons of his own for exercising caution, since he wanted to keep good relations with the Ernst Commission by following an initiative of the chairman of the Liberals in the Bundestag, Wolfgang Mischnick, who was pressing for territorial reform. However, this did not prevent Genscher, in his capacity as party chairman of the Liberals, to consider the chairman of the CDU as a potential future coalition partner. Since 1973 the name of that CDU chairman was Helmut Kohl, and he had been minister-president of Rhineland-Palatinate since 1969 (see Kubel 1981: 55). The sum total of these party-political factors of calculation on both sides was that nothing happened. The difference between this situation and that after the report of the Luther Commission was that the work of the Ernst Commission received universal praise. However, this did not affect the continuing lack of will for the implementation of the constitutional demand for reform that at that time still clearly existed.

The Constitution had become "inconsistent" by a demand contained *in* it but not implemented *by* it. In reality, however, the inconsistency had its roots in the lack of will by the decision-makers themselves to implement that clear demand into concrete measures of reform. This was demonstrated in the Lower Saxon territories of Oldenburg and Schaumburg-Lippe, when the obviously anachronistic and widely ridiculed referenda there for the restitution of these small historic Länder were successful. Many of those who had supposedly fought for their restitution had made it clear that the main motive of their efforts was that they did not really want the implementation of those anachronisms but that, on the contrary, their aim was to create a situation that would produce pressures for a general territorial reform.[6]

6. So in particular and very strongly the representative of the Oldenburg Committee, Dr. Cromme, in the hearing of the Bundestag Committee of the Interior on the Bill for the Act on the Land Affiliation of the Administrative District of Oldenburg and the County of Schaumburg-Lippe, 27 November 1975; Appendix to Minutes of Proceedings No. 89: 9–17.

But the political calculations of the parties on the federal level also continued to prevail after the change of the chancellorship from Willy Brandt to Helmut Schmidt. The weakening of the constitutional demand into a mere empowerment was now initiated together with the drafting of the Lower Saxony Act, on the basis of both that apologetical reasoning of the "inconsistency of the Constitution" and clear instructions by Helmut Schmidt, who had become chancellor in 1974. Those instructions, which aimed at the reform-preventing revision of Article 29, supported the constitutional theory approach of the minister in charge, federal Minister of the Interior Werner Maihofer. According to this theory, it was inadmissible in partial referenda on measures of territorial reform to subordinate the decision of a smaller territory to the will of a higher-ranking larger area in the way of an "octroi." In a politically entirely welcome manner just that theory then led to the currently valid version of Article 29. As has been explained above, simple majorities in the areas concerned are no longer sufficient for the outcome of such referenda. Instead, there is now the need for double majorities both in the partial territories concerned and in the areas superior to them, particularly in the Länder concerned, in order to effect changes. It would seem to require no explanation that with this effect Maihofer's "theory of octroi" led to a system of blockade (to be sure, one that was desired), which from the beginning leaves any project of territorial reform without any chance at all if it has to be achieved in this manner.

The instructions of the federal chancellor and the constitutional theory of his minister of the interior were at the same time the reasons for the subject of territorial reform not being introduced into the simultaneous deliberations of the Bundestag Commission of Inquiry on Constitutional Reform (Deutscher Bundestag, *Zur Sache 2/77*), which had been created in October 1970 and had been reconvened in February 1973. That Commission's ignoring the territorial reform issue was all the more surprising because this body had concentrated its attention mainly on the area of "Federation and Länder" (besides that of "Parliament and Government"). Specifically for this category of topics, it had instituted one of its only two working groups. Parallel to that working group a commission of the Länder sat with the same agenda for potential constitutional reform in the relations between the Federation and the Länder. Not only were those engaged in party-political calculations not interested in territorial reform; on the contrary, they did everything to postpone the issue indefinitely. Thus, they prevented any discussion of territorial reform in either of these two bodies.

However, when in 1990 German unification occurred, it became clear anew how necessary such reform had become, despite party-political strategies. The so-called Round Table in East Germany concerned itself intensively with the task of creating a rational Länder structure in the territory of the GDR prior to accession to the Federal Republic and before and after the first democratic elections there. Also, the federal minister of the interior, Dr. Wolfgang Schäuble, started a very serious and, in its first phase, also energetically organized an attempt to utilize the opportunity offered by unification for territorial reform in the current and future federal territory. (Schäuble was at that time in charge of the internal political coordination of the unification process on the side of the West.) His attempt, however, was soon caught in the web of resistance that confronted him in the Conference of the Minister-Presidents on the Western side. Finally, this attempt had to be given up, because the speed of the process of unification necessary for reasons of foreign policy did not permit its continuation.

On the other hand, Schäuble had been successful in negotiating and drafting the Treaty of Unification to the effect that Article 5 of that treaty provided for a merger of the two future Länder of Berlin and Brandenburg, if referenda in these two Länder would be in favor of such a measure. Many (and among them definitely also Schäuble) had hoped that a positive result of these referenda would create a decisive impetus, causing a chain reaction for the entire federal territory. As a result strong disappointment was widespread when, after difficult negotiations between the two Länder governments and the concluding of a state treaty between them, the two referenda failed in 1996. The reasons for those failures, however, were to be found much more in lingering East–West contrasts and resentments in the motivations of the voters rather than in any negative evaluation of the merger as such and its functional aspects. This fact was particularly reflected by a positive majority in the area of the former Land of West Berlin in contrast to a simultaneously rejecting majority in the former East Berlin and in Brandenburg. Only after this result and the analysis of these reasons did political elites generally become aware of the fact that the time for the merger had been chosen far too early in a phase of still insufficient integration between East and West and that the attempt had, therefore, been condemned to failure from its beginning (for details, see Leonardy 1999b: 288–89).

Nonetheless, particularly in the West, public discussion of the necessity of a general territorial reform of the Länder continued, contrary to all expectations, immediately after the general shock over the failure of the Berlin-Brandenburg merger (for details, see Leonardy 1999b: 289f.). That debate was even intensified by the controversies over fiscal equalization. Meanwhile, the debate has also revisited Berlin and Brandenburg, which have started serious deliberations regarding a new attempt at merging during this decade.

In conclusion, it should be noted that the creation of the Land of Baden-Württemberg in 1951–52 on the basis of Article 118 BL has been the only successful example of territorial reform. It should also be noted that the synergetic effects of merging the three previous Länder in the southwest led to the emergence of a Land that in its economic and financial potential has become the number one of all Länder, not only in the old but also in the new united Federal Republic.

The Continued Existence of the Need and Demand for Territorial Reform

Though the results of territorial reform since 1949 have been meager, there are three groups of legal, factual, and financial reasons for the need for territorial reform in the German federal system today.

Legally, reform is needed because the rational criteria for reform in Section 1 of Article 29 have clearly become superior to the emotional ones. This is demonstrated by the fact that the aims of territorial reform—"to ensure that each Land be of a size and capacity to perform its functions effectively"—have been upgraded from the original second sentence in Section 1 to the first sentence. As a result the revision of 1976 placed them in front of all further detailed criteria with the main aim of achieving sufficient potential of performance in the Länder structure. In addition, the revision of 1976 deleted, among those more detailed criteria, the rather nebulous notion of the "social structure" and replaced it with the much clearer criterion of "the requirements of local and regional planning" (mainly based on the report of the Ernst Commission). This once more emphasized clearly the functional significance of the need for territorial reform.

In fact, the federal necessities for territorial reform have indisputably become stronger. This can be shown most clearly by an identification of at least the main dangers that would develop into threats of a deformation of the federal system in Germany if the neglect of essential reform continues (Leonardy 1999b: 291f.)

In the first place, the efficient and comparable capacities of the Länder for the performance of their constitutional functions under the criteria of Article 29 would not be secured if territorial reform does not come about in the future. Second, the large number of Länder, which was already too high before German unification, would continue to make coordination between them as well as with the Federation all the more difficult, more complex, and less transparent, both in the domestic and in the European arenas. Democratic confidence in the federal state would continue to be the loser. Third, numerous existing Länder would hardly ever gain a chance to be sufficiently equipped for their increasing European functions, both within the Federal Republic and on the level of the European Union. For them the concept of a "Europe of (or rather with) the regions" would certainly never be a realistic one.

A fourth consequence would be that the far-reaching imbalances between the Länder in their economic and financial capacities, which have increased since German unification, would continue to be a focus of divide-and-rule strategies on the part of the Federation. Serious imbalances of the federal system would thus become permanent. Fifth, achieving the regional "equivalence of living conditions" (which, since the revision of Article 72 BL by the Constitutional Reform Act of 1994, has replaced the often misunderstood notion of the "uniformity of living conditions"[7] would be a task that would become increasingly dependent on the Federation. This would clearly imply a perversion of the federal idea, which in its nucleus presupposes sufficient capacities for the achievement and maintenance of interregional balance for all parts of the system.

---

7. The fact that the term "*uniformity* of living conditions" in Article 106 BL was not also replaced by "equivalence" can be explained by the decision of the Joint Constitutional Commission not to consider changes in the financial part of the Basic Law.

Last, but certainly not least, the particular problems of densely populated urbanized areas with high economic potential divided by Länder boundaries would remain unsolved, although Article 29 attempts to deal with those problems. Both economic development and intraregional balancing in those numerous areas would be hampered in the future.

In the financial field, recently revitalized needs for territorial reform have become visible. Above all, these needs have been made clear by the judgment of the Federal Constitutional Court in its new leading case on fiscal equalization of 17 November 1999 (key statements and reasoning in *Neue Juristische Wochenschrift* 2000). Financial needs remain valid, despite the difficulty in explaining rationally the fact that during the discussions regarding this judgment, the Conference of the Minister-Presidents of 24–25 March 2000 in Berlin denied any connection between it and territorial reform (see *Das Parlament* 2000a; *General-Anzeiger* 2000). This is especially surprising given the support by a number of heads of Länder governments for territorial reform in the entire Federal Republic, based on a clear reference to financial facts (for details, see the comments on the referenda in Berlin and Brandenburg in Leonardy 1999b: 289 f.). In this last judgment the Court did not repeat its previous statement that there is a close connection between territorial reform and reform of fiscal equalization (*BVerfGE* vol. 86: 148ff. [270]). Instead, among its requirements for a federal law on the definition of abstract standards (*Maßstäbegesetz*) to be passed by the end of 2002, the Court made numerous statements that are undeniably directly relevant to territorial reform.

The judgment pointed out clearly that on the basis of present legislation the so-called budget emergency grants for the Saarland and Bremen will have to be terminated in 2004 at the latest. It is not discernable how these Länder can continue to be viable after that date.

Above all, however, the Court clearly questioned previous elements of financial equalization that are directly connected to territorial factors. These include (1) the "costs of political leadership" in small Länder, (2) the privileged method for the counting of inhabitants in city-states, and (3) the financial privileges for seaports and financial costs for large airports.

The direct relationship between these factors for financial compensation and the size of the Länder affected by them can hardly be denied. With due respect for the Conference of Minister-Presidents, its denial of the relevance of such statements for territorial reform comes close to a contempt of the Federal Constitutional Court. The only "justification" for such a denial can be that those in favor of territorial reform among the minister-presidents fear the federal ship of reform being overloaded, if it has to carry financial and territorial reform simultaneously. This would seem, however, to overlook the fact that this ship has set sail already with the judgment and that the Länder have been presented with a double opportunity. Also, it would seem that there has been insufficient recognition of the fact that even in spite of this politically sensitive subject the judgment of the Court was unanimous. This would appear to indicate clearly that in the future, the Court will no longer be prepared to accept any more crippled solutions for fiscal equalization. To note this, however, then means at the same time that the Federal Constitutional Court has not only indirectly but also—despite not mentioning it *expressis verbis*—clearly come out in favor of the need for territorial reform.

Ways to Overcome the Failures of Parties and Institutions

Precisely this renewed attempt by state institutions to ignore a clear and central statement even of the highest court is more evidence that the territorial basis of the federal state can be reformed only on the condition that the parties and institutions are *forced* to face the issue and to put it on the political agenda. The question therefore arises of which political and legal initiatives must necessarily be taken in order to break the ice. A further question concerns what has to be done in order to avoid the danger of those deformations of the federal structure that were described above (Leonardy 1999a: 292f.).

Above all it appears to be necessary to introduce the dangers of such deformations into public debate. The political parties must be forced not to disparage territorial reform any longer in the interest of short-sighted tactical power plays. If the growing lack of financial resources and the demands for a "lean state" emanating from it are to be discussed honestly, then the necessities of such demands must permeate the field of that reform. Such honesty would also substantially help in diminishing general discontent with politics as such.

At the same time, the useless game with fancy maps for territorial reform must be brought to an end, because it only contributes to a discrediting of the project itself. Instead, a new independent expert commission should be convened in order to adapt the proposals of the Ernst Commission to the changed conditions following German unification.

Last but not least, a new model for the procedure of territorial reform should be discussed and developed. Such a model could make use of a solution that (though without success at the time) had been discussed already during the debates on the revision of Article 29 in 1975–76.[8] That model consisted of three main elements.

- First, at the beginning of the procedure there should be a general referendum in the entire Federal Republic on the question of whether or not a territorial reform of the Länder structure should take place. This referendum should be held on the basis of a first draft with alternative solutions emanating from the proposals of the suggested new independent expert commission. Its result should once and for all decide the main question of territorial reform, and it should in this manner avoid and end further dispute about it. In contrast to the original version of Article 29, therefore, a general referendum should have its place not at the end but at the beginning of the procedure on territorial reform.
- Second, under the condition that this referendum should show support for territorial reform, alternative concrete models should be developed by the federal legislature (and, as has been true since 1949, this should not require the consent of the Bundesrat). Those models should be worked out on the basis of the proposals of the independent expert commission, and

8. At that time initiated by the then vice president of the legislature (and former deputy minister-president) of Baden-Württemberg, Walter Krause, in the all-parties-group of Bundestag and Länder convened by Federal Minister Werner Maihofer. The initiative had been drafted by the author of this chapter. Krause had forwarded it in particular to Chancellor Helmut Schmidt, to Willy Brandt as the leader of the SPD, and to Herbert Wehner, the chairman of the SPD caucus in the Bundestag. He had also given the draft to the press (see *Frankfurter Allgemeine Zeitung* 1975; the author first published the model in Leonardy 1993: 1). The basic idea of the model—the inclusion of a general referendum into the procedure of territorial reform at its start—was more recently revived by the economics minister of Baden-Württemberg, Walter Döring (*Frankfurter Allgemeine Zeitung* 1998) and by the Berlin Minister (*Senator*) of Justice Erhart Körting (*Der Tagesspiegel* 1998; *Süddeutsche Zeitung* 1998).

they should take into account the regional results of the general referendum at the start of the procedure.

- As a third step, regional referenda in those areas directly affected by the reform project should finally decide which solutions are preferred within those alternatives. In contrast to the present procedural rules requiring double majorities (see above), such regional referenda should return in the new model to the principle of simple majorities in the areas to be restructured. The legal situation prior to the reform-preventing revision of 1976 should therefore be restored. Such simplified and directly result-related regional referenda should then end the procedure.

Methods to Force Acceptance of Reform by Parties and Institutions

As noted in the previous parts of this chapter, the political parties and the institutions of the state, on the level of both the Federation and the Länder, have until now failed to address the question of territorial reform, because they have not had the will to start and implement that project. Therefore, if one recognizes the necessity of territorial reform, nothing else will be left but to break this resistance. Irrespective of one's personal evaluation of so-called plebiscitary elements (direct democracy) in the Basic Law,[9] this will only be possible if those elements contained in the Basic Law for the purpose of carrying out territorial reform are utilized and mobilized. Plebiscitary elements would, indeed, be suitable for the initiation of a chain reaction for territorial reform. These can be found in the already quoted Section 4 of Article 29. As has been explained, this provision relates to the fact that in several parts of the federal territory there are "clearly defined and contiguous residential and economic area(s) located in two or more Länder and having at least one million inhabitants." The provision therefore refers to the fact that a number of

9. The general introduction of such elements beyond Article 29 is not favored by the author (see Leonardy 1989: 442–450); the opposite view is represented by, for example, von Arnim, whose views on territorial reform, however (54–59), coincide basically with those in this chapter.

large urbanized areas in the Federal Republic are divided by Länder boundaries in a manner that hampers their economic development.[10] It is indeed remarkable and certainly no accident that those possibilities contained in Article 29, Section 4 have been a "sleeping beauty" in the Basic Law until now, which is obviously relatively little known even to some constitutional lawyers and which on the political level has hitherto not been "kissed awake" by anybody for easily explainable reasons. This is all the more surprising as the Federal Constitutional Court already outlined the requirements for the utilization of these possibilities (in its so-called Franconia judgment of 1997).[11]

The decisive condition for initiating a chain reaction for territorial reform would seem to lie in a connection of the potential of this section and those of the new Section 8 (added in 1994), according to which territorial reforms can also be initiated by means of a state treaty between neighboring Länder. (Such a connection was also what the then Lord Mayor of Hamburg, Dr. Henning Voscherau, had in mind when he successfully proposed the instrument of a state treaty procedure in the Joint Constitutional Commission of Bundestag and Bundesrat.) How, then, could the constitutional implementation of such a connection between the plebiscitary potential in divided urbanized areas with those of state treaties in the territories concerned be organized?

It is no doubt correct that the implied question of the relation between Section 4 and the new Section 8 has not yet been sufficiently examined constitutionally (see Maunz and Herzog, *Grundgesetz* on Article 29). Regarding the idea of a chain reaction to be initiated by the potential of Section 4, a focus on legalistic nuances may not, however, be so important. It would appear to be much more relevant to imagine the probable course of political events that would most likely follow a successful popular petition under Section 4. On the basis of German constitutional practice and the assumptions closest

10. This refers to the urbanized economic areas surrounding the three city-states of Berlin, Hamburg, and Bremen as well as to the Rhine/Main and the Rhine/Neckar areas (Frankfurt/Mainz/Wiesbaden and Mannheim/Ludwigshafen), and further to the Leipzig/Halle area in the East.

11. On the more detailed criteria for popular petitions under Article 29, Section 4 BL and in particular on the delimitation of an area relevant for this, see the decision of the Federal Constitutional Court of 24 June 1997: BVerfGE 96, 139–52 (2 BvP 1/94); press release of the Court of 2 July 1997.

to reality on that basis, the ensuing sequence of events would probably be as follows.[12]

First, in the case of a successful popular petition under Section 4,
the Federation would most certainly select the second alternative of
this provision, which means that it would decide in favor of an advisory referendum. If it selected the first alternative, it would be changing Land boundaries by a federal law as a result of the relatively weak
indicator of a popular petition. In selecting an advisory referendum,
the Federation would also have the advantage of securing for itself
an exemption from liability for further consequences, that is, it
would be under no obligation to implement further steps even after
a positive result of that advisory referendum. Thus, it would not be
legally obliged to initiate a federal law for boundary changes for the
purpose of implementing the outcome of the referendum (Maunz,
Herzog, and Scholz, notes 86–89 to Article 29).

Second, if the advisory referendum would (as assumed here) have
a positive result, then the Länder concerned would most certainly
have a major interest from this moment in taking the matter into
their own hands and not leaving it to the Federation. If they did the
latter, they would run the risk that the Federation could still decide
in favor of federal legislation to change the boundaries.

At this stage, then, Section 4 would come directly into play. This
means that the Länder concerned would now have a rather serious
reason not only to think about concluding a state treaty under Section 8 but also to start negotiations between each other. Within all
categories of political logic, such a state treaty would then have to
accept the (presumably positive) result of the consultative referendum, if it is to avoid the risk of a denial of consent by the Bundestag
(which needs to give such consent according to the last sentence in
Section 8). Regarding the sequence of steps under Section 8, it would
quite obviously make no sense to assume that the consent of the
Bundestag would have to be sought only *after* the referendum, which
is necessary under the third sentence in Section 8. In case of a positive outcome of that referendum, the Bundestag would in actuality

12. This argumentation is derived from a letter from the author to Hans-Herbert
von Arnim, who had asked for an explanation of the author's proposals in Leonardy
1999a: 133–45, and who kindly referred to this letter in *Vom schönen Schein der
Demokratie* 2000: 334.

have to give its consent under the impact of that result, which would practically diminish its discretion to zero. In order to characterize the federal implications of the state treaty options in Section 8, the report of the Joint Constitutional Commission rightly refers to a "general federal component" in it (Deutscher Bundestag, *Zur Sache* 5/93: 88).

In summary, all of this means that the Länder concerned would have to respect the result of the consultative referendum when drafting a state treaty and that the Bundestag would also have to consent to such a state treaty, even though it is legally not obligated to do so.

These events in only one part of the federal territory, that is, in the divided urbanized area, would, of course, not necessarily be useful for and compatible with overall territorial reform in the entire Federal Republic. (On its necessity, see the so-called South-West-State judgment of the Federal Constitutional Court of 1956 [*BVerfGE* vol. 5: 39].) This would have to be dealt with differently. But exactly the problems connected with the requirements of a functionally consistent argument would in such sequence of events also promote public debate, and the need for an overall concept would therefore be made apparent. A wide and profound public discussion about reform would thus take place only after a sequence of events as described here.

Within such a debate it would be conceivable that the proposals outlined above for a new procedure to achieve territorial reform would gain relevance. The readiness within the parties and in the Länder to discuss such a new overall procedure would most likely grow rather quickly under the pressure of chain reactions, which would otherwise follow in the context of Sections 4 and 8. The motivation to develop a new general procedure would be derived from the fact that such a completely new revision of Article 29 would be the only way to avoid those otherwise no longer controllable chain reactions and to put a consistent, complete model in their place. This would then be an optimal, yet still obviously not quite improbable, result of a process that would begin with utilization of the potential in Article 29, Section 4.

In all of this opponents of territorial reform may see a mere playing with theoretical ideas that, in their evaluation, are not based in reality. However, this view can be dangerous for them. The facts are that presently there exist no fewer than three such starting points that could cause events like the ones described.

First of all, the deliberations regarding a renewed attempt at merging Berlin and Brandenburg have already resulted in continuous new talks and negotiations between the two Länder governments concerned. It is true that at the time being these contacts are concentrated on a repetition of the procedure under the rules of Article 118a BL, which came to be inserted into the Constitution after German unification (see *Frankfurter Rundschau* 2000; *Frankfurter Allgemeine Zeitung* 2000a; *Berliner Zeitung* 2000). However, a closer constitutional analysis could also lead to the conclusion that the potential of Article 118a was "consumed" by the unsuccessful attempt in 1996. In any case such an evaluation could not be simply excluded, and an exclusion could imply a legal risk in case of a renewed court dispute on the constitutional implications of the proper procedure for a merger.[13] In comparison, the utilization of the potential of Section 4 for the initiation of a popular petition in the urbanized area of Berlin would be rather more promising politically and thus generate strong pressure against opponents of reform.

A further area relevant for the potential of Section 4 can be located in the so-called AKK suburbs of Mainz in the northeastern Rhine/Main triangle. This refers to the towns of Amöneburg, Kostheim, and Kastel, which until the end of World War II were a part of Mainz. In drawing the boundaries between the American and French zones of occupation, these towns were incorporated into the Land of Hesse in the American zone and thus were separated not only from Mainz but also from the Land of Rhineland-Palatinate. In the meantime there have been several attempts by the residents to change boundaries with the aim of returning the three towns to Mainz, thus taking them out of Hesse and incorporating them into Rhineland-Palatinate. All such attempts have failed up to now, because Hesse resisted them. Since 1999 a new initiative has been proposed by all the local political parties that aims at a special federal law for a referendum in this area (see *Mainzer Rhein-Zeitung* 1999; *Allgemeine Zeitung* 1999; *General-Anzeiger* 1999; also a proposal for general territorial reform: Grebner 1999; Dörrlamm et al. 1995). As before, however, Hesse shows no readiness to seek a solution by a state

---

13. After all, the constitutional conformity of the state treaty between Berlin and Brandenburg and that of Brandenburg's ratification act (of 27 June 1995) had already been disputed before the Land Constitutional Court (VfB Bbg 18/95).

treaty. This would, therefore, be a typical situation for the mobiliza-
tion of the potential of Article 29, Section 4. The towns concerned
all belong to the urbanized area of Frankfurt/Mainz/Wiesbaden,
which both by its size and by structural criteria clearly meets the conditions of Section 4.

The utilization of the possibilities of this divided area would thus
offer two clear advantages. It would first avoid the disadvantages of
a merely local solution, which could easily be ridiculed. Further (and
more important) it would imply the chance of a test case for the initiation of a chain reaction leading to the much larger aim of general
territorial reform. The formulation of such an aim could then no
longer be ridiculed as a local matter. In addition, the removal of Länder boundaries in the urbanized Rhine/Main area would certainly
also meet with a high degree of interest from those affected as well
as very powerful economic forces which would have even better
chances of development in an area no longer divided by the boundaries between Hesse and Rhineland-Palatinate.

A third possible case for the application of Article 29, Section 4,
recently became apparent in the area of Bremen. The head of the
cabinet office of Bremen contacted the Lower Saxon counties bor-
dering on the city-state of Bremen, suggesting that a "regional corporate body" consisting of these counties and Bremen should be
created and that it should even be equipped with a parliament of its
own. He forwarded this proposal to the counties directly without
informing the Lower Saxon Land government in Hanover. Public
discussion of this political and administrative misbehavior had then
hardly started when the city government of Bremen (*Senat*) quickly
decided to take back the initiative.[14] However, that fact does not
eliminate the underlying problem, which is that the population in
the area surrounding the city-state would certainly not object to the
removal of an annoying boundary. Here also one finds all the characteristics of a divided urbanized area. If that were not the case, Bremen would certainly not have raised the issue. If the potentials of

14. The apparently confidential paper (or nonpaper?) of the Bremen Cabinet Office
(*Senatskanzlei*) entitled "Regional-Körperschaft Bremen-Unterweser: Neue Formen der
Zusammenarbeit zwischen Oberzentrum Stadtstaat und dem Umland-Region" is
known to the author. For the course of events regarding it, see *Hannoversche Allgemeine
Zeitung* 2000; *Frankfurter Allgemeine Zeitung* 2000b; *Das Parlament* 2000b.

Article 29, Section 4, would be utilized skillfully in this case, the Bremen initiative could well prove to be a boomerang against the city whose official representatives are well known for their particularly strong defense of their city's status as a separate Land.

Summary and Outlook

The analysis of all relevant factors shows that territorial reform of the Länder is neither an irrelevant nor an unachievable project in *Realpolitik*. Its necessary implementation requires mobilizations first of regional publics and then a step-by-step nationwide political debate.

Indisputably, efforts to implement this highly necessary reform for the German federal state would be costly in political energy. However, the price that would have to be paid for the failure to invest such energy would be much higher. Under the conditions of a large population in a flawed system of territorial division, the chance of maintaining a viable federal system would have to be questioned.

It should be noted that the constitutional system of the Basic Law mentions efficiency criteria only in the context of the Länder, and that it does not do so with regard to any other organizational unit in its system. At the same time, however, the Basic Law offers the solution to deficiencies in the criteria: the territorial reorganization of the structures in which federalism unfolds.

The task of territorial reform of the Länder receives its constitutional rank above all in the context of the larger task of securing the viability and the political force of conviction of the federal order. The federal system is under a permanent pressure of adaptation and modernization. The reason for this is the fact that the absolute protection, which it enjoys under Article 79, Section 3 BL, simultaneously implies the obligation for the federal state to maintain its organization and its instruments on the highest possible standards and to adapt them to changing conditions. That includes the federal legislature's implementation of the obligation under Article 29 BL. This means that it has to secure the viability of the federal state by the creation of an expediently structured and in itself balanced system consisting of efficient units. Only under that condition can the federal system give life to the advantages which justify its constitutional inviolability; and only then can it sufficiently fulfill its functions to protect liberty and to secure the division of powers (Bundesminister des Innern, Bericht 1973: 36 [no. 59]).

There is nothing to add to these assertions of the Ernst Commission in its report of 1972–73, which even today have lost nothing of their validity and their terseness. Indeed, one is startled by the contrast between this statement and that of the Conference of Minister-Presidents of 24–25 March 2001, which claims that in the context of the Constitutional Court's judgment on fiscal equalization, "no Land may be questioned in its existence." That statement can only be characterized as a renewed failure to confront the problem and, moreover, as a deliberate denial of the connections between fiscal equalization and territorial reform. As Adrian Ottnad has demonstrated, fiscal equalization and territorial status quo stabilize each other mutually (Ottnad 1999: 228ff.; Ottnad and Linnartz 1998: 658). Precisely this point is being overlooked, if one thinks that an "overloading" of the intended "modernization of the federal order" can or even must be avoided in reforming fiscal equalization and territorial structure simultaneously. There is no doubt that one cannot achieve both aims at the same time and with finality. But one should at least achieve the first and bring the second on its way irrevocably. Otherwise one will inevitably experience a failure with both.

Reports of the outcome of the recent new negotiations on fiscal equalization in June 2001 have clearly confirmed Ottnad's observation of a mutual stabilization between territorial status quo and fiscal equalization, because results make clear that the smaller Länder profited substantially more than the larger ones due basically to their disproportionate share of votes in the Bundesrat. Hans Pitlick of the University of Hohenheim derived the conclusion from this that the hidden cost in fiscal equalization is to be found in the relation between a Land's number of inhabitants and that of its Bundesrat votes. As a consequence he pleads for a more proportional distribution of those votes (*Frankfurter Allgeimene Zeitung* 2001; for an earlier plea to this effect, see Leonardy 1999b: 293–94). The underlying thesis that smaller Länder have a privileged position has also been demonstrated by the reasons for the compromise on the fiscal transfers. That compromise on the Constitutional Court's requirements became possible not only by simply ignoring some of them, but also by the Federation's paying no less than 1.5 billion DM into the equalization pool. Otherwise, the Länder by themselves would not have been able to arrive at an agreed settlement. This proves two basic and deplorable facts. First, the territorial status quo prevents the Länder from solving their problems with the federal system alone. Second, under the conditions of that status quo, the Federation can go on playing the game of divide and conquer with the support and to the disproportionate advantage of the smaller vis-à-vis the larger Länder. This is the opposite of what territorial reform of the Länder structure is aiming at in Article 29. One can only hope that ignoring these facts and contexts will not continue in the planned Joint Commission of Bundestag and Bundesrat for the "modernization" of the federal order.

If, despite all the evidence, the need to engage in territorial reform does continue to be ignored, then one should have the courage to confess one's denial of the territorial problem in German federalism and consequentially delete Article 29 BL entirely. In its present version as a reform-preventing concept, this article in any case does not add to the glory of the Constitution. If one wants to delete it, then it should be clear that in doing so one would deny and remove a peculiarity of the German federal system, which does not exist in this form in other federal states in the world. Article 29 of the Basic Law is the manifestation of an understanding of a functional system of federalism that is directed by equal potential for performance of its constituent parts. Precisely because of this particular characteristic of the German federal system, comparisons that point to the (alleged) nonexistence of a problem of territorial reform, for example, in the United States or Canada, are out of place, because in these and other federal states there is no such clear constitutional postulate demanding the equivalence of capacities for performance. The framers of the German Constitution did not come to that particular self-understanding by themselves, or by the admonitions of the military governors at the start of their deliberations on the Basic Law. Rather, that peculiarity was the result of a territorial German history full of changes and accidents. The aim was to correct the history of an extremely unbalanced Länder structure in a relatively small, densely populated, and highly industrialized geographical area by the approach of territorial reform. Nothing has changed in the reasons for this approach to reform since then. Indeed, those reasons have become stronger.

In all of the described attempts at reform since 1949, we have experienced the fact that the implementation of the German approach to reform has not been easy. That alone, however, does not justify ignoring it. The chairman of the Expert Commission for Territorial Reform of the Länder described the reason for the difficulty of reform in a dinner speech, when the Commission visited Bremen in 1972. Addressing the then government (*Senat*) of Bremen under its president, Lord Mayor Hans Koschnick, Werner Ernst said: "The problem of democracy consists in the fact that it presupposes a degree of human reason, which it must first create itself" (personal notes). Koschnick did not contradict that statement. One hopes that the democracy of the German federal state will be able to solve this problem as it has been able to deal with so many other problems since it came into existence.

Chapter 4

LÄNDER PARLIAMENTS IN THE FEDERATION

Some Remarks on the Division of Powers

~⊂⊃~

Franz Greß

Introduction: Identification of a Problem

"Do Länder Parliaments Have a Future?" was the title of an expert meeting in 1971 sponsored by the Deutsche Vereinigung für Parlamentsfragen, and in 1979 the leading scholar in the field concluded that the Landtage (state parliaments) "without any doubt have suffered a loss of functions and power" (Schneider 1979: 129). In the early 1980s, the presidents of the Länder parliaments in a joint resolution complained that the creeping erosion of competences of the Länder have "above all struck their legislatures" (Konferenz der Präsidenten der deutschen Landesparlamente 1983: 357). Länder parliamentarians and the concerned public have also discussed the topic in a growing number of conferences, and the number of publications about this subject has increased over the years (Landtag Nordrhein-Westfalen 1986; Bayerischer Landtag 1987; Hessischer Landtag 1990). The common denominator is that the Länder parliaments have suffered a serious "loss of power" (Eicher 1988) and the question often raised is, "Does the parliamentary system in the Länder have a future?" (Greß 1990).

The experts have identified two main reasons for this loss of legislative power in the Länder: first, the continuous extension of the federal competences in the cooperative system of German executive federalism; and second, the development of a new tier of competences on top of the German system (Klatt 1999). The federation and the European Community (later the European Union) became targets of severe criticism by Länder politicians for their part in the weakening of the system of federal division of powers. The basic argument is that cooperative federalism has developed into a federalism dominated by the executive, especially because the highly interlocked system of German federalism was never meant to be a federalism that strengthens autonomy and parliamentary responsibility, but rather one that enshrines consensus building based on a long-standing tradition of bureaucratic etatism and social paternalism. This tradition is most prominently expressed in Article 72 of the Basic Law, which in 1949 insisted on the establishment of "uniform living conditions" as a duty of the federal legislators, a provision that was softened somewhat in 1994 when it was amended to "equivalent living conditions."

The changes in intergovernmental relations from a "federalism of powers" (*Substanzföderalismus*) with limited competences for the states to a "federalism of codetermination" (*Beteiligungsföderalismus*) at the national level and to a certain extent at the European level was nicely described by then federal President Roman Herzog in 1996. In a speech commemorating the fiftieth anniversary of the parliament of North Rhine-Westphalia, he made very clear that the competences of the federal legislator have been "expanded with the consent of the Länder," that is, via the Bundesrat, and that they have been used by the federation for the realization of policies nearly without limits with the consent of the Federal Constitutional Court (Herzog 1996: 23). A similar process was identified in the development of European integration, which in general eroded the position of the national parliaments and delegitimized them. The "decline of parliaments" (von Beyme 1998) in this emerging European political system was even more explicit in the case of the Länder parliaments. The Länder governments have been the "winners" as they have been partially compensated for the losses of Länder competences by the growing importance of the Bundesrat in the decision-making in federal policies regarding Europe, while the Länder parliaments still have no formal right to decide on the government's position in the second chamber.

The Case for Land Parliaments

To give a fair picture, one has to underscore that in the debates about the loss of powers voices could always be heard which insisted on the continuing importance of the Länder parliaments within the power structure of the Länder. Case studies have demonstrated that the Länder parliaments have used their competences to "offer different political solutions within the Federation" (Hahn 1987: 29), that they have played their "original part" (Kalke 2001: 21) in the development of specific policies, and that even in the case of the application of model uniform laws, "one cannot speak of an unimportance of the legislation of the German Länder" (Wettach 1994: 313). It is interesting that the areas of legislation analyzed are not restricted to the classical competences of the Länder such as primary and secondary education where a longstanding tradition of limited competition exists. Quality standards and school organization are notorious areas of inter-Länder conflicts, mostly smoothed over by the coordination mechanism of the Ständige Konferenz der Kultusminister (Permanent Conference of Education Ministers). In other cases, the conflict is between the autonomy of the Land legislator and the preemptive quality of the Basic Law. The most recent example is the discord about the substitution of religious instruction by a new compulsory subject, Life-Formation, Ethics, and Religious Studies (*Lebensgestaltung – Ethik – Religionskunde* [LER]) in Brandenburg. This issue was brought before the Federal Constitutional Court by the Protestant and Catholic churches, concerned parents, and the Christian Democratic parties of the Bundestag based on Article 7, para. 3 and Article 141 of the Basic Law. Due to the complexity and the far reaching consequences of this case, the Court did not reach a final ruling in its decision in July 2001 but urged the conflicting parties to seek a mutually satisfactory agreement (*Frankfurter Allgemeine Zeitung*, 25 June and 23 July 2001). Other authors recently have emphasized that the federal structure has been successfully used by parties and voters to sharpen regional profiles and to give new parties access to the political arena (Sturm 2001: 81–90).

The German party system is a thoroughly federal one. This system includes simple features such as the growing importance of the Land organizations in the party structures (Poguntke 1997: 512) and complex structures such as the functionally or voluntarily restricted regional parties, the PDS or the CSU (Hrbek 2002). There is no question that there is a party system at the Länder level and that it has become more important since reunification (Schneider 1979; Birsl and Lösche 1998; Galonska 1999).

The Green Party started on its way to Berlin at the Land level, and in 1984 the first SPD-Green coalition was formed in Hesse with Joschka Fischer as minister for environment and energy (Greß and Lehne 1999). Parties of protest make their successful appearance in the elections to Länder parliaments, for example, the extreme right-wing DVU (Deutsche Volksunion) and the Republikaner, but they have been confined to this level. Single-issue parties have a chance to affect the political process within a limited electorate of a city-state, for example, the Schill Party (2001) and before that the Statt-Partei (1993) in Hamburg. Finally, elections at the Land level have been utilized to test the attractiveness of issues and personalities in the election campaigns. In 1998 Minister-President Gerhard Schröder and the Social Democratic Party defined the elections in Lower Saxony as a kind of "primary" or "plebiscite" for Schröder's candidacy for chancellor in the upcoming federal elections (Müller-Hilmer 1999). Similarly, the Christian Democrats (CDU) in 1999 in Hesse decided to test in the Land elections the issue of integration of immigrants, a move that helped to win the elections and proved the mobilizing effect of the issue at the polls (Schmitt-Beck 2000).

Both of these examples also strongly underscore the complex interrelation between elections at the Länder and the federal levels which is a further component of the cooperative German federal system (Renzsch 1998). All of this testifies to the fact that parliamentarianism on the subnational level gives voters a voice, and that opportunities exist to create coalition governments whose patterns are different from the national ones and therefore tend to sharpen their programmatic profile (Kropp and Sturm 1998).

This empirical evidence is significant enough to promote some skepticism about generalizations concerning the "loss of power" of the Länder parliaments. In spite of all the unitary trends which cannot be denied, the Länder parliaments do serve within a limited scope as "political laboratories" to test political innovations (Greß and Huth 1998: 54–57).

The New Länder: Members of Parliaments and Institutional Patterns

German unification offered an opportunity to experiment on the institutional level of the Länder insofar as the political will to overcome a dictatorial system by a federal and decentralized democracy resulted above all in the creation of representative institutions in the reconstructed Länder. The restitution of parliaments in the eastern Länder was a new beginning in various ways. It led to the creation of a new intergovernmental system with new Länder under new constitutions that were obliged to pass comprehensive legislation and recruit a new class of politicians (Patzelt 2000b: 542–68).

About 77 percent (N = 383) of the class of 1990 Land legislators (N = 509) were first-time legislators (Derlien and Lock 1994: 92). There was also, however, a significant difference in the composition of the Länder parliaments. The social profile of Länder parliaments in the East—contrary to the Western dominance of the teaching profession—was marked by the presence of scientists, technicians, physicians, and pastors. A consequence of these eastern patterns of political career has been problems resulting from "on-the-job training," ranging from simple deficits in technical knowledge to the lack of political routine usually provided by previous party socialization via party activities and office holding.

But these differences did not last. Empirical studies underscore the successful process of integration into the mainstream of parliamentary professionalization. With some delays and modifications in the East, the same patterns of parliamentary and political role behavior as in the West developed, and parliamentary socialization did work successfully. As early as 1991–92, 86 percent of the Land legislators saw themselves as full-time legislators, and only 6 percent rejected that understanding of their role (Patzelt 2000b: 545).

That this role adaptation is in large part an integration of elites can be seen in the case of Berlin. While the distinctive East-West profile in the electorate has become clearer in every election since 1990, the integration within the city's legislative institution has been successful, due to the "efficient functional logic of parliamentary structures" (Schöne 2000: 576), including the close interaction between party and members of parliament. The still discernible differences in the perception of parliamentarianism between a more idealistic Eastern and more realistic Western concept do not impinge on the day-to-day routine of the Berlin parliament which follows a pragmatic pattern.

The picture in the Brandenburg Landtag is similar. The prevalent parliamentary routines are similar to those in the West (Schüttemeyer and Lübker 2000). There are differences, of course, in the social structure of the members of parliament, with fewer members having a background in the teaching profession, with fewer public servants (after the election in 1999 the figure dropped to less than 30 percent), and more members with economic or technical backgrounds by training. Religious affiliation is significantly lower than in the West: of the new members after the 1999 election, only one-third belonged to a Christian denomination (Schüttemeyer and Lübker 2000: 589). But at the same time the interlinkage of the parliamentarians with party structures has increased and developed into Western patterns. The same is true for the selection of candidates. Incumbents nearly doubled their chances to get a safe place on the party's slate (1994 = 37 percent; 1999 = 63 percent). At the same time voting along party lines increased dramatically (see table 4.1). As noted by Schüttemeyer and Lübker, the members of the Brandenburg Landtag became realists of parliamentary craftsmanship (*Realisten des parlamentarischen Handwerks*) (Schüttemeyer and Lübker 2000: 592).

A very important consequence of this adaptation to parliamentary routine is the strong identification with the institutions of a purely representative democracy and a weak approval of plebiscitary

Table 4.1 Party-Line Voting in Brandenburg, 1990–99 (in percentage)

	First Term	Second Term
SPD	38.2	66.0
CDU	62.9	87.6
PDS	70.1	72.2

Source: Schüttemeyer and Lübker 2000: 585–98.

elements. When members of the Brandenburg Landtag were asked to assess representative democracy, the item that dealt with complementing parliamentarianism with plebiscitarian elements had an average score of 2.4 on a scale from 1 to 5 (Schüttemeyer and Lübker 2000: 597).[1]

These results are in stark contrast to the existing provision in Article 22 of the Brandenburg constitution, which guarantees citizens the right of direct and indirect initiatives and referenda as a means of political participation (*Gestaltung*). The institutional structures have taken root, and even without fellow MPs with a Western socialization, as in the case of the Berlin parliament, the Brandenburg Landtag after ten years of existence is "(nearly) a parliament like any other" (Schüttemeyer and Lübker 2000: 598). The reconstruction of democratic institutions in eastern Germany after reunification did not result in any new institutional developments; no "new method" (Patzelt and Schirmer 1996: 27) of parliamentarianism developed, only a slightly modified reproduction of the already established model. The smooth adaptation to the functional logic of parliamentarianism has many facets, but basically it proves the weight of institutional patterns; it reflects the dominance of the party state and, of course, the direct help from the West. All Land parliaments in the East started with a director of the Landtag administration from the "old" Länder, except in the case of Saxony-Anhalt. There was no time and obviously no need to risk making groundbreaking reforms at the level of the Länder parliaments in the new Länder.

While the majority of political scientists welcome this development and see it as a result of an effective transition to a working democracy at the Länder level, critics still insist that "the system recruits the type of politicians it needs" (Arnim 2001: 272). They take this development also as further proof of their broader criticism of a political system that is managed by a political class out of its own interest and in which federalism has fallen prey to the party state (Arnim 2000: 154–65). They see it as a system in which the justification for the Länder is primarily one of spoils, which includes well paid positions at all levels of Länder politics and

---

1. 1 = I fully agree, 5 = I think this statement is wrong. The figures for the different parties are SPD: 2.5 CDU: 3.6 PDS: 1.1. The wording of the item is: "Representative Democracy at the Land level should be complemented by plebiscitary elements."

administration, including the Länder parliaments with their high legislative compensations.[2]

The Vote in the Bundesrat

One of the sweeping reform proposals for the Länder parliaments is based on the idea of drawing consequences from the Länder parliaments' losses of competences or powers by the direct election of the prime ministers (minister-presidents) in the Länder. This change from a parliamentary to a presidential system at the Land level would introduce a true separation of powers with a tightened democratic control of the executive branch and strong parliaments. The presidential system is seen as a remedy for the lack of transparency and responsibility resulting from *Politikverflechtung* (interlocking of policymaking procedures) and as a means of balancing the strong position of the prime ministers in national politics via the second chamber or Bundesrat (see Werner Patzelt, chapter 5, this volume).

The highly interlocked German system of intergovernmental relations trades a "federalism of substance" (*Substanzföderalismus*) for a "federalism of participation" (*Beteiligungsföderalismus*) in an ever closer entanglement of the federal government and the Länder governments. The Länder parliaments have no formal way to instruct the Land vote in the Bundesrat, and in this sense the German system combines a strict dual component with a highly cooperative general practice. This can be justified on the basis of the functional logic of the parliamentary systems within the Länder; however, one consequence is a shrinking of the legislative function. The fact is that in parliamentary systems, structural instruments of control are weak, because normally the parliament divides along party lines with the majority forming and supporting a government (cabinet) and with the minority serving as opposition. This is the soft spot of parliamentary systems, especially in regard to their function of controlling the government and administration effectively.

---

2. The monthly basic compensation in July 2003 was €7009 for a member of the Bundestag in Berlin, €6401 for an MP in Hesse, €5861 in Bavaria, and €5403 in Lower Saxony. Even in the small Saarland, MPs received €4429 monthly (for salaries in DM in 2000, see Sturm 2001: 78).

This point is stressed not only by "outsiders." In September 1991 the Conference of the Presidents of the Länder Parliaments passed a resolution in favor of amending Article 51 of the Basic Law by a pro- vision that would provide that in case of the transfer of legislative competences of the Länder to the Federation, "the members of the Bundesrat in their votes are bound by the votes of the Länder parlia- ments" (Janssen 2000: 59). This should also be true in the case of a transfer of exclusive legislative competences of the Länder to inter- national organizations according to Article 24 (1) Basic Law. We will return to this European aspect later. Here it is important to note that when in a May 2000 discussion paper the Conference of the Presi- dents of the Länder Parliaments again put together their proposals to strengthen the Landtage, they did not refer to a binding mandate for the members of the Bundesrat. Only the working group of the admin- istrative heads of the Länder parliaments—that is, the directors of the Landtag offices, who meet regularly in a conference of their own (Huth 1988) and who prepare the Conference's position papers— agreed as a majority that a binding mandate is within the jurisdiction of the Land constitutions and does not need any changes in the Basic Law (Janssen 2000: 60).

This is a position not widely shared. First of all, the prime minis- ters insist on their privilege to determine the general guidelines of Bundesrat politics and show no sign of complying with the demands of the Landtage (Münch and Zinterer 2000: 665f.). The importance of this point is underscored by the incorporation of decision rules for the cabinet in all coalition treaties (Kropp and Sturm 1998; Kropp 2001). In the literature on constitutional law, the argument for the exclusive executive responsibility is well entrenched, based on the ruling of the Federal Constitutional Court in 1958 which established an executive privilege according to which the cabinet decides on the votes in the Bundesrat without formal parliamentary interference (BVerfGE 1958: 120).

The European Challenge

As already mentioned, the impact of European integration on the Län- der parliaments should not be underestimated. The creation of a new layer of competences on top of the Federation and the incorporation into a theater where the specific traditions and norms of German federalism were and still are often misunderstood is a real challenge for the Landtage.

The new political dimension for the Länder has two aspects that are two sides of one coin: information and the capacity to (re)act. Since the Single European Act went into effect in 1986, the Conference of Landtag Presidents has called repeatedly for the incorporation of the Landtage into the European decision-making process within the national framework of intergovernmental relations. The various joint resolutions emphasized especially the right of the Land parliaments to receive information and the possibility of exercising some influence on the formulation of the position presented by the Land government in the Bundesrat. As we have seen, these issues are still unresolved, and Article 23 BL, which strengthened the Bundesrat in the decision-making on European politics, has not been challenged by the Conference of the Presidents of the Länder Parliaments in their latest position paper. Analytical literature nevertheless sees Article 23 BL as not very successful in regard to the position of Länder parliaments. One observer has noted that their "growing unimportance has not been curbed by any of the rights of participation guaranteed to the Länder by Article 23 BL" (Oberländer 2000: 205).

Here again the perspective taken is decisive. When we accept that the emerging political system of Europe is on its way toward a new status for the multilayered system, the result is probably in the loss of autonomy and a steady growth of participation within integrated processes of decision-making (Johne 2000a: 365). Participation in these complex processes involving the Länder capitals, Berlin, and Brussels requires above all a sound basis of information. Since the Single European Act in 1986 and after the introduction of the "European Article," Article 23 BL, in 1994 in response to the Maastricht treaty, the Länder parliaments have focused on this access to information. Today the results show a fragmented picture. The right to get information from their government has been incorporated into the constitutions of eight Länder (Brandenburg, Bremen, Mecklenburg-Vorpommern, Lower Saxony, Rhineland-Palatinate, Saxony-Anhalt, Schleswig-Holstein, and Thuringia). The other Länder parliaments still rely on parliamentary motions or written agreements with the respective governments (Johne 2000a).

The general trend is in the direction of incorporating this right into the Länder constitutions. The Rhineland-Palatinate is the latest example where an agreement dating from 1988 between the prime minister and the president of the parliament concerning information on European affairs was transformed into Article 89 b (1), 7 of the revised constitution of March 2000.

To strengthen the flow of communications, the Conference of the Presidents of the Länder Parliaments and the president of the Bundestag agreed in 1995 to cooperate in European affairs, and the parliament of North Rhine-Westphalia commissioned a liaison person to take part in the meetings of the Bundestag Committee on European Affairs. This process gives committees on European affairs in the Land parliaments a fair chance of sharing information, but obviously not all potential recipients are really interested, depending often on the internal treatment of the information offered by the administrative offices of the parliaments.

Parallel to these efforts since the early 1990s, the Land parliaments established committees on European affairs as specialized instruments for dealing with this new political challenge. Between 1990 and 1998, fifteen of the sixteen Länder had reacted to the growing importance of Europe by creating specialized committees that could serve as an institutional base for an active role of the Länder parliaments in this field. There has been no clear pattern of development, though it seems that the more detailed regulations about parliamentary rights can be found overwhelmingly in the West. Looking at the institutional setting of the management of European affairs, Länder parliaments in the West and in the East follow the same functional parliamentarian logic.

Another front line where the Länder parliaments fought for European recognition is the selection of the members of the German delegation to the Committee of the Regions (CoR) at the European level. Here the Land Bremen has taken the lead in Article 101, Section. 3 of the Land Constitution, where the right to select delegates is given to the Bürgerschaft (parliament of the city-state). Still, in most cases the Land government (cabinet) selects delegates, even though there is a tendency to include more parliamentarians as deputy members of the CoR (Johne 2000b: 103ff.).

Looking at this institutional "arms race" between parliaments and governments, the question is whether different measures will really compensate the legislative bodies for their "downgrading" in the process of European integration. An empirical comparison of selected decision-making processes in the parliaments of Hesse and Baden-Württemberg concerning the preparation of the 1996 session of the European Council and the development of the Agenda 2000 program revealed that parliaments have not been the starting point of the political process in their respective Länder. Parliaments accompanied and corrected the process in both Länder, but the parliamentary role was one of confirming and legitimizing executive actions. The development of positions in the Länder and the decision on the final vote in the Bundesrat on both European subjects was clearly dominated by the executives of the Länder (Johne 2000a: 347). The main reasons for this sobering result are simply the lack of timely information and the lack of personnel at all levels of the parliamentary process. The analysis also stresses that highly formalized institutional channels—as in the case of Baden-Württemberg—and weak institutional arrangements—as in the case of Hesse—do not make a difference in practice; therefore, in this context institutional provisions do not really matter.

The Länder parliaments are still on their way toward becoming European players. But looking ahead to an enlarged EU that is admitting new members with no federal tradition and that comprises small nation-states that are often smaller than the German Länder, it is more realistic to predict that the troubled waters ahead will impinge negatively on German federalism and its parliamentary quality.[3] Together with the permanent extension of EU competences, this development will support a tendency toward "deparliamentarization" at the subnational level, which any future European constitution probably will not reverse.

---

3. Among the "Luxemburg Group" which are the six members of the first round of enlargement, the Czech Republic and Hungary have a population of about ten million, and three other states have fewer than two million inhabitants. In the second group (Helsinki Group) five out of six members have fewer than nine million inhabitants. These figures should be compared to the three Länder of the Federal Republic that have more than ten million inhabitants.

The Allocation of Responsibilities:
Reforms of Control and Legislation

The Länder parliaments have always been a locus of innovation and experiments, but especially since the late 1980s they have become active in modernizing the constitutional and procedural framework of the Länder. In several Länder parliaments, including the important commission of North Rhine-Westphalia, study commissions have been installed to create information and to provide proposals for institutional and political solutions to the role of Länder parliaments in the changed federal and European environment (Große-Sender 1990). Such commissions were also formed in 1996 in Rhineland-Palatinate and Hesse. In 1997 they agreed on an exchange of materials and results (Landtag Rheinland-Pfalz 1998), and in 1998 the Bavarian Landtag followed with a study commission targeting "Reform of Federalism—Strengthening of Länder Parliaments" (Männle 2001: 166–70).

Parliamentary reform is a continuous process often caused by a mix of external and internal developments, including the impact of European integration and globalization. This can be seen in the crisis of public finance and the need for reform of administration (Greß and Janes 2001). The provision in the Basic Law according to which "the Länder shall execute federal laws in their own right" (Article 83 BL) encourages the Länder to look for "new public management" and new instruments of governance, especially when in 1998 the Federation changed the budget law (*Haushaltsgrundsätzegesetz*) and gave the Länder time to adapt until 1 January 2001. Budgeting, outsourcing, public-private partnerships, and controlling in the area of public tasks help to cut costs and increase responsibility in the administration, but at the same time they impinge on the competences of the Landtage, especially with the development of "side budgets" (*Nebenhaushalte*), which are out of reach of parliamentary control.

In May 1999 the Conference of the Presidents of the Länder Parliaments drew attention to the fact that the privatization of state tasks is an important instrument for reaching "lean government" but that through privatization "the participation and control by the parliaments" (Landtag Rheinland-Pfalz 2001: 51) will be reduced significantly. Again in May 2000 the Conference underscored that "the greater freedom of the executive in spending funds has to be combined with appropriate instruments of control and steering" (Landtag Rhein-land-Pfalz 2001: 59).

The most decisive front line of reforms, the "big issue," is about the transfer of legislative competences from the Federation back to the Länder. The centerpiece of the argument is that the sharing of competences between the Länder and the Federation has led to irre-sponsibility, inflexibility, a lack of transparency, and it has eroded the position of the Länder parliaments. The topic became politically important in the deliberations of the Joint Constitutional Reform Commission of Bundesrat and Bundestag between January 1992 and October 1993, and various subjects for legislative devolution became earmarked and provisions discussed that would strengthen the posi-tion of the Länder parliaments (Deutscher Bundestag 1996). The amending act of October 1994 therefore puts restrictions on the use of concurrent and framework legislation by the Federation. It empowers the parliament of a Land to seek a Federal Constitutional Court ruling in the event of disagreement about the concurrent leg-islative power of the Federation (Article 93 [2 a] BL). Article 80 [4] BL provides that administrative regulations that Land governments are authorized to issue pursuant to federal laws can also be passed by an act of the Land parliament.

Great expectations were especially raised with the so-called open-ing clause (*Öffnungsklausel*) of Article 125a, [2] BL, which opens to the federal legislator the opportunity to provide that a federal law may be superseded by Land law. But it took nearly three and a half years to compile a final list of items that the Länder wanted. This work was done mostly by the Länder governments under the leadership of Bavaria, and here, as in other Länder, nobody seemed very eager to get competences back. Consequently, the joint Bundesrat initiative nearly did not pass the Bundesrat committees but instead fell prey to special interests which are especially strong in the administration at this level (Bocklet 1999: 376). In December 1999 only a watered-down version reached the Bundestag, and there it still rests. Länder parliamentarians who have been involved in this process are deeply disappointed over how things have developed. They criticize this sort of "executive federalism" but also complain that Länder politicians "hesitate to take over responsibilities" (Männle 2001: 165).

To give support to this process, the Conference of the Presidents of the Länder Parliaments has put the question of Länder legislation on its agenda. As already mentioned, in May 2000 the presidents discussed a report on "development and strengthening of federalism" prepared by a working group of the directors and made it available not only to the parliamentarians in the Länder but also to the interested public (*Zeitschrift für Gesetzgebung*, 2000: 5–39). In presenting these materials to the public, the presidents emphasized that three aims should guide further discussion:

1. strengthening the autonomy (*Selbständigkeit*) and responsibility (*Eigenverantwortung*) of the Länder and their parliaments;
2. improving transparency by disentangling political decisions; and
3. reforming the intergovernmental system of finances (*Zeitschrift für Gesetzgebung*, 2000: 4).

Without going into details of the proposals to amend the Basic Law in the areas of exclusive federal legislation (Article 73) and of concurrent federal/Länder legislation (Article 74), it can be said that the proposals are very limited in their scope. In general there seems to be a discrepancy between theoretical reasoning and the moderate changes deemed necessary. The basic argument runs along the following lines: constituent members of a federation without parliaments that are partners in "balance of interests in the domestic structure of the federation" are like "provinces of a unitary state, which are no longer Länder with their state quality " (*Zeitschrift für Gesetzgebung* 2000: 5); the distribution of legislative competences in Articles 73–75 BL should, therefore, be reformed, taking into account the principles of subsidiarity and the goal of developing a "competition among the Länder for better legislative problem solving (*Zeitschrift für Gesetzgebung* 2000: 6).

The proposals to reform the intergovernmental system of finances in order to create more autonomy for the Länder also challenge the status quo, even if they are not new. The disentanglement of the system as it stands now should lead to a certain responsibility for the Land parliaments, which today are "practically excluded from legislation on taxes" (*Zeitschrift für Gesetzgebung* 2000: 21). The principle should be that "he who orders has to pay the bill." The resolution here repeats the demand to abolish the joint tasks of Article 91a and 91b BL and to compensate the Länder by transferring to them the revenues that today are flowing from the federal budget. The practice of nonfunded mandates must be stopped, and the Länder must be offered the competence to introduce competitive elements into their share of the income tax and the right to create their own revenues in the fields of excise taxes and real estate taxes. The working group of the directors of the Länder parliaments concluded that this does not mean abolishing the intergovernmental system of fiscal equalization, but that system should be restricted to dealing with those circumstances that are beyond the reach of Land politics.

The bottom line is a call for the disentanglement of financial responsibilities, the strengthening of the parliaments by giving them a limited competence to decide on revenues, and stressing the principle that the Länder are the first in competences, in accordance with Article 70 BL.

Of course, this is not the only proposal on the table at the moment. Other interesting contributions to the discussion have been made by think tanks such as the Bertelsmann Foundation (Bertelsmann 2000) or the liberal Friedrich Naumann Foundation, which published several manifestos on the subject (the latest one in January 2002), including a proposal to have the members of the Bundesrat elected by the Länder parliaments. In its paper titled "Disentanglement 2005," the Bertlesmann Foundation makes innovative proposals for the strengthening of the Länder parliaments according to Article 72 [1 and 2] BL, especially when it proposes that in the transfer of legislative competences in concurrent legislation the principle should be that the Länder parliaments act and the federal legislators—Bundestag and Bundesrat—react within due time. The report also recommends the instrument of the "waiver" granted to states that want to deviate from federal standards. A last step could be to put the Länder and Federation on an equal footing in concurrent legislation and to develop a catalogue of criteria that support soft solutions such as waivers in case of conflicts instead of the rigid system in which federal law automatically supersedes Land law.

Summary and Outlook

An overview of fifteen years of reform proposals concludes with a chapter on "lethargical Länder parliaments" (Münch and Zinterer 2000: 667). I think this summary is unfair. The Länder parliaments have been and still are busy, but not (always) successful. Who counts the parliamentary documents, who tells us about the energy spent on legislative responsibilities? The results of any inquiry are mixed due to the very nature of the political environment.

- The parliamentary system is based on a special division of powers in which the government (cabinet) and the parliamentary parties of the majority are closely connected, the result of which is a structural dominance of the executive over the parliament.
- Land parliaments have been successful in the modernization of their institutional setting within the framework of the functional logic of parliamentarianism.
- The shifting of the federal balance and the transfer of legislative competences back to the Länder did not happen—and obviously will not happen in substantive form.
- Because the shift of the cooperative paradigm of German federalism toward a more competitive one did not occur, the powers of the legislatures of the Länder are bound to this pattern.
- Within these limits the parliamentary systems of the Länder offer a place for policy innovations and an administrative profile of their own.
- Last and most important, Länder parliaments serve as a testing ground that keeps the party system flexible and gives access to nearly unlimited possibilities of coalition building at the Länder level.

To focus the argument: It seems that the political legitimation for the Länder as entities with state status lies to a large extent in the fact that they provide institutional space for innovations in the party system; in this sense they serve as true laboratories of democracy (Detterbeck and Renzsch 2002: 69–81).

This raises questions about assertions that German federalism is simply a victim of the party state and that therefore direct democracy should be strengthened. The situation is more complex than this, for there is a dialectical tension between the state status of the Länder within the Federation, the party state, and the conditions of Länder politics. We have to take this interaction, including its shortcomings, into account when we hear the call for "more direct democracy" (Heußner and Jung 1999b), which is sometimes presented as a sort of populist miracle drug (Arnim 2000).

The opinion polls tell us a different story when we take seriously the concept of federal democracy and the preferences of the public toward institutions and processes. The figures reveal that only a minority of the population prefers to give the Länder more competences. Obviously unitary federalism looms large in Germany, and diversity is not valued very much. Interviewed in 1995 by the Institut für Demoskopie in Allensbach about their approval or disapproval of differences in living conditions in the Länder (number of schools and theaters, quality of administration), 54 percent of the population in the West and 57 percent in the East saw major differences, and 36 percent in the West and 49 percent in the East disapproved of them (Greß and Huth 1998: 137). Asked about their preferences for the distribution of competences between the Federation and the Länder, the population for all issues preferred a federal solution—contrary to the fact that the topics listed in the questionnaire are all within the legislative competence of the Länder (see table 4.2).

The supporters of a concept praising direct democracy as more responsive than representative democracy also should be aware of the discussion in the United States, where the National Conference of State Legislatures (NCSL), scholars devoted to an effective federalism (Rosenthal 1998), and journalists (Broder 2000) defend the reformed legislatures against the plebiscitarian challenge and are wary of the weakening of the system of checks and balances.

Table 4.2 Regulation by Länder or by Federation (in percentage)

	That should be regulated by the Federation	That should be a matter for the Länder
Equipment and organization of the police	52	42
Local voting rights for foreigners	53	32
Extension of the rail system	59	29
Regulation of school graduation	69	26
Speed limits on the Autobahn	73	19
Final decision on deportation of foreigners who have criminal convictions	75	19
University regulations/guidelines	71	18
Drug policy	78	14
Determination of criteria for drunkenness	85	7

Source: Greß and Huth 1998: 137.

But at the same time, when looking at the United States, we should not forget that the highly interlocked system of German federalism was never meant to be a federalism that protects and strengthens the autonomy of its constituent parts. The longstanding tradition of etatism and paternalism was never sympathetic to concepts that understood federalism not as a well-oiled political machine designed to coordinate administration but as an arrangement that promotes and protects the division of powers. Basically the German model of federalism offers an alternative to the traditional way in which representation and territory are linked. Rather than considering territory as a "package" in which individual voters exercise their choice in selecting the members of sovereign institutions, the Bundesrat offers an example of "an institution wielding general power in which the interests of territorial governments (defined as executives rather than legislatures) are protected by those very governments" (Sbragia 1992: 288). With this in mind, the development of changing patterns of party politics and the persistence of the institutional setting against reforms within German federalism may be understood as the expression of a conflict between the parliamentarian institutional structure and the dynamics of the party system— bound together, but not identical and still molded by historical conditions (Lehmbruch 2002: 53–110).

Chapter 5

GERMANY'S LATENT CONSTITUTIONAL CONFLICT

Werner J. Patzelt

New Evidence for an Old Issue

As long as four decades ago, political scientist Ernst Fraenkel made the point that Germans' open uneasiness with their new democracy might be due to the prevalent feeling that the new institutions would not fit what they instinctively conceived as "true" democracy (Fraenkel 1979: 101–10). Both ordinary citizens and intellectuals were complaining that the system of government was unacceptably distorted by political parties that were too strong, by too much parliamentary party group discipline, by a lack of a "true" separation of powers, and by an undue influence of interest groups. Basically, popular German constitutional thinking was seen to be at odds with the newly implemented constitution and the practices introduced in accordance with it.

If Fraenkel's analysis is correct, the usual German grumbling about the regime and the political class is not caused simply by alleged bad policy performance or by mistakes of political leaders (see Maier 2000). Rather, the very criteria on which popular judgments are based are a significant part of the overall problem. As a consequence, neither better policy performance by the system nor better political personnel would make political alienation disappear. In this case the choice would be either to adjust the structures of the polity to popular constitutional ideology or to invest in long-range political education.

Representative data collected by the author in 1995 confirm Fraenkel's diagnosis.[1] They show that most Germans have perceptions of central features of the German political system, especially of the role of parliament and deputies, that simply do not conform with the system's functional logic (Patzelt 1998a). Therefore, even an absolutely correct functioning of the system attracts criticism that is widely accepted but nevertheless misplaced. Unfortunately, other research[2] shows that a significant minority among German members of parliament share popular misunderstandings (Patzelt 1996: 502). Based on this new evidence concerning an old issue, Fraenkel's assumption can be expanded to the thesis that there is a double-sided conflict in Germany. On the one side is a contradiction between the actual structure of the parliamentary system and what the people wish this structure to be; and on the other side is tension between the majority of citizens and the majority of parliamentarians about the nature of the system and whether it works as it is supposed to. This conflict can be called a constitutional conflict, because an important part of Germany's constitutional structure is involved. This conflict is latent, because only its surface phenomena—political alienation or disenchantment (*Politikverdrossenheit*) and falling rates of trust in institutions and politicians—have attracted much attention during the last decades, whereas the basic attitudinal patterns have generally been ignored. Therefore, to speak of a "latent constitutional conflict"

1. This research was carried out in cooperation with the Allensbacher Institut für Demoskopie, IfD surveys 6015 and 6016. In both waves, weighted representative samples of approximately 1000 respondents each in West and East Germany were taken. Case numbers below n = 1800 are not due to missing cases, but to filtering questions and to a split-half procedure applied to several questions. For details, see Patzelt 1998a.

2. In 1994 a questionnaire was sent to all German members of parliament at state, federal, and European levels. The response rate was one-third. All following data on MPs are based on the (weighted) answers of 815 members of state parliaments and the Bundestag. Case numbers much lower than that are due to the fact that four versions of the questionnaire, each having a different focus, were each administered to a quarter of the MPs. For details, see Patzelt 1996, 1997. From the outset, the MP survey and the population survey mentioned in note 1 were designed to match each other. Both were funded by the Deutsche Forschungsgemeinschaft.

seems to be appropriate. It may be conceded that such a conflict might be common for many other political systems as well. But this diagnosis is always bad news, especially for representative democracy, that is, for a regime whose institutional setting is founded on public opinion and popular consent.

The Perceptions of Germans about Their Parliamentary System

Popular Assumptions about the Bundestag

Criticism based on solid knowledge and well-developed arguments must be taken much more seriously than criticism stemming from ignorance and prejudice. This applies also to the popular German critique of the parliamentary system of government. Surveys show that even the most visible among German political institutions, the national parliament (Bundestag), is the object of widespread misperceptions and of unfounded evaluations (see Holtmann 2001b; Patzelt 1994, 1998a; Schüttemeyer 1986). The basis is ignorance, and the consequence is the dominance of prejudices that fill the gaps in knowledge and understanding.

This becomes clear in the following findings (see Patzelt 1998a). Replying to an open-ended question, that is, without being prompted, 58 percent of Germans could not mention any structure or part of the Bundestag besides its plenary session, where the national parliament's work is accomplished. A fourth of the 42 percent who did attempt an answer gave uninformed responses such as constituency work, the Bundesrat (the Federal Council, i.e., second chamber; see Patzelt 1999a), or even state parliaments (Landtage). Only 27 percent referred correctly to committees, 12 percent to parliamentary party groups, and 6 percent to the policy-focused working groups of parliamentary parties. More comforting results were obtained when respondents were given a list of possible answers. In this case 85 percent claimed to know about the existence of parliamentary party groups, 80 percent of the plenary session, and 78 percent of parliamentary committees. Since 60 percent claimed to know even about the petition committee, some effort to appear better informed than one actually is seems to have played a role no less significant than the well-known difference between passive and active knowledge. Therefore, the real level of information about the Bundestag is closer to the knowledge disclosed by the open-ended question. But whoever is on such a level has little possibility of understanding what is going on in the Bundestag, how the parliament actually works, and why it plays which role in the overall institutional setting. Rather, erroneous assumptions about parliament, its elements, and their combined activities can be expected, and this is exactly what the findings show.

After 1994 Germany was marked by a stalemate between a Bundestag run by the governing center-right coalition and a Bundesrat dominated by the Social Democrats and their allies, who had the role of parliamentary opposition at that time. Therefore, the conference committee of both legislative institutions met quite often and had exceptional media coverage. This fact is reflected by the finding that 39 percent of Germans called the conference committee "particularly important" (mean on a three point ranking scale: 1.6). Another 39 percent (mean: 1.7) called the plenary session of the Bundestag "particularly important," 34 percent (mean: 1.7) referred to the parliamentary party groups, 28 percent (mean: 1.8) to the parliamentary committees, and 23 percent (mean: 1.9) to the policy-focused working groups of the parliamentary parties. But in German parliamentary reality, the rank order of practical importance is the other way around, with policy-focused working groups on top, followed by committees and the meetings of parliamentary party groups. The plenary session of the Bundestag is usually not much more than the site of formal decisions and ritual debates, and the conference committee will be an important player only under exceptional conditions. But these "details," which are rather fundamental, are not known to ordinary citizens. Therefore, they have quite limited opportunities to really understand parliamentary measures and procedures when presented in the news. And because German state parliaments get much less media coverage than the Bundestag, knowledge about them will certainly not be better than the level of understanding of the national parliament. As a consequence, the following findings reflect assumptions that Germans make about their parliamentary system at large.

The central feature of this system is that cabinet emerges from parliament, with the chancellor (or the Land prime minister) being elected (and/or possibly removed) by a parliamentary majority that may be formed, according to electoral outcome, by one single parliamentary party, by a coalition, or by exceptional support from parliamentary parties that do not join a coalition but "tolerate" the cabinet and support it as long as agreement can be reached on separate issues. In Germany an "action unit" formed by the cabinet and its supporting majority usually can be forged. As a consequence, this "government camp" tries to provide political leadership in a steady, and more often than not mutually disciplined, confrontation with the parliamentary opposition parties. In fact, Germany's whole political life is shaped by this "new dualism" between the government camp and the opposition, that is, by the parliamentary system's form of horizontal separation of powers. Under such conditions, the central and never ending task of parliament is the formation and maintenance of a majority that is willing and able to support the cabinet and its policies. Electing—and keeping in office—the chancellor or prime minister as head of government is the cornerstone of this system. Only those who understand these connections and their corresponding institutional mechanisms will be able to make sense of the numerous political and tactical details reported by the mass media. Otherwise, they will have no chance to interpret the political game as it is experienced and played by politicians or to formulate evaluations that really focus on what is practically important to political actors.

Unfortunately, but as expected, table 5.1 shows that Germans are not in a good position to understand the logic of parliamentary politics. It is true that 74 percent of Germans know about the election of the federal chancellor by the Bundestag. But only 39 percent of respondents personally thought this task to be "particularly important." The precondition of any chancellor's election, and the very basis of his subsequent power, was known to even fewer respondents; that is, only 30 percent claimed to know that creating and maintaining a stable parliamentary majority in support of the cabinet is a task of the Bundestag, and no more than 42 percent thought this task was "particularly important." Therefore, there is an enormous difference of 44 percentage points between those who know about the Bundestag's central electoral function and those who are aware of its preconditions and the very important systematic consequences thereof.

Lack of understanding and, as a result, misperceptions of parliament's role in the parliamentary system become even clearer in column 4 of table 5.1, where data from columns 2 and 3 are compared. Column 2 displays personal evaluations of the Bundestag's functions, whereas column 3 shows how respondents perceived the actual

Table 5.1 Popular Perceptions of the Bundestag's Tasks

Task	Known	"Particularly important" according to the respondent's personal opinion (percent or mean)	"Particularly important" in political practice (percent or mean)	Surplus of importance in practice (in percent)
	(1)	(2)	(3)	(4)
Deciding on bills	84	51 or 1.5	57 or 1.4	+6
Electing the chancellor	74	39 or 1.8	49 or 1.7	+10
Drafting bills	72	42 or 1.6	50 or 1.5	+8
Controlling the cabinet	66	65 or 1.4	62 or 1.4	−3
Presenting arguments and standpoints to the public in plenary debates	63	36 or 1.8	37 or 1.8	+1
Introducing citizens' desires and points of view into politics	60	61 or 1.4	63 or 1.4	+2
Deciding against the will of a majority among citizens if MPs believe this to lead to a better decision	42	18 or 2.1	23 or 2.1	+5
Deciding in accordance with the will of a majority among citizens	39	55 or 1.5	57 or 1.5	+2
Maintaining a stable parliamentary majority supporting the cabinet	30	42 or 1.7	47 or 1.6	+5
None of the above	1	—	—	—
Respondents	1,762	*219 to 688*	*269 to 750*	*219 to 688*

Notes: Shown are either percentages based on the case numbers indicated below or means based on three-point rating scales, with 1 = particularly important, 2 = important, 3 = less important. Case numbers vary because of split-half and filtering procedures.

Source: Patzelt 1998a: 733.

importance of these functions in political practice. A look at column 4 reveals that in practice, too much weight seems to be given to electing the chancellor, to maintaining his parliamentary majority[3] and to—mostly cabinet-initiated—legislation, whereas the Bundestag's control function appears to be stunted. In reality, the internal control processes within the government camp are simply not recognized by the public (see Patzelt 1999b), whereas failures of opposition initiatives shape public perception as well as intraparliamentary party discipline in nearly every vote taken on the floor. What Walter Bagehot toward the end of the nineteenth century called the "efficient secret" of a parliamentary system of government (Bagehot 1891), that is, that the cabinet emerges from a parliamentary majority that may be difficult to create and to maintain, is obviously still a mystery for most Germans today. However, if this central feature of the overall system of government is not understood, then its consequences—such as intraparty group discipline (see Patzelt 1998b) and coincidence of leadership in party, parliament and cabinet—will not be understood, either.

Best known by far is parliament's legislative function. This fact fits quite well with the popular, traditional, and—citing Montesquieu— "canonized" way of referring to the Bundestag, or to a Landtag, as a "legislature" thought to be opposed to the executive branch of government. Based on a list of the Bundestag's possible tasks, 84 percent of respondents claimed to know about decision-making on bills (drafting bills: 72 percent), and 51 percent (and 42 percent, respectively) personally would call this task "particularly important." Slightly less known is the Bundestag's function of executive oversight. Two-thirds of Germans know about it, and 65 percent personally think that this task is "particularly important." Sixty-three percent know about the expressive function of the Bundestag (36 percent believe this is particularly important) and 60 percent know of the Bundestag's task of being responsive to popular wishes.

Introducing people's desires and opinions into policymaking, an essential part of representative democracy, is regarded as "particularly

---

3. Closer analysis displays that only every second respondent—at the most— either accepts personally or at least sees the factual connection between electing the chancellor as the cornerstone of the cabinet and securing his parliamentary majority; the respective correlation coefficients are $r = 0.40$ and $r = 0.32$.

important" by 61 percent of Germans. As a normative principle, this sounds to them very much like a rule for decision-making according to popular preferences. Thirty-nine percent clearly saw this as one of the Bundestag's tasks, and 55 percent evaluated this task personally as "particularly important." In contrast, only 18 percent were personally convinced that decision-making in opposition to popular preferences, even if motivated by the deputies' own convictions, would be a "particularly important" task—although 42 percent recognized this as a leadership task of the Bundestag. Decades ago, Ernst Fraenkel called this task "improving the empirically detectable popular will," and he regarded this option as one of the central advantages of representative democracy. Germans, however, still tend to think and judge in terms of what Fraenkel called "vulgar democratic theory," that is, they want their representatives to act as the people's delegates rather than as trustees, but they suspect that the trustee role prevails (see Patzelt 1998a: 749).[4] This can also be seen in column 4 of table 5.1. Clearly more Germans think that their deputies actually decide against popular preferences than accept the argument that such decision-making may be based on good reasons. Inferring from all findings discussed so far, it may safely be stated that a considerable number of Germans certainly have knowledge about their country's parliamentary system of government, and about its working structures and their functions. But this is not the majority by far. On the contrary, the majority's knowledge and understanding is shallow and full of gaps. The latter are conveniently filled with common sense assumptions and with prejudices that lead to a bias against the functional logic of the established parliamentary system.

Judgments about the German System of Government

The functional logic of the parliamentary system should be known much better to success-oriented persons acting within its institutional framework than to ordinary citizens, especially if the latter are no more than casual spectators. These have no major incentives to become well acquainted with the rules of the game, whereas parliamentary actors can hardly afford to follow personal impressions

---

4. On how MPs see their roles themselves, see Patzelt 1996, 1997.

Table 5.2 Judgments about the System of Government: Citizens and MPs Compared

Which type of system ...	... does exist in Germany?		... is desired?		Difference of percentages
	Citizens[1]	MPs[2]	Citizens[1]	MPs[3]	Citizens
	(1)	(2)	(3)	(4)	(5)
Presidential	18	6	33	53	+15
Parliamentary	61	84	40	70	−21
Neither/nor	6	10	8	45	+2
Undecided, don't know	15	—	19	—	+4
Respondents	**938**	**205**	**938**	**208**	

Notes: Column percent shown except in column 4; see note 3 below.

1. The wording of the question is given in footnote 5 below.
2. The choices were: "The Cabinet should be confronted by parliament as a whole" = presidential system; "The Cabinet should be supported by a parliamentary majority generated for this purpose; this unit of cabinet and supporting majority should be confronted by the parliamentary opposition" = parliamentary system; "The Cabinet, coalition parties and opposition parties should act independently from each other" = mixed type.
3. The choices given in note 2 were to be rated on five-point scales with 1 = fully agree and 5 = fully disagree. Shown are answers with values of 1 and 2.

Source: Patzelt 1998a: 739.

rather than practical observations. This is why a comparison of citizens' and deputies' judgments will be so telling. In fact, tables 5.2 and 5.3 display considerable normative disagreement between representatives and constituents about the very structure of the German system of government.

It is true that 61 percent of citizens know that Germany has a parliamentary system.[5] But only 40 percent really want to have such a

5. It should not be expected that ordinary citizens can handle concepts such as "parliamentary system of government" or "presidential system of government." Therefore, respondents were given a sheet that contained descriptions of two states. State A was characterized as follows: "The Cabinet and parliament are independent from each other. Parliament as a whole, i.e., all members are controlling the cabinet." State B was described as follows: "In parliament, some parties join to form a majority and to elect the cabinet. There is a single political camp formed by the cabinet and its supporting deputies, and this camp is controlled by the opposition." Respondents were asked to pay special attention to the relations between cabinet and parliament in both

system. Instead, 33 percent favor a presidential system of government.[6] This means that by 21 points fewer Germans appreciate a parliamentary system than know such a system exists in Germany. By the same token, more Germans wish by 15 points to have a presidential system than erroneously think they possess it already. So, the parliamentary system can hardly be asserted to have extensive roots in popular German political thought. Quite the contrary, 41 percent of citizens definitively prefer an alternative; a further 19 percent have no clear opinion and, therefore, are susceptible to ad hoc criticism of virtually every kind. This is all the more disturbing, since detailed additional analyses show that many popular evaluations of the German system of government are in conformity with the basic preference for either a parliamentary or a presidential type of system (Patzelt 1998a: 739 passim).

Obviously, "new dualism" and the parliamentary system's guiding principles and functional logic appear strange to most Germans. Instead, every third citizen perceives a presidential system with the separation of powers along institutional lines as the proper form of balancing parliament and cabinet. This "old dualism," brought into its republican form by the framers of the U.S. constitution more than two centuries ago and made well known along with America's rise to world power, was typical of German constitutionalism in the nineteenth century. Therefore, it may be inferred that so many Germans' inclination toward "old dualism" is only the tip of an iceberg of "old institutional thinking" conveyed over generations in millions of everyday conversation and in thousands of lessons taught by teachers, journalists, and even politicians.[7] By the same token, the acceptance of the parliamentary system's "new dualism" by a mere minority may mean that German political common sense is simply lagging

---

descriptions. Then, one half-group was asked in which state they would prefer to live; the other half-group was asked to say in which of both states—A or B—the relations between cabinet and parliament would resemble the actual relationship in Germany. Of course, state A is a model of the presidential system's "old dualism," and state B is a model of the parliamentary system of government.

6. An additional sobering indicator of the quality of political knowledge is the fact that 18 percent of respondents believed Germany to have a presidential system of government.

7. For a detailed discussion, see the section on German constitutionalism and its legacies.

behind the establishment of this country's much more modern political system. Thus modern institutions are evaluated by old-fashioned standards, and their functioning is criticized mainly not because of bad performance but because of inadequate criteria of evaluation. Actually, this is the shortest formula for the first dimension of Germany's "latent constitutional conflict."

No less important is its second dimension, where the tension line runs between political actors and observers. Fortunately, only 6 percent of German MPs believe they are involved in a presidential system; a large majority, 84 percent, are aware of the institutional setting in which they operate. Acceptance of the parliamentary system also prevails clearly among parliamentarians; 70 percent support the existing "new dualism," while only 11 percent oppose it. But it is certainly disturbing that 53 percent of the members favor a presidential system at the same time, with only 23 percent strictly rejecting it. Obviously, many deputies simply do not recognize the mutually exclusive character of these system types. Thus, even among MPs only a minority really seem to understand the parliamentary system.

Still more disturbing is that large majorities among constituents and representatives do not agree about which type of system Germany should have. Things become even more dramatic when two important corollaries of the parliamentary system are considered. The first is the nearly "natural" compatibility of parliamentary mandate and cabinet office, which was famously called an "efficient secret" by Walter Bagehot. The second is the usual coincidence of parliamentary mandate and a—mostly regional—party leadership position. This coincidence stems empirically from the fact that in a system with strong parties only party leaders (and occasionally persons at least supported by party leaders) will have a good chance of receiving either a safe district or a safe position on a party list. Normatively, responsible party government, as one of the most efficient ways to organize representative democracy, simply calls for MPs to be held personally accountable by voters for their parliamentary performance; and within the framework of systems of proportional representation, this is most easily accomplished by giving the same persons responsibility for intraparty and intraparliamentary decision-making, that is, by electing party leaders into parliament. Seen this way, an MP's forced electoral responsiveness as a party leader is nothing else but a highly desirable counterweight to his "free mandate" that might otherwise allow for purely personal voting. Unfortunately, this rational means of combining representation with democracy seems still to be unknown, or at least rarely understood, among most Germans and many of their politicians. Instead, there is, as table 5.3 shows, deep disagreement between representatives and constituents on both issues.

Although some 90 percent of German cabinet members on the state and federal level have a seat in parliament and keep it during their time in executive office (see Kempf and Merz 2001: 21–24), this current practice is accepted by only 52 percent of German MPs,

Table 5.3 Corollaries of the Parliamentary System: Evaluations of Citizens and MPs Compared

Compatability between parliamentary mandate and …	Cabinet office		Party office	
	Citizens[1]	MPs[2]	Citizens[3]	MPs[4]
	(1)	(2)	(3)	(4)
Desired or accepted	16	52	29	52
Undecided	27	12	21	26
Rejected	57	36	50	22
Respondents	*1,876*	*211*	*1,876*	*597*

Notes: Column percent shown. Case numbers among MPs depend on the number of questionnaire versions where a question was included.

1. Question: "If a member of the Bundestag becomes a minister: Do you think it is better if he hands over his seat to a successor, or do you think it is better if he is a member of parliament and minister at the same time?"
2. Respondents were asked to rate the following statement on a five point-scale: "It is good if MPs can become cabinet members and if cabinet members can remain members of parliament." Codes: 1 = fully agree, 5 = fully disagree. Values 1 and 2/ 4 and 5 are combined; answers with value 3 are shown as "undecided."
3. Question: "Do you think that a member of the Bundestag or of a Landtag should be allowed to hold a party office at the same time, for instance, as chairman of the district or Land organization of his party, or do you think both positions should be separated, which would mean that a deputy should not be allowed to hold party offices as long as he is member of parliament?"
4. Respondents were asked to rate the following statement on a five-point scale: "An MP should be grounded in his party by holding leadership functions on the same organizational level (district, Land, Federation) for which he bears responsibility based on his parliamentary mandate." Codes: 1 = fully agree, 5 = fully disagree. Values 1 and 2/4 and 5 are combined; answers with value 3 are shown as "undecided."

Source: Patzelt 1998a: 741.

with 36 percent opposing such quite typical compatibility. Only a slight minority is really prepared to accept what actually is in full correspondence with the functional logic of Germany's parliamentary system. Of course, advocates of the parliamentary system tend to be advocates of compatibility as well (r = 0.32), whereas supporters of a presidential system are inclined to be supporters of incompatibility (r = -0.23).[8] Among citizens a majority reject system-conforming compatibility: 57 percent of respondents definitively do not want members of the cabinet to remain members of parliament, whereas only 16 percent accept what is neither wrong nor detrimental in a parliamentary system. Thus, the people and their representatives are clearly at odds on this important issue. As far as legitimacy is concerned, this is really bad news.

The same structure of conflict can be found with regard to the usual coincidence of party office and parliamentary mandate. Ninety percent of German deputies have leadership positions on the different organizational levels of their parties, among them roughly 60 percent on the constituency level and 20 percent on the state level (see Patzelt 1996: 488–89). Thus, German members of parliament are overtly party leaders. But again only a slight majority of 52 percent among MPs accept this current and politically rational combination of positions. A remarkable 22 percent oppose it. Among the citizens even 50 percent reject combining party and parliament positions, thus harshly criticizing common practice. Only 29 percent of Germans are in favor of MPs' holding party leadership positions. So once more representatives are at odds with the people they represent. It can be argued that popular criticism would be even more severe if citizens were better informed. Actually, only 22 percent of Germans suspect MPs of having party leadership positions, whereas 42 percent think they are rank-and-file party soldiers. By the same token, only 17 percent of citizens believe that deputies have a significant voice in intraparty policymaking, whereas 40 percent are convinced that they have to defend party positions formulated without their participation. Misjudging so clearly the real party role of deputies entails serious misunderstandings of how party discipline is generated in parliaments and is no proper basis for an evaluation. Centered around the erroneous but popular concept of "*Fraktionszwang*" (i.e., forced party group discipline), such misunderstandings

8. The same pattern can be found in the population data.

lead to important further reproaches against the established parliamentary system (see Patzelt 1998b).

The Structure of the Latent Constitutional Conflict

The point is that Germans do not complain at all that MPs might not have enough influence in their parties; after all, table 5.3 shows that they even dislike MPs' holding party leadership positions. Rather, citizens are more likely to object to the allegedly too dominant party role in representative democracy. Although Germans are in favor of democracy, many of them expressly dislike parties and do not believe them to be one of the central organizational means of making democracy work in a mass society. Along with their aversion to parties, citizens dislike the parliamentary system, which necessarily is run by parliamentary parties. It is true that Germans elect parties or party candidates because their electoral system is based on proportional representation. But in popular political thought, representative democracy appears as something that ought to be disconnected from political parties. Where the functional linkages between parliaments and party politicians cannot be fully ignored, as is the case with MPs, these very connections seem to be improper and arouse criticism of parliament and parliamentarians. Obviously, many Germans ignore the fact that representative democracy and responsible party government may be two sides of the same coin and that they are entirely appropriate in a parliamentary system.

Hence, it will not come as a surprise that acceptance of and opposition to the combination of party positions and parliamentary mandate is connected with citizens' other orientations toward the German system of government. Such coincidence is appreciated less by those who also reject compatibility between executive office and parliamentary mandate ($r = -0.34$), and by those who think that Germany has a presidential system of government. There seems to exist a syndrome of closely intertwined perceptions and attitudes lying behind the commonly ascertained surface attitudes toward the parliamentary system and its political class, and the basic pattern of this syndrome is quite similar among citizens and MPs. In this respect, deputies are true representatives of the people.

But their "median attitude" within this pattern is quite different. The average citizen still adheres to what might be called a "classical" doctrine of separation of powers, that is, as few connections as possible are desired between the two "political" branches of government. And he or she adheres to a concept of representation that reflects preparty politics. "State institutions" such as parliaments should be separated to the greatest possible extent from "societal organizations" such as parties and interest groups. The idea hardly occurs to such a citizen that these ties may serve as efficient means of control: the deputies' close party links as part of a chain of control between citizens' constant evaluation of parties—and party leaders—via polls and various electoral and institutional ties between a "legislature" and the cabinet as a means of internal parliamentary control of the executive branch of government by its—not unconditionally—supporting majority. On the contrary, most Germans see combining parliamentary mandate with executive office or with party leadership positions only as an additional source of the MPs' personal influence, which ought to be reduced for the sake of democracy and separation of powers. Obviously, ordinary citizens think predominantly in the terms offered by "old dualism" and made plausible by institutional imaginations from preparty history.

Among MPs the "new dualism" of the parliamentary system is much better rooted than among citizens. Table 5.2 shows that they widely appreciate its basic principle, and, according to table 5.3, a majority of deputies even accept its unpopular corollaries. Seen in this way, most parliamentarians seem to have advanced beyond ordinary citizens in their understanding of the parliamentary system and of its functional logic. Though strong, only a minority among parliamentarians share the citizens' central prejudices. Yet ordinary people get repeated confirmation from this minority—instead of criticism—for their misleading assessments. Moreover, many citizens simply do not accept the idea of MPs' having a more advanced understanding of political issues. Rather, they accuse *them* of seeing things the wrong way and of displaying unacceptable behavior.

Thus, the German parliamentary system attracts popular criticism exactly when it works as it should. This criticism is a result of the citizens' fusing of correct, but isolated, observations into a faulty picture of the whole. And because ordinary people do not have much systematic or background knowledge, they explain whatever seems incomprehensible in that picture as a defect of the system or as a result of unacceptable pressure, be it the staged character of debates in the Bundestag's plenary session or the normal voting discipline practiced by parliamentary party groups.[9] This popular stance of most of the German public resembles people watching European soccer while believing they are seeing American football. But as long as the spectators truly believe they are watching football, no commentator will have the chance to prevent them from getting angry and from blaming players for "irregular play"—although the real problem definitively is not the players' behavior but the spectators' expectations and interpretations. Exactly this is the frustrating irony of Germany's latent constitutional conflict.

German Constitutionalism and Its Legacies

Incompatibility of Constitutional Ideology and Constitutional System

Where does this conflict come from? Ernst Fraenkel referred to the quite different sources of German democratic "constitutional ideology" on the one hand, and of the Federal Republic's constitutional structure on the other hand (Fraenkel 1979: 13–31, 113–51). According to him, German "vulgar democratic theory" was imported from the French Revolution in the form of Rousseauist ideas of direct democracy. Of course, any form of representation will appear as a lessening of democracy to anyone who thinks in Rousseauist terms. So, if installing a parliament cannot be avoided, then the assembly must at least be reduced, for democracy's sake, to the role of finding and expressing the general will of the people. As a first consequence, strong parties and significant interest groups that represent competing social interests and serve as an intermediary between citizens and government are considered to be normatively unacceptable, although their practical emergence cannot be prevented. As a second consequence, a deputy's "free mandate" should have no other purpose than to protect him or her from repeatedly attempted, but illegitimate, influence by parties and interest groups. In addition, the cabinet and the executive branch of government appear to have no other purpose than to execute the general will. This will is either

9. For a more detailed analysis, see Patzelt 1998b.

found in parliament by deputies who do not succumb to particular interests but rather follow their "personal conscience," or—preferably—the popular will is determined by "direct democracy," that is, by means of frequent plebiscites.

However, the core of the Federal Republic's institutional structure, its parliamentary system, was not shaped along Rousseauist ideas, but is an "imported" result of England's constitutional history. There, the political role of estate assemblies developed organically, and without the interlude of absolutism, into the parliamentary system. Yet estate assemblies were not based on abstract principles but comprised exponents of social classes and differentiated group interests who based their actions on rational calculations of give-and-take compromising. In the Houses of Parliament, they wanted to influence the policies of the crown, not to separate powers. Developing institutional mechanisms for this purpose, the English system went a long way from "king in parliament" to a crown reduced to a national symbol and to a monarch limited to the role of his prime minister's dignified spokesperson. Rooted in society ever since the House of Commons came into being, and even more so after the electoral reforms of the nineteenth century and the development of modern parties, the English Houses of Parliament were eager not to check and balance but to command the executive branch of government.

According to Fraenkel, this type of parliamentarianism was always strange to continental constitutional thinking. There, revolutionary ideas of people's sovereignty as well as the aftermath of the French Revolution had parliaments seeing themselves as liberal or even democratic antipodes, but by no means as heirs of estate assemblies. As a consequence, parliaments wanted to be acknowledged—like the crown—as one of the highest organs of the state devoted to the common good, but not as assemblies where competing social interests were represented by their exponents. This brought parliaments to seek rather the role of an opponent or critical partner than of a possible creator of the chief executive's power. Therefore, the idea would not appear convincing that a single and sole source of democratic legitimacy could suffice, that is, that even a chief executive's legitimacy might be derived rather from parliament than from general elections. Finally, Montesquieu's partly mistaken interpretation of England's constitution in the eighteenth century became an apparently everlasting doctrine that could justify mutually opposing roles of an "executive" and a "legislative" branch of government, with a base of legitimacy for each as the compelling postulate of the timeless classical theory of a "true" separation of powers. Combining such a French democratic theory with an English parliamentary system places Germany in a conflict between the living and the imagined constitution.

Fraenkel's analysis and explanation are still valid. There cannot be any doubt that German constitutional theory was—and still is—deeply marked by theorems on separation of powers that are canonized by attributing them to Montesquieu (see Schütt-Wetschky 1984, 2001). They justify "old dualism" as possibly the best, if not the only, sound institutionalization of checks and balances. In the 1980s an analysis of textbooks used in German higher education detected that such theorems were still conveyed with some success like self-evident truths to young people living in a thoroughly parliamentary system (Oberreuter 1985). The data discussed above show that a majority of Germans still think along the lines described.

As further evidence, in reflections on desirable reforms of the German constitution that became quite popular after reunification, nothing seemed to be more evident than Germany's alleged suffering from a lack of "direct democracy." Therefore, direct elections of the federal president and of the Länder prime ministers were demanded, demands that would transform Germany and its Länder at least into semipresidential, if not presidential, systems according to the hallowed doctrine of a "true" separation of powers. Even more popular was, and still is, the hope that introducing plebiscitary elements might be an important step toward solving various modernization problems.[10] Behind those desires, Rousseauist arguments can easily be found, even though they are often distorted (Holtmann 2001a). And while the influence of interest groups used to be the focus of some criticism in the Federal Republic (the *locus classicus* is Eschenburg 1956), the disgust directed at political parties became fully fashionable more recently when it was encouraged by

---

10. Actually, after reunification plebiscitary elements were introduced or improved in all Länder constitutions and in nearly all Länder laws regulating local government. At present, the federal level is the only level of government without plebiscitary means of decision-making.

a federal president's invectives (see Hofmann and Perger 1992), by a constitutional lawyer's investigative research (Arnim 1991, 1995), and by party financing scandals in the early 1980s and late 1990s. Not surprisingly, one of the goals pursued by the promoters of plebiscites and "direct democracy" is to break the power of parties and "party politicians."

The Legacy of German Constitutionalism

Although Fraenkel's analysis explains to a considerable extent both the findings presented above and an important part of actual discussions on the German constitution, it should be complemented by some further observations on the legacy of German constitutionalism. The central fact is that not only German constitutional theory but also Germany's constitutional history itself was marked by "old dualism" until the end of Imperial Germany. In nearly all German states, and later on the level of the Bismarck Reich, leadership and executive authority were invested exclusively in a monarch, assisted by a prime minister or a cabinet of ministers appointed by him. This executive branch of government was confronted by an essentially bicameral legislature possessing powers of legislation and budget control but lacking any significant influence in cabinet formation and short-term policymaking (see Kirsch 1999; Kühne 1989; and Ritter 1962). This nineteenth-century tradition of regime structure was mirrored and fixed by German constitutional theory in the concept of the "monarchical principle." It meant that all prerogatives and the prevailing legal powers belonged to the monarch. He was vaguely responsible to God, to history, or to "the country," but in no way to any institutional body. Legislative powers were shared with the legislature because the crown had deigned to grant this when decreeing the constitution. A corollary of this principle was the understanding of separation of powers as a means of keeping parliamentary power—not executive power—in narrow confines. Any active attempt on the part of a legislature to influence the crown's decisions with regard to cabinet formation, or even to think about a deputy's possible right to become a member of the cabinet while retaining his seat, was interpreted as an attempt to exceed the "legitimate" limits imposed on a "legislature" by the "true" understanding of separation of powers (see Boldt 1980; Schönberger 1997). It is one of the ironies of German constitutional discussions that the postulate of incompatibility of parliamentary mandate and cabinet office, which stemmed from a thorough executive-friendly interpretation of the separation of powers doctrine, has now gained credibility as a way of enhancing parliament's power—just as if the "new dualism" would have reduced parliament's power instead of increasing it.

No less consequential was the fact that both political parties and systematic constitutional thought about their proper role emerged only after both the system and the theory of German constitutionalism were established, that is, in the second half of the nineteenth century. The central problem is that representative assemblies without significant powers of policymaking and patronage necessarily turn out as dead ends for pragmatic party politics. Therefore, political parties simply could not work as efficient transmission belts for electoral preferences within the system of German constitutionalism. Rather, they concentrated on highly ideological debates on policy choices far beyond their own reach. As a consequence, they could be regarded as useless if not outright "dysfunctional" elements of the political system. Even the theory of political representation could not define a positive role for parties in the framework of the German constitutional monarchy (see Schütt-Wetschky 2001). Typically, and for reasons disclosed by Fraenkel, a representative assembly was meant to represent the people as a whole, not primarily its divergent interests. Therefore, it was supposed to work—hand in hand with the monarch and his prime minister—for the common good as defined by "the state" and not by a contentious society and its always quarreling organizations. Of course, the legislature was only demeaning itself when it engaged in "merely political" give-and-take compromises. As a consequence, the ideal of a nonpartisan member of parliament complemented the overall conception of a state hovering above society and of a cabinet concerned with the common good and not with party support.

Mistaken and biased as all these ideas may be, and although their effect was to make German constitutionalism a living lie, such thoughts and reflections were highly popular in their time and taught generations of Germans how to think about the proper working of their political system. Because there was no significant empirically minded political science until the Weimar period, constitutional

lawyers—deeply rooted in such biased, but often theoretically bril-
liant, constitutional theory—successfully maintained the monopoly
on defining how the political system ought to work and how it would
certainly work if not run poorly and for egoistic purposes by the
despised class of "party politicians." Their lessons, none of which
were based on systematic legislative research, were conveyed to
teachers, public servants, intellectuals, and even politicians themselves from Imperial Germany until the early decades of the Federal
Republic. As a consequence, after 1945 German democratic thought
often did no more than simply put an additional layer upon that old-
fashioned scheme of constitutional thought. Thinking in terms of
"old dualism" even survived the creation of Germany's "new dualism" in the Länder constitutions after 1946 and in the Basic Law of
1949. Montesquieu's theory seemed to be the final word on "separation of powers," and the United States with its presidential system of
government, the (direct) democratic form of the "old dualism," was
admired as the best possible model of stable democracy. In the form-
ative years of the West German Federal Republic, there was also no
popular incentive for placing political parties in higher regard. The
shortcomings of the party-driven Weimar Republic and vivid experiences with party-based dictatorship both in Nazi Germany and the
Soviet occupation zone nourished the traditional German anti-party
effect going back to Imperial Germany. As a consequence, (West)
Germany had received a modern parliamentary system on both the
Länder and national levels, but its constitutional thinking, both academic and popular, was—and still is—lagging far behind this institutional innovation.

It is true that Manfred Rauh has offered remarkable arguments to
support his view that there has been a continuous parliamentarization of already Imperial Germany (Rauh 1977). But his thesis has
provoked many objections. Christoph Schönberger (2001) has convincingly shown that the power of the Reichstag certainly increased
between 1871 and 1914, but that there was nothing like a "parliamentarization" leading away from the German type of "old dualism."
First, Schönberger directs attention to several important factors hin-
dering Germany's transition toward a parliamentary system. These
included the existence of an efficient and mostly benevolent bureaucracy under the control of the crown, which made governing appear
to be a form of administration, not a challenge for policymaking. In

addition there was the legacy of Germany's delicate biconfessional-ism and the reaction to the equally delicate equilibrium of political forces in Imperial Germany, which led to the prevailing preference for negotiated agreements rather than majority decisions. Finally, Germany's federal structure was an insurmountable obstacle to effi-cient policymaking based alone on parliamentary majority decisions. All of these reasons still play an important role today and explain why Germans have some difficulty accepting the ways in which their established parliamentary system has functioned.

In a second line of argument, Schönberger shows that the rising power of the Reichstag, especially in the form of oversight of the budget and of well-informed debate on legislative proposals, turned this institution into the bureaucracy's competing partner and made it a "legislature" in the sense of "old dualism" rather than transform-ing it into an assembly seeking access to executive power. The legacy of this experience is Germany's "working parliamentarism" of today, with its notorious weakness for making clear to the people that their opinions and desires are represented in the Bundestag. Taking their cues from the "classical" doctrine of separation of powers, and inspired by anti-English and anti-French attitudes, leading parlia-mentarians—and also constitutional lawyers—even opposed devel-opments that might have led the Reichstag beyond its role as a "legislature" in the framework of the "old dualism." They asserted that "German parliamentarianism" corresponded to the "true" form of separation of powers, represented the "true" form of parliamen-tarism, and, therefore, was superior to its English and French "rivals" (see Redslob 1918; Schönberger 2001: 645–46). Such convictions were to become widespread during the Weimar period with its semi-presidential system. Even today they lie beneath much popular striv-ing toward "a more perfect parliamentarianism" and are a major source of inspiration for criticism raised against the "English" parlia-mentary system that has been "exported" to Germany.

In a third part of his argument, Schönberger makes the point that in Germany—quite in contrast to England or France—democ-ratization preceded parliamentarization and rather hindered than promoted it. In England and France, parliamentarism was well estab-lished under aristocratic or plutocratic conditions before democracy and its intermediary institutions emerged. Thus, parliamentary structures and procedures could "gain experience," and a reliable and even trustworthy parliamentary culture could develop before the challenge of democratization and mass party politics was to be met. But in Germany it was exactly the other way around. Democratic elections were introduced and parties developed before a resilient parliamentary culture could emerge. Especially the liberals were weakened by Germany's democratic electoral system. Therefore, instead of undoubtedly patriotic liberals in England and France, strong parties suspected of being "internal enemies of the Reich"—namely, the Zentrum (Catholic Center) Party and even the Social Democrats—would have gained access to executive power if there had been a parliamentarization of the Reich. In this context, voluntarily refraining from seeking such access meant avoiding enormous political stress. On the one hand, this permitted German parties to avoid the burden of real political responsibility. Thus invited to a demagogic style of political competition, they poisoned Germany's political culture. This in turn helped to discredit parties and party politics in popular German political thought.

On the other hand, such a restricted parliamentarianism, embedded in the pro-monarchical setting of German constitutionalism, could look like an obstacle to "real" democracy itself. Seen in this way, parliamentarianism could pass as a historically necessary but soon to become—if not already now—an outdated form of the bourgeois state. Therefore, parliamentarianism could now be opposed for the sake of democratization—in this case not because of Rousseauist but communist and (national-)socialist ideas. This is why constitutional lawyers and political theorists often handled "parliamentarianism" and "democracy" as mutually exclusive ideas in late Imperial Germany and during the Weimar period. Even today, when "parliamentary democracy" has become quite a common concept in German political language, parliamentarianism is discussed frequently as only a second-rank form of democracy. Therefore, this legacy of German constitutionalism carries consequences up to the present time. These were especially virulent in the late 1960s, when—particularly among an academic audience—the leftist "anti-parliamentary opposition" demanded a soviet system for the Federal Republic. In the Soviet occupation zone, this legacy was to lead later to the GDR's very special form of "socialist parliamentarianism" (see Patzelt and Schirmer 2001).

Consequences?

Given this brief historical review, the evidence for today's latent constitutional conflict in Germany is not surprising. Of course, analogous data from other countries would be helpful for a more complete interpretation. Are other nations, whatever their history of constitutional structure and ideas, also suffering from criticism and misunderstandings that are similar either in type or degree? Unfortunately, comparable surveys of citizens and representatives have not yet been carried out in other countries, and so we do not yet have an answer to this important question.

What can be done with what is known so far? Of course, the findings and their explanation may be ignored. Politicians may assert that the discussion above is essentially an "academic problem" and political scientists may reject a "latent constitutional conflict" as a label and even discount the argument for its existence. If there is nothing new or important in these findings, then, of course, no special action needs to be taken. But if there really is a latent constitutional conflict in Germany, then *laisser aller* will promote a continuing grumbling among Germans and nourish a further loss of trust in their parliament and the parliamentary system. Of course, avoiding political scandals and securing better policy performance by the political class is required in any case. But, in addition, a clear choice ought to be offered.

Germans might accept that the parliamentary system, because of all the legacies discussed above, will continue to have difficulty gaining popular acceptance, in which case they really should change the system. In this case, presidential systems should be introduced at both the national and Länder level, complemented by extended plebiscitary elements in favor of minorities, and by a first-past-the-post electoral system leading to a two-party system with clear alternatives. Or German politicians and political scientists who think they have good reasons to believe that Germany's parliamentary system has worked quite well in the past and suffers mainly from ignorance and misunderstandings by most citizens and by a significant part of the German elite should invest heavily in political education in schools, adult education, and the mass media. The goal would be to overcome the legacies of German constitutionalism and to modernize popular constitutional thought. No concessions to popular desires should be made as far as system structure is concerned; especially shifts toward semi-presidentialism must be vigorously opposed.[11]

But it would be appropriate to implement plebiscitary elements on the federal level. Plebiscitary elements now exist on all subnational levels of government. Because they have not done any damage to the German polity, and because other countries have not been ruined by national plebiscites, either, there are no compelling arguments to reject their use for decisions on the federal level. Plebiscitary elements appear to be desired by most Germans, and continually rejecting them is more harmful than any potentially sobering experience with them might be. Even on the federal level, rational plebiscitary procedures will not change the system very much.

Having plebiscitary elements on all levels of government and using them from time to time while firmly maintaining the parliamentary system would help to reconcile, even for less informed people, what unfortunately has been separated in the history of German political thought: democracy and parliamentarianism. Complementary and continuous introduction in the differences between the "old" and "new" dualism, with the explanation that they are equally valid ways of realizing separation of powers and a *gouvernement modéré*, could first persuade the better educated people and later the rest of the citizenry that the parliamentary system is a more modern institutionalization of society's influence on political decision-making. Therefore, one minor institutional change and an enduring major effort in civic education could lead to an end of Germany's latent constitutional conflict. However, the precondition is to take this conflict seriously and to treat it as a real and debatable issue.

11. Any "compromise" leading to a semipresidential system should by firmly rejected. In contrast to either a presidential or parliamentary system, such a system has no straightforward logic of functioning and is likely to suffer from many system-induced problems. Therefore, its popular acceptance, based both on understanding and system performance, will be even more problematic than the current acceptance of the parliamentary system.

Chapter 6

THE CHANGING PARTY SYSTEM AND THE CHALLENGE OF DIRECT DEMOCRACY

Peter Lösche

Without a doubt, more than ten years after unification it is still accurate to characterize the German political system as a "party state," for it is the parties that are the most important institutions in forming the will of the people. They are the most significant mediators between state and society and the main selectors of the political elite in the parliamentary system of government.

Nevertheless, we can witness an ongoing discussion about how parties and the party system as a whole are in a state of deep crisis. Annoyance, dissatisfaction, and frustration regarding political parties have become some of the most popular catchwords in the 1990s. Some commentators have begun speaking and writing about political apathy, even about a general political discontent. However, the political reality looks quite different from what journalists have tried to project: never before in the history of democracy in Germany has political participation been as intensive and extensive as in the 1990s and today. Citizens' action groups, all kinds of ad hoc organizations and informal groups flower vigorously while political participation continues to increase. It is becoming more and more obvious that parties do not have a monopoly on political participation. They are not the only institutions forming the political will of the people. This should come as no surprise, for although the German political system has been interpreted again and again as a pure and simple representative democracy, means of direct democracy have been discovered and are used on the local and regional (Länder) levels. Further, there are dozens of proposals to attach elements of direct democracy to the federal constitution.

Are the German party state and representative democracy compatible with direct democracy? What kinds of changes have come about in the German party system recently, promoting or restricting the implementation of elements of direct democracy? What are the challenges with which the German party system and the individual parties are confronted? Would direct democracy provide German parties with tools they could use to respond to current challenges? These are the questions that will be addressed in the following essay.

The Changing Party System

On the surface, and especially as compared to parties and party systems in countries such as Italy, France, Belgium and the Netherlands, continuity and stability are the dominant characteristics of the German party system and of the individual political parties in Germany. However, beneath the surface, fundamental changes have come about. This process of permanent change not only alters single parties, but it also transforms the entire party system at the same time. German unification and the ongoing integration of the different political cultures in the old and new Länder have accelerated this process. The following points will illustrate what I mean by this contention.

Alliance 90/the Greens are on their way to becoming a clear-cut left-liberal, libertarian-ecological, human rights-oriented party, emancipating themselves from their old roots of communist sectarianism and ecological fundamentalism. Behind the backs of the actors and without the public noticing, the old split within German liberalism has arisen again—the split between a left-liberal party on the one side and a market-oriented national-liberal party on the other, a split that was thought to have been overcome when the FDP was founded in 1948. Today, there are two liberal parties in Germany: the economically neoliberal Free Democrats and the left-liberal ecological Greens. From a national perspective, both liberal parties can be seen as regional West German parties, both being based socially on different segments of the middle classes.

At the same time, the Party of Democratic Socialism (PDS), successor party to the Socialist Unity Party (SED) of the German Democratic Republic (GDR), can be seen as a regional East German party. Although the PDS remains the party of the old guard and communist cadres, it also functions as a party of social protest and dissatisfaction. Furthermore, the party has a grassroots foundation in East German neighborhoods, with party members active in former so-called mass organizations such as Volkssolidarität, Demokratischer Frauenbund, and Demokratischer Kulturbund.

When looking at East German parties, one should not be misled by what can be seen on the surface: East German parties and the regional party system are no simple extensions of their West German counterparts, but rather they are different in terms of structure, organization, and culture—and that not only because of the PDS.

Whereas two big catchall parties, the Christian Democratic Union (CDU) and the Social Democratic Party (SPD), and two small liberal parties, the FDP and the Greens, dominate the party landscape in the old Federal Republic, a party system of three equally successful parties, the CDU, SPD, and PDS, can be found in East Germany.

All East German parties are influenced heavily, even determined, by their specific and respective GDR histories. The CDU and PDS (as well as the FDP, although irrelevant in the new Länder today) developed out of GDR regime parties. In contrast, the SPD (as well as Alliance 90/the Greens, also of negligible importance in this region) emerged out of the citizens' rights groups that opposed the communist regime. There is no continuity between the current SPD and the old milieu party, the community of solidarity of the Weimar Republic. Nevertheless, GDR history and political culture are engraved in both the former regime parties and the citizens' rights parties, differentiating them from their West German counterparts.

As compared to West German parties, low numbers of party membership and party activisms as well as organizational weakness typify political parties in the new Länder. Even the numerically strongest party, the PDS, is losing members dramatically because of the party bases becoming older and gradually lessening their political participation. Those who join a party in East Germany are expected to run for party and/or local office, while "multioffice activists" can be found in all parties today. Half of all party members in the new Länder have to be considered activists, while in West Germany the proportion of members participating actively in party affairs is as low as 10–15 percent. Proportionate to the absolute number of party members, more full-time party professionals, so-called party secretaries, are employed in East Germany than in West Germany.

Furthermore, the social position of party members, party activists, and party delegates in local representative bodies differs in the East and West. The share of those with a university degree, especially in engineering, natural sciences, and medicine, and the proportion of those who belong to the educational elite in general is clearly higher in East Germany.

East German members of the Bundestag and Länder parliaments have a different understanding of how to serve their districts and how to act in the legislature than their West German colleagues. They tend to be more responsive to the demands of their constituencies and less accountable to their respective parties. In other words: party discipline in parliament is less rigid in the new Länder than in the old.

Finally, referring back to the GDR citizens' rights movement, in comparison to the old Länder, more elements of direct democracy have been implemented in East German state constitutions and in state, regional and local party statutes and by-laws.

Regardless of the labels "party of mass integration," "catchall party," and "people's party," both the CDU and the SPD are in a process of fundamentally changing their organizational structure, programmatic approach, and the functions they fulfill in the political system. An end to traditional membership and the activist-run party seems to be coming about. A new type of party is emerging, identifiable according to the following three categories.

- *Media party:* The national party leadership communicates increasingly with the party membership via print, and especially via electronic media. However, this is not a one-way street. Rather, opinion polls taken on the grassroots level are a new way of inner-party political participation. This process leads to a dissolution of the traditional delegate system, for party activists are circumvented, causing them to lose influence and power. In this way, inner-party democracy in general is gaining new meaning.

- **Professionalized party:** Party activists, that is, amateur politicians, are replaced by highly professional political consultants who are either self-employed or—as is generally the case in Germany—employed by the party. The professional party performs three functions: it runs election campaigns, selects the political elite, and governs, that is, it acts within cabinets, parliaments, and bodies of local government.
- **Caucus party/party in public office:** The center of power and the organizational core is shifting with the emergence of a new type of party. The traditional party structure is being reorganized to become a "party in public office." Organizational and decision-making bodies independent from elected representatives are being replaced with a structure in which party activists are holders of public office at the same time. Party members who are also members of Bundestag or Länder legislature caucuses are becoming more important for inner-party decision-making. Cabinet members and representatives in local legislatures simultaneously govern and set the course for party policy. In this way, officeholders are becoming more important for party organization and decision-making. At the same time, those who hold key positions within the party are members of parliament and/or executive bodies. Power has become more focused in the hands of those who accumulate positions in public and party offices simultaneously.

Current Challenges to Parties

New and myriad challenges have arisen for German parties due to the transformation processes in which all parties are currently involved. I have already mentioned some of these challenges implicitly. In the following I would like to outline more explicitly the problems with which political parties in Germany are confronted. These are some of the new problems and challenges for which party leadership will have to find answers in the near future.

The traditional sociocultural milieus that traditionally served as the foundation of the SPD and CDU/CSU, the democratic socialist and Catholic milieus, are eroding. The old ideologies of integration, the *Weltanschauungen,* are on their way out. A general decrease in citizens' identification with particular parties can also be observed. Nevertheless, when election day comes around, traditional party supporters are still very important, and they have to be convinced to turn out to vote rather than stay at home. Of course, parties rely on accumulating votes in order to win elections. Thus, they have to negotiate the split between those who identify strongly with the party and the floating voters. However, making a split between different segments of the electorate almost always leads to a blurring of the party's programmatic profile and the image of the party in general. As a consequence, some voters may be put off by the wishy-washy nonsubstance of election campaigns.

Parties are not only losing members and activists, but the remaining party members and party activists are also growing older. Parties are confronted with what one could call "ossification." Ossification in terms of social structure implies that the old guard remains, including especially public employees. It is the public servants who dominate the local and regional party meetings, and since they are growing older, retiring from civil service, a danger of "pensionization" arises. Most of the few young people who join parties are attracted because of job opportunities, consequently leading to a tendency of "patronagization," namely, of the parties becoming patronage machines. Yet another danger may be pointed out in this context: within some of these old-age patronage machines, some local and regional organizations are reluctant to admit outsiders. The established balance of power within the organization is defended against young people from other segments of society who, were they to be admitted, might call the status quo into question.

New organizational behavior is becoming apparent among the younger generations. Instead of joining traditional mass organizations like the above-mentioned catchall parties, trade unions, or churches, they organize more informally. Younger people are more likely to participate in environmental or citizens' action groups and diverse ad hoc groups, all of which emerge and dissolve erratically and easily. Professionalization has divided implications for parties: on the one hand, it leads to parties' becoming more efficient, enabling them, for example, to run successful American-style election campaigns. On the other hand, the old guard of traditional party activists who used to serve as the ideological and organizational backbone of the milieu parties are becoming increasingly frustrated. A widespread tendency can be observed that political consultants, the staff of members of parliament, committees and subcommittees, and local officials are emerging as the new political movers and shakers. They take the place of and contribute to the frustration and discontent of the good old "comrades" or "party friends."

In summary, some authors, especially political journalists, argue that German parties are in a process of steady decline, not in the least because of ossification, pensionization, and patronagization. What is needed is for young, dynamic, and highly motivated people to join the parties. However, it is exactly this type of person who is avoiding political parties.

What is to be done? What course of action can be taken to revitalize parties and make them more attractive for young people? Obviously, young people are politically motivated, and they are politically active on the local and the regional levels. However, they generally do not become party activists or even members of a party. What effect would introducing measures of direct democracy into lame-duck parties with a disproportionally older membership have? What can be expected from introducing elements of direct democracy into the political system of the Federal Republic? These questions will be taken up in the following section of this essay.

German Parties and the Challenges of Direct Democracy

The discussion of whether elements of direct democracy should be introduced is always accompanied by normative connotations. Therefore, at the beginning of this section, I will indicate my own position on this matter. I am somewhat skeptical about implementing elements of direct democracy in the German party system. It is not the Weimar experience, cited quite often in this context, that nourishes my doubts, but rather current examples of direct democracy in countries such as the United States and Switzerland that lead to my skepticism. I will argue that in a specific, territorially limited context, direct democracy does make sense. In contrast, in the larger arena of national parties or the German political system as a whole, it is not the idealism usually associated with direct democracy that is likely to be realized but rather other unintended "isms."

Implementation of Elements of Direct Democracy and Political Parties

I would like in this section to focus on three elements of inner-party direct democracy, namely, closed primaries, open primaries, and inner-party plebiscites.

CLOSED PRIMARIES/CAUCUSES

According to current party statutes and election laws, in some cases it is already possible to nominate candidates for the Bundestag and Länder legislatures in caucus-like membership meetings. This is true if and when they run in single-member districts. For small political parties such as the FDP or the Greens, it is no problem whatsoever to assemble all party members living in a certain district at the same time, hold discussion sessions on issues and goals, and then take a vote. Parties such as the SPD or the CDU face the technical problem of arranging to have the several thousand members in a single member district meet at the same time and place. In that kind of district, candidates are commonly nominated by delegate conventions. However, the number of districts in which candidates are nominated in closed primary/caucus style has increased in the last decade. Nominating candidates according to proportional representation on Länder lists (for the Bundestag, for example) poses a technical problem. Furthermore, German federal election law and the law on political parties do not allow for the nomination of party candidates by ballot. Of course, these laws could be amended. National party law does, however, permit ballot elections for the nomination for the party's chancellor candidate on the national level or the party's prime minister candidate on the state level. At the same time, the election of national or state party chairpersons by ballot is not permitted by the current law on political parties. These regulations illustrate the complex, sometimes confusing situation regarding elements of direct democracy.

Legal aspects aside, I would argue against membership ballot elections for nominating candidates for Länder or national office and for electing national or Länder party chairpersons on the basis of political rationality. Measures of this kind would fragment parties into personalized clientele organizations, forced to run permanent campaigns and to invite pressure groups to finance candidates, thus increasing their influence on inner-party decision-making processes. On the other hand, of course, one could argue that this kind of nominating procedure would motivate and mobilize party members, electrifying the party altogether for a successful general election campaign.

OPEN PRIMARIES

In April 2000 the secretary general of the SPD, Franz Müntefering, proposed several organizational reforms to revitalize his party, among them open primaries. According to this proposal, all voters would be entitled to nominate candidates for public office. When the Social Democratic executive committee decided on the reform package, not one vote was cast in favor of Müntefering's idea, for good reason: introducing measures of this kind to German parties would result in opening up the parties in order to destroy them. First, according to current American experience with open primaries, this nomination procedure leads to a situation in which party members and party activists can no longer be held responsible and accountable for those nominated to run under the party banner. Second, open primaries would be regarded by losing candidates as an incentive to keep inner-party campaign machines working permanently in order to be more successful in the next primary election. Third, interest groups would move in, supporting certain candidates and fragmenting parties even further. Fourth, inner-party conflicts during primary campaigns would provide ammunition and arguments for candidates from outside the party in the general election campaign. Fifth, aspirants in primary campaigns would move to the left or right, depending on the type of party, to seek support of convinced party members and sympathizers. In contrast, in the general election campaign, the candidate would have to move back to the center to reach out to the floating vote. The impression of flip-flopping and opportunism would arise, promoting public frustration and annoyance with parties and politicians. Finally, the parties' most important incentive to attract new members—namely, participating in the inner-party decision-making process, and especially nominating candidates—would disappear.

INNER-PARTY PLEBISCITES

Several parties have introduced and carried out membership referenda, particularly on the regional level, in the last ten years. For example,

Social Democrats in Rhineland-Palatinate voted on their state election platform, and FDP members voted nationwide to determine the party's stance on obligatory military service. Plebiscites provide a chance to mobilize party members and to engage them in party affairs. This is true only insofar that such referenda remain rare events, used not more than every other year. On the other hand, referenda can be abused by executive committees that want to get rid of unpopular positions supported year after year at the party convention. Here the party leadership circumvents the delegate system and takes an issue to the members directly, as the FDP did a few years ago.

Implementation of Elements of Direct Democracy and the Political System

There are two elements of direct democracy that are common in the German political system and which—according to some citizens' initiatives—should be expanded: the popular election of public executive officers on the local level and local and regional plebiscites.

The tradition of electing mayors directly by the citizens of a city or town is common in southern Germany. This tradition has been adopted by some Länder in the North, such as Lower Saxony and North Rhine-Westphalia. There is no doubt that direct democracy has been very successful on the local level. Nevertheless, proposals to expand this model to elect state prime ministers the same way that mayors are chosen not only do not make sense, but they also contribute to the growing frustration with parties. What do I mean? Ours is a parliamentary system of government in which the chief executive officer is elected by a majority of members of the legislative body, thus ensuring that the cabinet, headed by the prime minister, is in control of a working majority in parliament. Separation of powers between the executive and the legislative branches of government does not exist. Instead, a balance of power is achieved on the one hand through the governing majority, encompassing the cabinet and the majority in parliament, and on the other through the opposition, the minority in parliament. If, however, the prime minister were to be elected by popular vote, elements of the presidential system of government would be introduced into an otherwise parliamentary system of government. The possibility of divided government, stalemate between the legislative and executive branches of government, would be imported. Situations such as a prime minister whose budget is not passed by parliament because of divided government could arise. Not only gridlock but also public discontent regarding parties and politicians would be the result.

Referenda that work on the local and regional levels do not work on the Länder and national levels. This is one of the lessons to be learned from the experience in the United States and Switzerland. Quite often it is interest groups that influence, finance, decide, and manipulate referenda. Furthermore, emotions, prejudices, and even "appeals to base instincts" are mobilized in this kind of referendum campaign. A politics of fear is one possible consequence, as can be seen in the recent example of the referendum on the fusion of the city-state Berlin with the Land Brandenburg.

General Reservations Regarding Direct Democracy

My doubts about the practicality and ramifications of direct democracy are based on more general reflections. Political institutions in representative systems of government are locations for solving conflicts, give and take, negotiations, mediation, and compromise. That is what political institutions are all about. When conflicts are resolved elsewhere, for example by popular vote, political institutions are weakened, even emptied of their original purpose. Furthermore, incentives to run for public office could be lessened.

By using public referenda to solve conflicts, the opportunities to maneuver and make compromises disappear. People either have to say "yes" or "no" when voting on a proposition. An unjust reduction of complexity, even political polarization, could be the effect. Since ours is a *coordination democracy*, based on compromise, referenda would not work and would even call our political culture into question.

As already indicated, past and present examples in Germany as well as in the United States tell us that referenda campaigns might be converted into exercises of mobilizing sentiments, resentments, prejudices, intolerance, and xenophobia, especially in times of upheaval, anxieties, and popular resentment. In real political life, direct democracy has been used successfully by the (populist) right, not by the left. It is one of the great misunderstandings in the history of democracy that plebiscites are instruments of enlightenment and belong to the politics of the left. The Hessian campaign against double citizenship in early 1999 is just one example among many of how the politics of fear works.

Usually direct democracy functions in a socially selective manner. It is the more affluent and better educated who participate more intensively and extensively while the less educated and the lower classes are, to some extent, excluded. Direct democracy does not promote the "power of the people," but rather increases the influence of those who already know how to play complex and differentiated political hardball.

Furthermore, direct democracy could be regarded as a game in which the rules are made for interest groups. While political institutions act as filters for unjustified and illegitimate political power of organized interests, unlimited organizational and financial resources can be invested by pressure groups into referenda and primary election campaigns, even to the point of buying members of parliament or state assemblies or paying for single votes on particular decisions. California is a hothouse for this kind of direct democracy. Again, it is not "the people" or "the party members" who decide or nominate candidates, but rather specific interests.

Finally, and returning to the point where we started, elements of direct democracy such as open primaries and national membership referenda will fragment and eventually destroy our parties. American parties provide a negative example. Today, parties in the United States are trying to reduce the importance of primaries as a part of their efforts to strengthen parties organizationally and politically. At the same time, the discussion about implementing elements of direct democracy into political parties is taking place in Germany—and we call it "Americanization." This seems to be an irony of history. Perhaps the German equivalent of the American Political Science Association, the Deutsche Vereinigung für Politikwissenschaft, will publish a paper ten years from now written by party researchers with the title "Toward a More Responsible Party System."

Conclusion

The Federal Republic of Germany already has a kind of "mixed constitution," a political system that encompasses representative democracy as the dominating structure on the national level and elements of direct democracy on the local, regional, and Länder levels. It is obvious that representative democracy on the one hand and direct democracy on the other are compatible. The same is true for political parties: representative democracy is the guiding principle, but elements of direct democracy are practiced in all parties more or less extensively, restricted only by current election laws and the law on political parties.

However, the relevance of direct democracy in curing some of the problems that parties currently confront has been exaggerated. Ossification, pensionization and patronagization cannot be treated successfully with the magic pill called direct democracy. Parties have to attract young people by means other than plebiscitary democracy. Taking positions on current issues, even on programmatic questions, rediscovering political strategies and pursuing coherent policies, and convincing voters by arguments and not only by PR campaigns may be of great importance. Involving members in decision-making processes within the parties, such as nominating local and regional candidates for public office, the Länder legislature, or the Bundestag, as well as using inner-party referenda to decide on local, regional, and Länder issues might draw young people into parties again. However, instruments of direct democracy have to be regarded as questionable for political parties. When applying elements of direct democracy, parties have to be aware of the dangers: a further fragmentation and segmentation of their organizations; emotional, irrational, and prejudiced campaigns; illegitimate influence of interest groups; and the development of a narrow-minded, arrogant, and elite politics.

Chapter 7

DIRECT LEGISLATION IN UNITED GERMANY

⟨∞⟩

Hermann K. Heußner

Introduction

This chapter deals mainly with direct legislation, that is, "the process by which voters directly decide issues of public policy by voting on ballot propositions" (Magleby 1984: 1). In Germany the term *Volksgesetzgebung* is common, but it does not include legislative propositions placed on the ballot by the legislature (Heußner 1994: 41). In a narrower sense, this chapter focuses on the initiative that occurs when "a specified number of voters petition to propose statutes or constitutional amendments to be adopted or rejected by the voters at the polls" (Magleby 1984: 1). In Germany the citizen petition is called *Volksbegehren,* and the popular vote at the polls on these petitions is called *Volksentscheid* (Heußner 1994: 12–14). During the past ten years and even longer, direct legislation has become popular among Germans, as has been demonstrated in several polls. There are several reasons for this development.

From the very beginning of democracy in Germany in 1918–19, direct legislation was—at least on the level of constitutional theory and law—an important element. Inspired by Swiss and American examples of direct legislation (Heußner 1994: 58–59), the Weimar

Constitution—among other elements of direct democracy—permit-ted the initiative on the federal level (Article 73, Section 3; Schiffers 1971; Jung 1989, 2001b). In practice only two initiatives qualified for the vote at the polls: the 1926 initiative *Enteignung der Fürstenver-mögen* (expropriation of the property of the princes) launched by the Social Democrats (SPD) and the communists (KPD), and the 1929 initiative *Freiheitsgesetz* of right wing parties, including the Nazi Party, against the Young Plan, both of which failed (Jung 2001b: 18, 20–24, 37–38).[1] Most states (Länder) also adopted the initiative after World War I (Jürgens 1993: 250; Hernekamp 1979: 247–51).

After World War II, the constitutions of many Länder provided for the *Volksbegehren* and *Volksentscheid*.[2] Such provisions also could be found for a few years after the war in the states of the former German Democratic Republic (GDR), although the communists already had taken over so that these rights existed on paper only (Hernekamp 1979: 319–21). The 1949 constitution of the GDR formally included the initiative, too, although it was never used (Hernekamp 1979: 321; Hufschlag 1999: 194–202).

Nevertheless, the authors of the (West) German Constitution, the Basic Law or *Grundgesetz*—except for some territorial issues—chose not to create direct legislation on the federal level, partly because of the belief that the Weimar initiative (in the case of the *Freiheitsgesetz*) had proved useful to the Nazi Party,[3] but mainly in order to prevent the communists from using the initiative for their purposes (Bach-mann 1999: 76; Hufschlag 1999: 100–101; Jung 1994: 329–37).

In contrast to the Federation, the constitutions of the Länder were generally open to initiatives. Because of the distinctive prohibitive

---

1. The initiative *Enteignung der Fürstenvermögen* lost, although it received the sup-port of 36.3 percent of all eligible voters and 96.1 percent of the votes cast. However, Article 75 of the Weimar Constitution allowed initiatives to pass only if a majority of all eligible voters actually voted. The *Freiheitsgesetz* received 13.8 percent support of all eligible voters and 94.5 percent of the votes cast.

2. 1946: Bavaria and Hesse; 1947: Baden, Bremen, and Rhineland-Palatinate; 1950: North Rhine-Westphalia and Berlin. In 1952 Baden, Württemberg-Baden, and Würt-temberg-Hohenzollern joined to form the new state Baden-Württemberg, which intro-duced the initiative in 1974. The Saarland introduced the initiative in 1979. In 1974 Berlin abolished direct legislation (Heußner 1994: 62, 480; Jürgens 1993: 59; Jung 1994).

3. See, for example, the contribution of Theodor Heuss in the proceedings of the Parlamentarischer Rat (Parliamentary Council) 1948: 264.

requirements, however, the use of direct legislation in the Länder was very low. The exception was Bavaria (Heußner 1994: 461–65).

In 1989, however, German unification produced a strong push for direct democracy. The popular cry "Wir sind das Volk" (We are the people) in the former GDR manifested a strong and intensive democratic self-confidence that sought to influence political decisions not only through the representative form of democracy but also through devices of direct democracy (Heußner 1994: 2). Accordingly, direct legislation was embodied in the draft constitution of the so-called *Runder Tisch* (round table) of the former GDR, which included all relevant social groups after the peaceful revolution had succeeded (Heußner 1994: 2).

In the democratic Western Federal Republic of Germany on the other hand, a growing distance emerged in the first half of the 1980s between the established political parties and considerable parts of the population. As an example, the peace movement called for a referendum on NATO's decision to deploy Pershing II and cruise missiles. Also supporters of the environmental protection movement showed an interest in direct legislation (Heußner 1994: 1).

A uniquely inglorious milestone in the development of *Parteienverdrossenheit* (party alienation) was the so-called Barschel affair in 1987. In this political scandal just prior to the state elections, the prime minister of the northern state of Schleswig-Holstein, Uwe Barschel, spied on his rival from the opposition, Björn Engholm, and spread lies about him (Sontheimer and Bleek 1997: 68; Hübner and Rohlfs 1988: 258ff.; Skierka 1992: 332ff.). This affair was the impulse for a new constitution in Schleswig-Holstein that contained provisions of direct legislation innovative in German terms of direct democracy (Jung 1993: 32ff.; Jung 2000a: 84; Jung 1999b: 105).

It should also be noted that the continuing process of European integration and enlargement reinforces the desire of many citizens to decide directly on the various steps of European integration (Heußner 1994: 2; *Süddeutsche Zeitung*, 2–3 and 5 September 2000, 5–6 September 2001).

Direct Legislation on the Local Level

On the local level until 1990, direct legislation existed only in the southern state of Baden-Württemberg (Geitmann 1999: 241–45).

Then within only nine years all other states except Berlin followed, beginning with Schleswig-Holstein in 1990 and ending with Hamburg in 1998 (Jung 1999b: 107–8; Schiller 2000: 86). Interestingly enough, in Bavaria (Hahnzog 1998: 47; Seipel and Mayer 1997) and Hamburg (Efler 1999: 208, 212, 219) the people themselves through successful initiatives overcame the ruling parties' parliamentary resistance against these new devices.

The citizens are now using the new devices quite frequently. For example, in Hesse, North Rhine-Westphalia, and Schleswig-Holstein more than a hundred initiatives have been launched in each of these states.[4] About 30 to 40 percent of these initiatives have been adopted either by the local parliament or by the voters at the polls (Schiller 2000: 97).

According to Otmar Jung, in Bavaria we have a "revolution within the (participatory) revolution" (Jung 1999b: 115). Because of the relatively high number of municipalities in this state, direct legislation activity on the local level is higher than in all other states combined (ibid: 115; Schiller: 92). Within only four years, more than seven hundred initiatives have been launched, and more than four hundred had been voted on by the people.[5] Indeed, these figures express a strong desire of many citizens to participate directly in local matters. In 8.6 percent of all Bavarian communities, a local initiative has been proposed every year. In North Rhine-Westphalia the proportion is 7.5 percent.[6]

Direct Legislation on the Länder Level

There has been a direct legislation boom at the Land level during the last ten years. Although many Länder allowed the initiative even

---

4. In Hesse 116 initiatives were launched from April 1993 to October 1999, in North Rhine-Westphalia 143 from October 1994 to August 1999, and in Schleswig-Holstein 146 from April 1990 to October 1997 (Schiller 2000: 92).

5. From 1995 to November 1999, 789 initiatives were proposed and 426 have been voted on (Gebhardt 2001: 159, 164).

6. In Hesse: 4.2 percent; Schleswig-Holstein: 1.7 percent; Lower Saxony: 1.6 percent; Baden-Württemberg: 0.9 percent; Rhineland-Palatinate and Saxony: 0.6 percent; Mecklenburg-Vorpommern: 0.2 percent (Schiller 2000: 92–93).

before 1990, the practice was very uncommon.[7] This was due to the fact that, except for Bavaria, all states required signatures of 20 percent of all eligible voters to be gathered before the initiative could be voted on.[8] In Baden-Württemberg the requirement is almost 17 percent (one-sixth) of all eligible voters (Heußner 1994: 271). These signature threshold requirements are prohibitive preconditions (Jung 2000b: 441–42).

Only in Bavaria was the signature threshold 10 percent of all eligible voters (Heußner 1994: 271). Consequently, it was the only state in which some significant form of direct legislation activity could evolve, so that by 1989 three initiatives had qualified.[9] In the following elections the proponents of these initiatives succeeded at least partially (Heußner 1994: 271; Jürgens 1993: 176, 178–79).[10]

Constitutional Reform

Since 1990 eight states have adopted new constitutions. All of them include important provisions for direct legislation (Jung 1999b: 105). As already mentioned, Schleswig-Holstein adopted a new constitution

---

7. Except for Bavaria, not until 1978 in North Rhine-Westphalia did an initiative against a special form of comprehensive schools qualify for a vote at the polls. The Landtag (legislature) adopted the initiative, so the vote did not take place (Jürgens 1993: 194–95; Heußner 1994: 306).

8. This was the case in Bremen, Hesse, North Rhine-Westphalia, Rhineland-Palatinate, and the Saarland (Heußner 1994: 271).

9. Two in 1967–68 concerning school matters and one in 1972–73 concerning broadcasting matters (Jürgens 1993: 174–79; Heußner 1994: 282, 461–62).

10. P. L. Dubois and F. Feeney, *Lawmaking by Initiative* (1998: 64, footnote 64), describe the Bavarian initiatives as follows:

The Free Democratic Party and the Social Democratic Party each proposed initiatives in 1967 to create nondenominational schools alongside the existing denominational schools. The ruling party (Christian Social Union) responded with a proposed initiative of its own. The FDP proposal failed to get enough signatures, but both the SPD and the CSU proposals qualified. The SPD and CSU then reached a compromise agreement. The two original initiatives appeared on the ballot, alongside a constitutional amendment recommended by the legislature embodying the compromise. The two initiatives failed, but the compromise passed.… In 1972 the Bavarian legislature passed a law giving the government greater control over what was said by government-funded radio and television stations. A citizens group responded with an initiative proposing freedom of speech. The legislature rejected the proposal as unconstitutional but reached a compromise with the proponents. The initiative died because the legislative determination of unconstitutionality was not appealed. The compromise was approved by the voters.

in 1990, followed by Brandenburg, Saxony, and Saxony-Anhalt in 1992, Lower Saxony in 1993, Mecklenburg-Vorpommern and Thuringia in 1994, and Berlin in 1995 (Jung 1993: 32–35, 41, 45–61ff.; Jung 2000a: 39–64). Constitutional revisions including important reforms of direct legislation also took place: 1994–97 in Bremen, 1996–2001 in Hamburg, and 2000 in Rhineland-Palatinate (Jung 2000a: 66ff., 69–74; Hamburgisches Gesetz- und Verordnungsblatt [HGV] 2001: 105; Präsident des Landtags Rheinland-Pfalz 2000). Now direct legislation in one form or another is present in all states of Germany, and in various states the signature thresholds have been substantially lowered. In North Rhine-Westphalia—the state with the largest population—both the ruling coalition parties of SPD and the Greens and the opposition parties of Christian Democrats (CDU) and Free Democrats (FDP) favored substantial reforms (Neumann 2001: 35), which were introduced in 2002 (GV NRW 2002: 108).

Thirteen states allow not only the use of the direct legislation procedure for statutes but also for constitutional amendments.[11] There is some dispute in Hesse and North Rhine-Westphalia whether the constitutional initiative is allowed (Heußner 1994: 29–31, 33–34, 57–108; Muckel 1999: 109–33).

Experience with Direct Legislation in the Länder

From 1989 until the end of 2000, ten citizen petitions qualified: three in Bavaria; two in Schleswig-Holstein; two in Hamburg; and one each in Lower Saxony, Saxony, and Thuringia (Jung 2000b: 440; *Zeitschrift für direkte Demokratie* [ZfDD] 2001, vol. 50: 52). Two of the Bavarian initiatives also succeeded at the polls: the 1995 initiative that created direct legislation for cities and counties and the 1998 initiative abolishing the Bavarian second chamber, the Senate (Hahnzog 1998: 164–65; Gebhardt 2001: 54). In 1991 the citizens rejected an initiative sponsored by environmental groups concerning solid waste and voted in favor of a parliamentary counterproposal. Still, this counterproposal was a compromise including certain aspects of the citizen petition (Jürgens 1993: 166–73; Heußner 1994: 312).

---

11. Baden-Württemberg, Bavaria, Brandenburg, Bremen, Hamburg, Mecklenburg-Vorpommern, Lower Saxony, Rhineland-Palatinate, Saxony, Saxony-Anhalt, Schleswig-Holstein, and Thuringia (Arnim 2000: 304–11). Since 2002 also North Rhine-Westphalia.

In Hamburg the introduction in 1998 of direct legislation on the local level also was successful at the polls. In the same year the constitutional initiative to reduce the exclusion of financial matters in direct legislation, to lower the signature threshold to qualify an initiative for the ballot from 10 to 5 percent, and to abolish the requirement of the affirmative vote of 50 percent of all eligible citizens to amend the constitution and of 25 percent of all eligible citizens to adopt a statute through direct legislation failed, although it got 74 percent of the votes cast (Efler 1999: 214; ZfDD 1998, vol. 41: 9). This failure was due to the fact that only 45.5 percent of all eligible citizens voted in favor of the initiative (Efler 1999: 218). Still, this initiative was not entirely fruitless, for it was an important impulse in pressuring the legislature in 2001 to lower the signature threshold to 5 percent and to reduce the requirement for the passage of statutes to 20 percent of all eligible voters (Efler 1999: 220–21; HGV 2001: 105).

Also in 1998 in Schleswig-Holstein the people adopted an initiative prohibiting the introduction of the Spelling Reform, which was introduced by all state governments in order to simplify orthography at school (Kliegis and Kliegis 1999: 287–306).[12] In Saxony an initiative was introduced that would secure the independence of the municipal savings banks. But only after a lawsuit was filed did the Saxon government accept the fact that the initiative got sufficient signatures. In 2001 the people adopted the initiative at the polls (ZfDD 2001, vol. 53: 24). The vote on the initiative in Thuringia, which also qualified in 2000, was prohibited by the Constitutional Court of Thuringia (ibid.: 23).[13] The initiative introduced in 2000 in Lower Saxony, which deals with the equipment, personnel, and financing of kindergartens, finally was adopted by the legislature (ZfDD 2002, vol. 56: 19). The state government had tried unsuccessfully to stop the initiative. The State Constitutional Court declared the initiative to be

12. In 1997 the initiative against the abolishment of a particular Protestant holiday failed. Although the initiative got 68.2 percent of the votes cast, which equaled 19.9 percent of all eligible voters, the initiative lost because the threshold is 25 percent of all eligible voters (Schimmer 1999: 269–86).

13. The purpose of the initiative was to reduce the signature requirement from 14 to 5 percent, to abolish the quorum for the adoption of statutes, and to reduce the threshold to amend the constitution through direct legislation from 50 to 25 percent of all eligible voters (ZfDD 2000, vol. 47: 19). The court ruled that the initiative made it too easy to pass a law through *Volksgesetzgebung* (ZfDD 2001b, vol. 53: 23).

in accordance with the law (ZfDD 2001, vol. 53: 26). In summary, five out of ten initiatives that qualified from 1989 until the end of 2000 have been successful at the polls.

Within the same time period, there were sixteen citizen petitions that failed to garner sufficient signatures (Jung [2000b: 440] lists sixteen, including the Saxon initiative; Mehr Demokratie [2000] reports another in Bremen in 2000). Prior to a vote or collection of signatures, fifteen additional citizen petitions were declared invalid by parliament, the executive branch, or (ultimately) the courts because of constitutional or other legal violations (Jung [2000b: 441] lists twelve, including the initiative in Lower Saxony; Mehr Demokratie [2000] reports three more in 2000). Frequently the problem was that the proposal was an improper constitutional amendment or conflicted with subject matter restrictions such as budget items (Jung 2000b: 441).

On the other hand, the effect of threatening initiatives must be taken into account. Frequently just the filing or even announcement of an initiative petition will spur legislators into action. This was the case on at least five occasions during the last ten years (Jung 2000b: 441). For example, in 1994 in North Rhine-Westphalia the ruling SPD approved the direct election of mayors, which it had opposed before (Arnim 2000: 263–64).

In comparison with the use of direct legislation in some American states, the German experience described above is modest.[14] This is due to the relatively high legal thresholds for direct legislation in Germany, which are described below. Furthermore, and at least as important, the legislative powers of the German Länder are much smaller than those of the American states (Heußner 1994: 8, 108–11; Currie 1998: 513).

Constitutional and Legal Provisions for Direct Legislation

David Magleby has noted that how states structure direct legislation influences the extent to which the process is used and how it is used (Magleby 1984: 35). Therefore, the structure of direct legislation has

---

14. For example, from adoption of direct legislation at the beginning of the last century until 1996, Oregon saw 292 initiatives placed on the ballot, California 257, North Dakota 170, and Colorado 153 (Dubois and Feeney 1998: 30). In 1998 alone the people of California put twelve initiatives on the ballot (Allswang 2000: 268–69).

to be dealt with in greater detail. In many German states the constitutional and legal provisions for direct legislation show some characteristics that differ from the Swiss and/or American model. In Germany there is a very important subject matter restriction. Initiatives concerning budgets, taxes, and government salaries are generally not allowed to be considered. That means, according to most of the courts, that all initiatives substantially (*wesentlich*) influencing the budget are banned (BVerfGE 1999: 244, 269; BVerfGE 2000, Absatz nos. 81–99). This formula is not sufficiently precise; it depends very much on each particular case, and it leaves too much room for restrictive decisions (Heußner 1994: 177–90; Przygode 1995: 395–409). Consequently, for example, various initiatives designed to improve the public school system have been declared invalid (Jung 2000b: 441). If direct legislation is intended to give the people real legislative power, financial subject matter restrictions should be abolished or at least essentially reduced (Jung 2000b: 446; Heußner 1994: 198–99).[15]

Furthermore, the Länder have a comprehensive preelection review of proposals. Mostly the executive branch reviews proposed initiatives for deficiencies of form and for constitutional or other legal violations. When these authorities determine that the proposal violates some provisions of law, proponents may take the issue to court (Heußner 1994: 239–45; Arnim 2000: 206–7, 304–11; Przygode 1995: 58, 73ff.). In contrast, in most American states there is no extensive substantial judicial preelection review (Dubois and Feeney 1998: 43–45). The result is that in Germany many initiatives are eliminated at the beginning of the direct legislation procedure (Heußner 1994: 247–48; Jung 2000b: 441). This comprehensive preelection review seems preferable to American practice because it puts less pressure on the courts and diminishes the risk of passing unconstitutional laws that could be dangerous especially for minorities (Heußner 1994: 247–50; Dubois and Feeney 1998: 43–45).

A major difference between the United States and Germany can be found in the signature requirements. For example, whereas in California the signature requirement is 2.25 percent for all eligible voters for statutory initiatives and 3.6 percent for constitutional initiatives

15. The Bavarian Constitutional Court has rejected the use of *Volksgesetzgebung* to abolish the exclusion of substantial budget matters (BayVerfGE 2000: 911, 913).

(Heußner 1999b: 120; Dubois and Feeney 1998: 110), in Germany only Brandenburg requires about 4 percent and Hamburg and Schleswig-Holstein require 5 percent (Arnim 2000: 304–11; Hamburg Constitution, Article 50, section 2). In most states the percentage is between 10 and 16.67 percent. In Bremen (for constitutional initiatives), Hesse, and the Saarland, the percentage is still an extremely high 20 percent.[16] Except for Bremen the signature threshold is the same for statutory and constitutional initiatives (Arnim 2000: 304–11). Signature thresholds as low as in California are inadequate. They should be somewhat higher in order to prevent placing large numbers of measures on the ballot and overburdening the competence of many voters (Heußner 2001: 81–82; Dubois and Feeney 1998: 109–11).[17]

Procedures for the collection of signatures in most German states are restrictive. Only in six Länder can—as in the United States and Switzerland—the signatures be collected on the street, house-to-house, near polling places on election day, and through ads in newspapers (Heußner 1994: 256–64; Dubois and Feeney 1998: 55–56). In the other German states, petitions must be signed in designated governmental offices (*Amtseintragung*) (Arnim 2000: 304– 11). Furthermore, in six states the gathering period is only two weeks.[18] This period is definitely too short (Heußner 2001: 84). But the German practice of separating the solicitation of signatures from the acquisition of signatures is a good idea. In "free" collections the "emphasis is on efficiency rather than on disseminating information" (Cronin 1989: 62). When "confronted face to face," the voters "have no opportunity for private reflection about whether they wish to lend their signature to an initiative effort." Therefore, it is claimed that the "initiative industry" and paid petition circulators can "buy a place on the ballot" for "anyone willing to put up the funds" (Loewenstein and Stern 1989: 199–200). Through the *Amtseintragung* the integrity of the process is protected (Dubois and Feeney 1998: 107). It is more likely that the voters have to be convinced by

16. For signature requirements in all the Länder, see Arnim 2000: 304–11 and Jung 2002: 293. For North Rhine-Westphalia, see GV NRW 2002: 108.

17. In 1996 in California seventeen initiatives qualified for the ballot (Allswang 2000: 267–68).

18. In Rhineland-Palatinate it is now two months (Constitution, Article 109, Section 3).

the measure itself in order to motivate them to go to a governmental office (Heußner 2001: 83; Heußner 1994: 276).

In Germany direct legislation and legislative legislation are closely connected. This means that in all German states—as in Switzerland—we have only the indirect initiative (Möckli 1994: 101–4; Dubois and Feeney 1998: 91; Heußner 1994: 292–304; Arnim 2000: 208), whereas in most American states the direct initiative can circumvent legislatures (Dubois and Feeney 1998: 27–29). "With an indirect initiative, once the requisite number of signatures is gathered, the measure goes to the legislature for consideration. Generally the legislature has a fixed period of time to adopt or reject the measure. If the measure is adopted, it becomes law. If the measure is rejected (or if the legislature fails to act within the specified time), the measure goes before the people ..." (Dubois and Feeney: 35; see also Heußner 1994: 293–98, 353; Arnim 2000: 208, 304–11). The legislature also has the power to put forward a counterproposal to an initiative on the same subject to accompany the initiative on the election ballot (Arnim 2000: 207, 304–11).[19] One effect of the indirect initiative is that this type of direct legislation needs a relatively long period of time, between about five months and two years (Jürgens 1993: 138–43). This leaves time for deliberation and serves as a cooling-off period (Heußner 1994: 305–6; Heußner 1999b: 92). Another effect of the indirect initiative is that the deliberative capacities of the legislature have influence within the process of direct legislation. Parliamentary compromises, including the wishes of disadvantaged minorities, can then be heard in a separate proposal (Heußner 1994: 89, 305–6; Heußner 1999b: 92).

The structure of proposition campaigns shows at least four important differences between the United States and Germany.

1. According to the treaty of the Länder on the regulation of broadcasting, political commercials on radio and TV are generally outlawed (Hesse 1999: 101–2; Heußner 1994: 346–48). In contrast to the United States (Cronim 1989: 116–24; Dubois and Feeney 1998: 178–79; Heußner 1994: 326, 338–39), this extremely important and necessary provision reduces significantly the impact of the financial power of special interest

---

19. This is also possible in Bremen (Przygode 1995: 62, footnote 122).

groups through electronic media in direct legislation campaigns (Heußner 1994: 325ff., 346ff.).

2. In five Länder there is a system of public reimbursement for reasonable campaign costs (Jung 2000b: 442), which partly enables financially weak groups to participate in direct legislation. In the United States such a system for direct legislation does not exist. Only Oregon gives tax credits (Dubois and Feeney 1998: 178–79; Heußner 1994: 337–38).

3. On the other hand, no Land thus far appears to have adopted requirements for disclosure of campaign contributions and expenditures in propositions campaigns (Heußner 1994: 350). In the United States these provisions are common (Dubois and Feeney 1998: 189ff.). They should be adopted in Germany, too (Heußner 1994: 350).

4. Several U.S. states prepare voter information pamphlets with a wide range of information.

> California, for example, provides voters with the full text of each measure, an official title and summary prepared by the attorney general's office, votes in the legislature for and against a legislatively-referred measure, 500-word arguments for and against a proposed measure and accompanying 250-word rebuttals on each side, and an "impartial analysis" prepared by the office of the legislative analyst that includes an assessment of the fiscal impact of a measure on state or local governments. (Dubois and Feeney 1998: 165–66)

Unfortunately, no state in Germany provides the voters with voter information pamphlets of this kind (Heußner 1994: 316–17; Hartmann 2001: 783).

In contrast to the American states (Heußner 1994: 360), in Germany—similar to the situation in Switzerland on the federal level (Möckli 1994: 94)—initiative elections not always but generally take place on a different day from candidate elections (Hartmann 2001: 783; Heußner 1994: 353). Generally, this seems to be appropriate in order to reduce the number of decisions a voter has to make on election day.

Finally, an important difference between most American states and Switzerland vis-à-vis Germany exists in the majorities required to pass an initiative at the polls. In most U.S. states (Magleby 1984: 38–39, 46) and in Switzerland (Gross 1999: 91) only a majority voting on the issue is required for passage of both constitutional and statutory initiatives. In Germany constitutional initiatives require the affirmative vote of 50 percent of all citizens eligible to vote except in Bavaria, which requires 25 percent. Additionally, in five states a vote of two-thirds in favor of the amendment is required. In five states statutory initiatives need the affirmative vote of 25 percent of all citizens eligible to vote. Baden-Württemberg, Berlin, Mecklenburg-Vorpommern, and Thuringia require one-third; in Berlin there is also a 25 percent threshold but only if fewer than 50 percent of the eligible voters vote. In the Saarland an affirmative vote requires 50 percent of the eligible votes. Rhineland-Palatinate requires that 25 percent of all citizens eligible to vote participate in the vote on the particular initiative. Only in Bavaria, Hesse, North Rhine-Westphalia and Saxony is a simple majority voting on the statutory proposition sufficient (Arnim 2000: 304–11). These thresholds—when set at a reasonable level—can be useful tools to ensure that only initiatives become law that are based on a sufficiently large proportion of voter support (Heußner 1994: 86–87, 369; Heußner 2001: 88–90). However, many observers of direct legislation are opposed to these thresholds for being too high (Arnim 2000: 229–31; Jung 1999a: 863–98).

Reforms, Legal Problems, Court Decisions

As already mentioned, the signature thresholds in some German states have a prohibitive impact. Therefore, one of the main reform projects aims to reduce these hurdles, for example, by halving them from 20 percent to 10 percent as happened in Berlin, in Bremen (for statutes), Rhineland-Palatinate, and North Rhine-Westphalia (Neumann 2001: 35; Jung 2000b: 442). The efforts of direct legislation groups aim especially at thresholds of only 5 percent or less and free signature gathering within periods of several months. To the same extent, the elimination of special majority requirements for the passage of initiatives is a main concern of direct legislation groups.[20]

---

20. For example, efforts in Thuringia in 2000 and in Bremen and North Rhine-Westphalia in 1999 (Kampwirth 1999: 184; Neumann 1999: 23).

On these issues some adjudication already exists. For example, the Bavarian Constitutional Court decided that the Bavarian constitution requires that constitutional initiatives need the minimum consent of 25 percent of all citizens eligible to vote for passage (BayVerfGE 1999: 28–32). For some people this is a highly explosive decision, for it alters a fifty-year-old adjudication of the same court that expressly did not require a special majority for constitutional initiatives (Jung 2000b: 443).

The exclusion of almost all important financial measures is also a reform target of high priority. In several Länder there have been efforts to abolish these restrictions through constitutional initiatives.[21] Nevertheless, several executive branches and constitutional courts of these states declared these efforts unconstitutional. The Bavarian Constitutional Court is of the opinion that the unalterable constitutional right of parliament to decide on the budget would be infringed upon (BayVerfGE 2000: 911, 913).

Finally, the problem of amending and repealing initiative statutes should be mentioned. Whereas the law in some American states expressly deals with this question and places various limits on the power of the legislature (Dubois and Feeney 1998: 78–81; Heußner 1994: 96–99), in Germany this problem is not mentioned in the constitutions or statutes at all (Heußner 1994: 100–101; Przygode 1995: 427). In 1999 the legislature of Schleswig-Holstein repealed the above-mentioned Spelling Reform initiative statute passed by referendum one year before (Möllers and Ooyen 2000: 461). This was heavily criticized (Jung 2000b: 445); however, the Federal Constitutional Court refused to adjudicate the constitutionality of the issue (Jung 2001c: 150; BVerfGE 1999, Absatz No. 8).

Direct Legislation on the Federal Level

Direct legislation does not exist on the federal level. Nevertheless, in the constitutional discussions after German unification, the introduction of direct legislation on the federal level was an important subject. Consequently, in 1993 the majority of the Joint Constitutional

21. For example, the initiatives in Bremen and North Rhine-Westphalia in the note above or the initiative in 1998 in Hamburg (Efler 1999: 214) and in 1999 in Bavaria.

Commission of Bundestag and Bundesrat voted in favor of the *Volks-begehren* and *Volksentscheid*. However, the necessary two-thirds majority of the members of the commission was lacking (Heußner and Jung 1999a: 16–17).

The coalition of Social Democrats and Greens that came to power in 1998 decided to work for the introduction of direct legisla-tion (see coalition treaty in *Zeitschrift für Rechtspolitik* [ZRP] 1998: 499), and in February 2001 the Social Democrats presented a pro-posal to that effect (for details, see Jung 2001a: 61–75). There is also a citizens' campaign called "Menschen für Volksabstimmung" (Peo-ple for direct legislation) with the object of introducing direct legis-lation at the federal level (Weber 2001a: 31–32; Kurz 1999: 363–76). According to opinion polls, large majorities of the people are in favor of the initiative.[22]

In response to the political contribution (donation) scandal sur-rounding the former CDU chancellor Helmut Kohl during 1999–2000, the call for direct legislation became even stronger. Now, some influential Christian Democratic politicians, such as Jürgen Rüttgers, CDU Chairman in North Rhine-Westphalia, are also in favor of more decision-making by popular vote (*Rheinische Post*, 21 February 2001; Mehr Demokratie web site; Prantl 2000: 555–56). The politi-cal contribution scandal of the CDU is a very good example of the potential importance of the refinement of the parliamentary system through devices of direct legislation.

During the last decade the CDU, especially former chancellor, Helmut Kohl, did not disclose the sources and names of contribu-tions and contributors of millions of deutsche marks, thereby violat-ing the transparency rule of the constitution (Basic Law, Article 21, section 1) and the party law *Parteiengesetz* (Leyendecker 2000; Prantl 2000). Punishment of the violators is quite complicated, because there were no personal sanctions, especially for the violations of the transparency rule of the constitution and the party law. This is not surprising, since the potential or actual violators of the disclosure rules—the politicians and political parties—make the law. If the cit-izens themselves have the power to enact laws, at least some hope might exist that clear and strict personal sanctions, especially for the

---

22. In 1986: 66 percent; in 1991: 69 percent; in 1999: 70 percent; and in 2000: 75 percent (Heußner 1994: 2; Heußner and Jung 1999a: 17; Weber 2001b: 7).

violation of the disclosure rules, will be enacted. Thus direct legislation is necessary in order to correct *Parlamentsversagen* (parliamentary failure) (Heußner 1994: 76–80).

To a certain extent this can be demonstrated by the case of California legislation. In this state, the so-called Political Reform Act established by the people through an initiative in 1974 requires that the names of all contributors of $100 or more be disclosed (Diamond et al. 1975: 454, 463–64), while in Germany the threshold provided in the party law is about €10,000 (20,000 DM). A violation of this provision in California is a special misdemeanor, whereas such a special personal criminal sanction is lacking completely in Germany. In addition to other penalties provided by law in California, a fine of up to $10,000, or three times the amount the person failed to report properly, may be imposed upon conviction for each violation (California Government Code title 9, para. 91000a). Similar penalties exist in Germany only for the political parties. In California a violator can be banned from candidacy for any elective office for a period of four years, whereas such a provision is lacking in Germany. Now, following the scandal involving the former chancellor, the political parties can no longer prevent reforms of the party law, including personal sanctions for violators of the disclosure rules (*Süddeutsche Zeitung*, 16, 19, and 21–22 July 2001; para. 31d *Parteiengesetz*).

In Germany, political alienation is widespread (Gaiser et al. 2000: 12ff.). Everything has to be done to prevent this alienation from being transformed into a distrust of democracy. Direct legislation is one—but of course not the only—step to cure this problem. So it is no wonder that in Switzerland the trust in democracy is much higher than in Germany—in 1997, 88 percent versus 66 percent (Linder 1999: 64). And in California—despite all deficiencies of direct legislation in this state—72 percent of the people said in 1997 that direct legislation is a good thing for the state (Allswang 2000: 236).

Conclusion

In united Germany, on the local and Länder levels direct legislation has become a firm component of the political system. To the extent permitted by the legal preconditions and especially by the relatively small legislative powers of the Länder, direct legislation can help to reduce political alienation and parliamentary deficiencies. However, the center of legislative power is at the federal level. Therefore, in order to reduce political alienation and parliamentary deficiencies effectively, it is necessary to introduce direct legislation on the federal level. To amend the constitution (*Grundgesetz*), a two-thirds majority in both the Bundestag and the Bundesrat is required, that is, a large majority of members of these two legislative chambers must agree to share legislative power with the people. In several Länder the necessary majority of members of parliament were willing to make this decision. This has not yet happened in the Bundestag (and Bundesrat), but one can assume that sooner or later a similar conclusion will be reached.

Chapter 8

THE GERMAN SYSTEM OF EU POLICYMAKING AND THE ROLE OF THE LÄNDER

Fragmentation and Partnership

⌒⌒⌒

Udo Diedrichs

Germany: A Fragmented System of EU Policymaking

The German system of EU policymaking has traditionally been described as highly fragmented, complex, and multilayered (Bulmer et al. 1998: 26ff.; Huelshoff 1999: 220f.; Maurer 2002). This is due not least to the federal character of the German political system, including a multitude of actors on different levels already in the national arena with only limited centralized steering capacities (Katzenstein 1997b: 26). Especially compared to the French and British systems of government, Germany appears less efficient and effective with regard to its decision-making capacity and its ability to voice interests at the European level.

Different Principles of Decision-Making in Ministries, the Cabinet, and the Chancellory

Different principles interfere when decision-making in EU affairs is concerned. On the one hand, each ministry enjoys a rather high level of autonomy in defining its position, with each minister holding the political responsibility for his or her department (Streinz and Pechstein 1995: 145f.; Wessels 2000: 302ff.). Further, the chancellor can issue fundamental political directives that guide the general work of the ministries, but these normally do not touch upon the daily routine management of decision-making (Wessels 2000: 315ff.). Finally, following a third principle, conflicts between ministries are to be solved at the cabinet level, which means that interministerial coordination takes place (Maurer 2002).

Traditionally, there has been a weak or absent hierarchical structure in the routine coordination of German EU policy (Bulmer et al. 1998: 28). The competent ministries try to define their positions in relative autonomy and have to undergo a process of discussion and clearing with other ministries. The result is a high degree of institutional pluralism in which coordination between several departments becomes crucial for the day-to-day life between Berlin and Brussels (Bulmer et al. 1998: 28). Unlike other countries such as Great Britain and France, Germany does not have a clear and unified decision-making center that would provide guidance by exerting a steering function with regard to the different institutions and actors involved in EU affairs, thus ensuring a strong coherence of German positions across different policy fields.

The chancellor tends to play a major role in the fundamental direction of German EU policy. His position is strengthened by involvement in the European Council and his subsequent ability to shape constitutional decisions at the highest level. The fact that the European Council has in the last years taken over initiatives in an increasing number of policy matters stresses this tendency even more (Bulmer et al. 1998: 27). Especially Helmut Kohl intensively used his leadership role based upon the guidance competence—without regularly invoking it—for shaping the EU architecture, often in cooperation with other member governments such as France, a fact that further reinforced his position with regard to domestic pressures. However, the chancellor is not involved in fixing detailed technical or routine positions, especially in the day-to-day management of EU policy (Bulmer et al. 1998: 16).

The nitty-gritty work in the Council of Ministers, the COREPER (Committee of Permanent Representatives), and the working groups and committees is handled by the ministries and their administrative staff. Meanwhile, each German ministry disposes of one or more divisions for European affairs. However, some ministries are more active and more important than others in dealing with EU matters. Initially, the Ministry of Economics held a leading coordinating position—for different reasons—in the European Coal and Steel Community (ECSC) and European Community (EC) matters. In 1958 an agreement was reached between the Ministry of Economics and the Foreign Office in dealing with the newly created EC. In the 1960s, especially the Ministry of Agriculture and to a lesser extent the Ministry of Finance developed specialized departments for EC matters (Bulmer et al. 1998: 78f.). Since 1998, with the new Schröder and Fischer government in office, competences for coordinating EU matters have been shifted from the Ministry of Economics to the Ministry of Finance and to the Ministry of Foreign Affairs. But this did not mean that a more centralized handling of EU issues would then take place.

Growing Involvement of Numerous Actors in EU Affairs

Over the last decades, the amount and variety of ministerial involvement in EU affairs has increased considerably. Meanwhile, in addition to the traditionally strong ministries (Foreign Affairs, Economics, Agriculture, and Finance), nearly all ministries deal with EU affairs. Especially telling is, for example, the increasing activity of the Ministries of the Interior; the Environment; and Youth, Family and Health in the last ten years (Bulmer et al. 1998: 29). This seems to be a reaction to the expanded policy agenda of the EU itself, which has covered ever more areas since the beginning of the Treaty reform period with the Single European Act in 1987 (Maurer 2002; Maurer and Wessels 2000).

Commission draft proposals are passed from the Permanent Representation in Brussels to the Ministry of Finance—before 1998 to the Ministry of Economics—and are then handed over to the leading department depending on the policy concerned (Maurer and Wessels 2000: 293ff.). Thus, each ministry carries out its work on EU matters from the early stages of EU decision-making. An important role in coordinating different positions from the relevant ministries is assumed by the Interministerial Committee of State Secretaries for European Affairs, bringing together the representatives of the four traditional EU-relevant ministries (Foreign Affairs, Finance, Economics, and Agriculture), as well as the responsible State Minister of the Chancellery and the German Permanent Representative. Other ministries can be invited to take part (Streinz and Pechstein 1995: 138f.). The new government decided in 1998 to shift the chair in the Committee from the Ministry of Economics to the Foreign Office, thus strengthening the role of the latter in coordinating EU matters. The central function of the committee lies in settling controversial issues between the different actors and preparing the German position in the Council of Ministers and its bodies. Decision-making is by consensus.

Apart from this body, there are further groups composed of civil servants from the different ministries that deal with issues on the working group level and in COREPER. These activities are coordinated by the Ministry of Finance and the Ministry of Foreign Affairs. Consensus and compromise prevail as the central modes of interaction. There is no hierarchical order that could force any department to accept solutions against its will.

Until 1998 a cabinet committee also existed for European affairs, but it was dissolved after a rather irrelevant existence and extremely rare meetings in the last decades. The cabinet as a whole tends to discuss EU matters once they reach the interministerial arena.

Finally, when conflicts arise that cannot be solved at the working group or state secretary levels, either the relevant ministers, the cabinet, or, in the last resort, the chancellor can settle the issue. But in this process, several issues must be taken into account. Apart from the described principles (ministerial responsibility, cabinet principle, and guiding competence of the chancellor), the "arithmetic of the coalition" also must be respected, which then constrains the government's possibilities of deciding and acting (Bulmer et al. 1998: 31f.). Although EU matters are generally not considered as controversial among the different parties, certain decisions can be heavily influenced by their preferences, such as the nomination of EU Commission members or policy-specific issues, such as environmental matters.

The Role of the Bundestag: Growing Effectiveness without Disturbing EU Policy

Since the coming into force of the Maastricht agreement (Treaty on European Union [TEU]), the role of the Bundestag was strengthened especially by the creation of the Committee on European

Union Affairs (CEUA). It safeguards the rights of the German Bundestag as regards information on and participation in matters relating to the European Union. Its predecessor, the EC Committee, had been regarded as a rather weak tool for influencing the German position and interest definition in Brussels. It includes not only members of the German Bundestag (who, as a rule, also belong to a specialized committee), but also German members of the European Parliament (EP) without voting rights (Hölscheidt 2001: 126ff.).

The CEUA fulfills three main roles: it serves as an "integration committee," as a "horizontal committee," and as a "specialized committee for European affairs" (CEUA 1998). In its quality as integration committee, the CEUA is the central locus for dealing with fundamental EU matters in the Bundestag; in this regard, it considers ratification of treaty reforms and important institutional developments such as Agenda 2000, and it submits recommendations to the plenary session or opinions to the government. As a horizontal committee, the CEUA takes responsibility as the leading committee in cases where several sectors are dealt with in a planned EU legislative proposal, making it difficult to name a specialized committee of the Bundestag as mainly responsible for dealing with the matter. Its function as a specialized committee for European affairs comes into play when it provides additional expertise on an item dealt with by a specialized committee of the Bundestag. In these cases it may focus on institutional aspects or the general integration dimension of a given proposal. Generally, the CEUA is not responsible for considering the implementation of EU law; rather, this is a matter for the specialized committees of the Bundestag.

According to the new Article 23 Basic Law, the federal government shall inform the Bundestag and the Bundesrat as quickly as possible about EU matters (Streinz and Pechstein 1995: 146). It also shall take into account the opinion of the Bundestag when defining its negotiating position. If the federal government deviates, or intends to deviate, from the position of the Bundestag, it shall account for this decision and provide the reasons. Further legal acts such as the cooperation law between the government and the Bundestag and changes to the rules of procedure of the parliament contributed to strengthening the role and function of the CEUA.

The CEUA is entitled to exercise the Bundestag's rights with regard to the government and can address its opinion immediately to the government unless there is opposition by another committee. The CEUA is also responsible for receiving all EU-related documents and handing them over to the other committees. It is even able to exercise a "parliamentary scrutiny reserve" with regard to the voting on legal initiatives and proposals by the government.

The scrutiny and control of planned EU legislation, but also implementation of EC law, requires a constant process of consultation and information between the government and parliament. Ministers or even the chancellor appear before the CEUA, informing it about coming or recent important events at the EU level, especially European Council or important Council of Ministers meetings. The state minister of the Foreign Office attends the CEUA sessions on a regular basis. Apart from this, domestic and foreign experts and politicians are invited to the committee, especially members of the EU Commission or the European Parliament, as are academics and representatives of civil society.

The CEUA is engaged in contacts with other parliamentary bodies in the EU. In this respect, cooperation in the framework of COSAC (Conference des Organes Specialisés dans les Affaires Communautaires et Européennes des Parlements de l'Union européenne), which brings together representatives from EU committees of member states' parliaments and of the Constitutional Committee of the EP, plays a special role. It serves as a mechanism for exchanging information and experience between members of the European Parliament (MEPs) and also elaborates positions and recommendations with regard to institutional issues concerning the European Union. So far, COSAC has not developed into a decisive focal point for increasing national parliaments' influence in the EU, but discussions after the conclusion of the Nice Treaty and the next intergovernmental conference (IGC) might inject a new impulse into this process.

In general, the role and weight of parliament in defining the German position in the EU have been strengthened, but they did not fundamentally change the distribution of influence between the different actors (Streinz and Pechstein 1995: 146f.). They further increased the coordination and consultation reflex already in play. Since the majority within the Bundestag supports the government, the Bundestag does not act as a further impediment to a smooth EU decision-making process. The existence of a broad cross-party consensus about the basic principles and goals of European integration further contributes to a rather uncontested process of parliamentary deliberation, avoiding major problems for the government in pushing through its European policy.

The Interplay between the Federal and the Regional Levels

Growing Involvement of the Länder in EU Affairs: In Search of Lost Competences

Since the mid-1980s, especially with the coming into force of the Single European Act (SEA), the challenge of integration has affected the German Länder in an increasing and ever more substantial manner. Hence, they tried to get more closely involved in the decision-making process concerning EC affairs, considering it a compensation for lost competences (Gunlicks 1999: 189). The Länder had belonged to a certain extent to the victims of the ongoing integration process: "For the Länder, then, European integration has meant, among other things, further erosion of Land powers" (Gunlicks 1999: 188).

Since the beginning of the integration process, the Länder have been present via the institution of the Observer of the Länder (*Länderbeobachter*) who is stationed in Brussels and is even allowed to attend Council of Ministers meetings. He or she passes information to the Länder and the Bundesrat on EU issues (Dette-Koch 1997). In 1979 an improvement of the Länder influence was achieved by the "participation procedure," which was further strengthened and specified after the ratification of the SEA (Blume and Rex 1998: 33f.; Streinz and Pechstein 1995: 146).

The demands of the Länder for a strengthened status vis-à-vis the federal and European levels were then heavily supported in the early 1990s through the extraordinary situation created by German unification and the IGC leading to the TEU (Gunlicks 1999: 190f.). Both processes which were in certain ways interrelated, offered opportunities that were seized by the Länder in order to redefine their roles in EU affairs.

A substantial step in the direction of increasing Länder participation in EU policymaking was made after the conclusion of the Maastricht treaty, especially with the new formulation of Article 23 of the German Basic Law and subsequent legislation and arrangements related to it (Gunlicks 1999: 190f.; Streinz and Pechstein 1995: 147). First of all, Article 23 defined the principles of federalism and subsidiarity as fundamentals of the EU as a whole and linked German participation in the integration process to these values. Further transfers of sovereignty would need the approval of both the Bundestag and the Bundesrat. In cases where the establishment of the EU, amendments to its statutory foundations, or regulations that amend or supplement the contents of the Basic Law were concerned, a two-thirds majority in the Bundesrat (as in the Bundestag) would be necessary (Zeh 1999: 41f.). Especially the interaction between the Bund and the Länder was redefined and explained in more detail.

A central position in this context has been reserved for the Bundesrat as the representative organ of Länder interests. The Bundesrat is kept informed about EU proposals and can voice a position on them (Zeh 1999: 41f.). According to the different degrees of impact on the regional level, the Länder are able to participate in the formulation and definition of the German position in Brussels. This includes:

- involvement in the deliberations aimed at defining the German position in the Council of Ministers; here, varying cases have to be distinguished:
  - where the Federation has exclusive legislative jurisdiction, or in other respects has the right to legislate, and the interests of the Länder are affected, the federal government shall take into account the opinion of the Bundesrat;
  - where essentially the Länder have legislative powers, or the establishment of their authorities or their administrative procedures are affected, the federation shall give due consideration to the opinion of the Bundesrat, that is, it shall prevail;
- participation of Länder representatives in the negotiations taking place within the EU Commission or Council committees or groups—except the COREPER (Zumschlinge 1999: 55f.); this has already been established with the SEA; special provisions still exist for IGC and the accession negotiations; and
- the representation of the German position by representatives of the Länder either in Commission or Council groups or committees or even in Council sessions where essentially the exclusive jurisdiction of the Länder is affected (Streinz and Pechstein 1995: 147).

Separate rules apply for provisions based upon the implied powers in Article 308 of the revised Treaty of Rome in cases where the Länder enjoy exclusive competence or the approval by the Bundesrat is necessary to pass domestic legislation. In such cases the government shall come to an agreement with the Bundesrat before defining a position in the Council.

For dealing with EU affairs, the Bundesrat created the European Union Affairs Committee in 1993 in order to discuss EU-related documents and prepare decisions by the plenary session. Further, a freshly created EU Chamber of the Bundesrat is able to exercise the rights of the plenary session in urgent circumstances.

Meanwhile, all Länder governments have established special posts for dealing with EU affairs either at ministerial or state-secretary level (Streinz and Pechstein 1995: 140ff.). The single ministries also have desk officers for EU affairs. The Länder have also opened offices in Brussels that gather information and establish links between the European, federal, and regional arenas (Zumschlinge 1999: 60ff.). One important task is to maintain regular contacts with the Commission on issues of importance such as regional or competition policy. With the creation of the Committee of the Regions (CoR), the Länder offices in Brussels developed a preparatory scheme for the CoR meetings in this new organization.

The Committee of the Regions: A Regional Chamber in the Making?

The creation of the CoR by the TEU in 1992 was a major achievement for the Länder, although this new body did not satisfy all of their expectations (Degen 1998: 103ff.). Especially the inclusion of local authorities was not appreciated by many of the regions. Further, limited legislative rights—consultation in several policy fields—contributed to the impression of a powerless discussion circle. On the other hand, the regions for the first time disposed of an institutionalized voice in the EU arena, providing a forum for the Länder, especially the prime ministers, to project their views and ideas at a European level.

After two quite chaotic years of finding itself, the CoR gained a certain momentum and routine in its internal working structures and its relations with other institutions (Degen 1998: 110). At Nice it was decided that CoR members in the future must either hold an elected mandate or be responsible to an elected assembly, and the future number of members was restricted to 350 in order to ensure its working capacity. The Länder furthermore favor the proposal that the CoR be given the right to appeal to the European Court of Justice in order to protect its institutional rights, but this does not seem to be a viable choice for the future.

Although the hope that the CoR would emerge as a powerful and effective player within the EU has not been realized, the German Länder regard their participation in the CoR as one element in their European strategies. It represents one way of influencing the EU agenda, but so far it is less meaningful than the cooperation with the federal government in EU matters. Nevertheless, the method chosen by the Länder was to push for incremental improvements of the CoR powers and its structure, for example, the extension of policy fields on which it has to be consulted, or the establishment of an independent administrative setup.

It appears that in recent years the Länder have reduced their interest and appreciation of the CoR in favor of other important issues at the latest IGC, without, however, giving up their insistence on upgrading this institution. One of the main problems lies in the heterogeneity of the regions in Europe, the inclusion of local authorities (Magiera 1999: 26f.), and the sometimes highly cumbersome decision-making process within the CoR. The Länder feel closer to regions with proper legislative competences, such as those in Belgium, than with more administrative units, as in France. This differentiation might lead to a permanent tension within the CoR.

Interaction So Far: Tensions without Disturbances

Since the coming into force of the new provisions related to the Länder participation in EU affairs, ever more Länder civil servants have been appointed either to the Council working groups or the Commission comitology committees (Rometsch 1996: 85). Their interaction with federal civil servants is reported to be quite cooperative, avoiding major conflicts or clashes.

Regarding the activities of the Bundesrat, the impression prevails that its engagement in EU affairs has not created major disturbances, although there is a built-in tension between the Länder interests in further participation and the federal government's attempts to save its autonomy in Brussels. Where requested by the Bundesrat, the government accepted in most cases representation of the German delegation in the Council by the Länder, or where doubt persisted, often joint membership in the delegation was chosen. So far, conflict has arisen so far especially in cases concerned with educational policy, such as the Socrates or the RAPHAEL programs, leading to a discussion between the Bundesrat and the government as to whether a representation by the Länder was appropriate. Both sides agreed then on a consultation and conflict solution procedure that proved feasible simply because both wanted to avoid an institutional or even constitutional quarrel about these issues (von Dewitz 1998: 77f.). As there is no general rule, this process is characterized by constant negotiations between the federal and the regional levels. Even in cases of divergence, as, for example, regarding the issue of whether a simple or a two-thirds majority in the Bundesrat was necessary, no enduring conflict has emerged, as the legal acts so far were passed by unanimous vote.

The interplay between the Bund (Federation) and the Länder in EU affairs is thus generally characterized by a high degree of complexity and differentiation. The formulation of the German negotiating position is—more than in most other EU countries—the product of a cumbersome negotiation and discussion process, both between players of different levels and of different horizontal branches.

The Interplay between Bund and Länder at the Intergovernmental Conference

Germany at the IGC: Defending National—and Regional—Interests

A situation where the formulation and defense of national interests becomes highly prominent is in IGCs. On the one hand, fundamental constitutional changes of the EU system are at stake, which require definitions of what the member states basically want to achieve, while, on the other hand, it is the national governments that act as the central players in this process.

The German negotiating position in the IGC is the product of a series of consultations and deliberations taking place at different levels and across different branches, revealing an increasing role of the Länder in influencing and even shaping what German interests finally turn out to be. From the IGC on the Treaty of Maastricht, where central—but by far not all—demands of the Länder were taken into account, to the recent European Council at Nice, the Länder governments have had a considerable impact on the German negotiations and even on some outcomes of the treaty reform process. In central areas the German position can thus be realized as a combined and interconnected package taking into account different levels of government. Further, it can generally be stated that despite certain tensions and differences between the Bund and the Länder, the interaction between both in IGCs has worked quite smoothly. No major conflicts have been reported so far.

There are three relevant levels of Länder involvement at the IGC (Blume and Rex 1998: 39f.):

1. consultations and deliberations among the Länder themselves, in the European Ministers' Conference, or their working group, or the Conference of the Minister-Presidents, or finally in the framework of the Bundesrat;
2. coordination of the Länder positions with the federal government at different levels; and
3. participation at the IGC itself, either on the level of the personal representatives or even the ministers.

The result is again a highly complex and differentiated game whose main axis, however, is the link that exists between the Länder and the Bund. Only by coming to terms with the federal government would the regional claims have a chance to be realized.

Two special representatives for the IGC are appointed by the Bundesrat (from Baden-Württemberg and Rheinland-Pfalz at the 2000 IGC) and are closely involved in the negotiation process, for example, by participating in the IGC meetings at the ministerial or personal representatives' level. During the IGC negotiations, the Länder observe this process quite closely, are kept informed by the government, and can raise their voices in case of concern, which actually happened several times. The chancellor is engaged in a dialogue with the representatives from the Bundesrat and the Land prime minister for the IGC. Apart from that, the Länder ministers for

European affairs, as well as the prime minister, regularly discuss the ongoing negotiation process (Fischer 1998: 21ff.). Länder representatives are also members of the German delegation at the final European Council meeting for concluding the IGC.

The Länder as the Winners of the IGCs?

The Bundesrat seized the occasion when the ratification of the Maastricht treaty took place in order to underscore its further priorities. These included demands for a continuing institutional reform that would secure effectiveness and transparency of the EU especially with a view to enlargement, the further reduction of the democratic deficit of the EU, a clearer division of competences between the Union and the member states, a more precise definition of the subsidiarity principle, and the transformation of the CoR into a truly regional chamber with concrete powers. Further resolutions in the wake of the 1996 and 2000 IGCs (which finally led to the Amsterdam and Nice Treaties) stressed and specified these positions (Hrbek 2001). From the very start, it was clear that to enforce their interests the Länder would need to rely on close consultation and cooperation with the federal government.

In 1996 it became apparent that not all claims and demands would be equally shared and supported. The federal government made it plain that it would not be willing to defend a new formulation of the subsidiarity principle in the Treaty on European Union, or a catalogue of competences similar to that found in the Basic Law. Instead, it was ready to push for the adoption of a protocol on subsidiarity that offered a more precise orientation and provided for stricter rules of application than those to be found in the Treaty on European Union. Further, the federal government rejected the idea of a right of appeal to the European Court of Justice (ECJ) for the Länder and favored only a limited right of the CoR to appeal to the ECJ for protecting its institutional interests. Although the Länder were not able to fully realize their positions, they adopted a pragmatic approach involving small steps while not losing sight of their strategic, longer-term goals.

Interestingly, the focus of attention of the Länder during the 1996 IGC shifted increasingly toward issues that had initially not attracted so much attention, such as the public savings bank system or the status of public broadcasting—two cases where the Länder have specific interests that they see threatened by Commission actions in recent years. The federal government adopted these issues as part of the national position of Germany, and, as is known so far, the chancellor himself endorsed and defended them under difficult circumstances at the IGC in 1996 (Fischer 1998: 23).

The fragmented and pluralist structure in German EU policymaking allowed for cross-cutting coalitions at the IGC that were made responsible for certain patterns of behavior of the delegation from the Federal Republic. The resistance of certain Länder governments in line with the stance maintained by several ministries accounted for the German veto of proposals to allow qualified majority voting in a number of policy fields, such as in industrial and environmental policy at the Amsterdam summit (Bulmer et al. 1998). So, the possibility of varying institutional constellations is one of the features of the multilevel system, even where the chancellor plays a dominant role at the Intergovernmental Conference.

As a further point, it was not always possible to identify issues affecting the Länder as a whole. A process of increasing differentiation took place, as was shown in the case of employment policy, where a majority of the Länder agreed to a Bundesrat resolution calling for a European initiative in this policy field, leaving other Länder in a minority position (Hrbek 2001: 103f.). Here, party politics clearly influenced the behavior of regional governments, leading to more open approaches by Social Democrats, while Christian Democrats revealed a hesitant stance. Thus, different interests of the Länder governments led to a lack of consistency in defining common positions. Also, smaller or eastern German regions did not commit themselves as strongly to the claims made by the larger Länder, such as Bavaria, North Rhine-Westphalia, and Baden-Württemberg. One reason lay in the different capacities for exploiting further competences and opportunities for participation at the EU level (Hrbek 2001: 103).

At the 2000 IGC, the Länder again presented themselves in a rather coherent way. Here, especially the issue of demarcation of competences and services of general economic interest were high on the agenda. The treaty revision at Nice in December 2000 can be regarded as essentially satisfactory for German regional interests (Minister für Bundes- und Europaangelegenheiten des Landes Nordrhein-Westfalen 2000; Konferenz der Ministerpräsidenten der Länder 2000). Perhaps the main achievement has been that in 2004 a new IGC will be convened, which will focus also on the distribution of competences between the member states and the EU. This has become a major concern for the Länder. Also, unanimity has been preserved in some areas of interest to them, such as the promotion of culture, or town and country planning in the environmental sphere, thus preventing the danger of major intervention by the EU.

The results of the Amsterdam and the Nice Treaty reforms were considered largely as successes for the Länder (Hrbek 2001). Without achieving the optimal maximum outcome, the Länder nevertheless have made important points in central issues of concern to them (Fischer 1998; Blume and Rex 1998: 39ff.).

The problems concerning services of general economic interests, however, remained unsolved. Here, a major source of conflict arose between the Commission and the Länder—which were supported by the federal government—concerning especially the public banking system. In July 2001 an arrangement was reached between the Commission and the Federal Republic of Germany, avoiding a major legal conflict to be settled by the European Court of Justice. The European Commission urged the German government to propose a solution to the long-standing problem of state debt guarantees that benefit the country's powerful state-owned banks. According to the Commission, the guarantees are illegal state aid because they allow the banks to borrow more cheaply than their commercial competitors. After a transitional phase of four years, the German public savings banks will have to adapt to EU competition policy, thus reforming the traditional system of guarantors' liability. This will entail a major structural reform that will fundamentally change the German banking system (*Handelsblatt*, 17 July 2001).

Conclusions: German Interests in the European Union—More Fragmented, but Also More Effective?

Given the complex and segmented structure of German EU policymaking, what conclusions can be drawn? First, one must differentiate between German interests on a strategic and a tactical level (Bulmer et al. 1998: 14f.).

A rather broad but nevertheless substantial result is that Germany has been quite successful in achieving strategic goals, but it is considered to be less effective in tactical issues. The fundamental decisions of EU policy since the 1990s, such as the creation of the Economic and Monetary Union (EMU) and the stability-oriented approach in maintaining it, the strengthening of political union, the definition of a Common Foreign and Security Policy (CFSP), and enlargement of the Union belong to the essentials of German EU policy.

Certain elements known from the German model of decision-making are "transferred" to the European arena. The model of the Bundesbank has been applied to the European Central Bank system and its principles. Yet more fundamentally, the basic feature of the EU as a multilevel system of negotiation and problem solving resembles the German model of decision-making at the national level, providing the actors with a great deal of experience and familiarity in dealing with these matters (Bulmer et al. 1998: 14ff.). At the same time this has made it possible for the Länder to adapt to this system and define their role in the EU arena.

The fact that the Länder play a more important role could thus be quite smoothly digested and integrated into the broader framework of German EU policy. Länder positions partially become "nationalized" and then "Europeanized," as the Committee of the Regions, or the subsidiarity principle or finally the issue of the division of competences have shown. Claims and demands for participation addressed to the national political system by regional actors are not considered as alien or detrimental to the German position in Europe, but rather become part of it and are subsequently introduced into the EU arena where they may shape the constitutional and institutional structures.

The Länder involvement in EU affairs on the one hand puts pressure on the federal government, but on the other hand it can be regarded as a major contribution to the overall development of the EU as a multilevel system of governance. However, one central problem in the interaction between the Bund and the Länder lies in the fact that the erosion of Länder legislative competences in the wake of European integration has so far been compensated mainly by the participation of the regional executives, especially via the Bundesrat, leaving the parliaments at the margin. A new formula for the distribution of competences foreseen at the 2004 IGC might open a path for addressing this problem at least partially. Contributions from several Länder representatives seem to indicate that they strive to change substantially the established legal setup of the EU, leaving more space for national and regional decision-making. The former North Rhine-Westphalian minister-president, Wolfgang Clement, made a plea for the transfer of competences back to the national arena, especially in the case of agricultural and regional policy (Hrbek 2001: 110ff.). The German Social Democrats seem to endorse such positions by recommending a financing system in these sectors, as reflected in the "Schröder Paper" of March 2001 (see *Leitantrag* 2001).

Further, German Länder take sides with other regions. In a declaration by several constitutional regions from Germany, Belgium, Spain, Austria, and Great Britain in May 2001, a number of claims were made for the post-Nice process preparing the future institutional reform of the EU. Especially a strengthening of the subsidiarity principle, a review of political responsibilities between the EU on the one hand and the member states and their regions on the other, and a better system of delimitation of powers were recommended. The role of the Committee of the Regions should be strengthened, and constitutional regions should be able to go directly to the Court of Justice in case their prerogatives are harmed (*Political Declaration of the Constitutional Regions* 2001).

It remains to be seen to what extent the federal government will adopt these positions and defend them during the next treaty revision. Given the experience with recent reforms of the EU, one could expect a differentiated strategy that attempts to focus on key elements. The future of the working relationship so far between the federal government and the Länder will especially depend upon coherence of the positions of the regional governments and also upon their pragmatism, making it advisable to concentrate on core issues (such as the delimitation of competences) and not on maximum goals. Close coordination with the federal government will be indispensable for a successful result.

Chapter 9

GERMAN LÄNDER PARTICIPATION IN EUROPEAN POLICY THROUGH THE BUNDESRAT

Elisabeth Dette-Koch

Introduction

Anew political order has been taking shape in Europe since German reunification (Rogoff 1999: 415–30). As the process of
integration in the EU continues, national legislation is increasingly
being influenced by regulations approved in Brussels. It is estimated
that on average 50 percent of German laws are influenced by European law, and in single fields, for example, economic areas, the proportion is roughly 70 percent. This means that daily life is increasingly
influenced by Europe. Since January 2002, when real euro coins and
bills were introduced, everybody—not only in the member states of
the Economic and Monetary Union (EMU)—has taken notice.

Pursuant to Article 23, Paragraph 2, of the Basic Law, the Bundestag and the states (Länder) participate through the Bundesrat[1] in
affairs of the European Union. As a civil servant of one of the German
Länder, Baden-Württemberg, I work as a representative of that Land

---

1. The Bundesrat (the German Federal Council) is composed of members of
state governments.

Grüß Gott – ich komme vom Deutschen Bundesrat
(Good afternoon, I come from the German Bundesrat)

(state) to the German federation and in European affairs as head of the unit, European Affairs, EU-Committee of the Bundesrat. I am the so-called *Sitzungsvertreterin* (Commissioner) of Baden-Württemberg on the Committee on European Affairs of the Bundesrat.

One purpose of my presentation is to attempt to make clear that participation by the German Länder in European affairs is not so confused and fragmented as the cartoon above would have us believe.

As Udo Diedrichs has already indicated in the preceding chapter, during the negotiation of the Maastricht treaty, pressure by the Länder led to the amendment of the German Basic Law in 1992 by the addition of Article 23, which replaced Article 24 (1) as the special article on Europe.[2] The amendment was part of a deal between the

2. Concerning the structural safeguard clause of the new Article 23 of the Basic Law, see Oschatz and Risse 1995: 427–28.

federal government and the Länder. It was the "price" the Federation (Bund) had to pay for the Bundesrat's consent to the Maastricht treaty law (so-called ratification law).

Article 23 (1) authorizes the Federation to transfer by statutory law sovereign powers to the European Union with the consent of the Bundesrat. Article 23 (2) provides that "through the Bundesrat, the Länder shall be involved in matters concerning the European Union."[3]

3. See the English version of "Basic Law" published by the Press and Information Office and available from the German Embassy: Article 23 (The European Union).

(1) With a view to establishing a united Europe the Federal Republic of Germany shall participate in the development of the European Union, which is committed to democratic, social and federal principles, to the rule of law, and to the principle of subsidiarity, and ensures protection of basic rights comparable in substance to that afforded by this Basic Law. To this end the Federation may transfer sovereign powers by law with the consent of the Bundesrat. The establishment of the European Union as well as amendments to its statutory foundations and comparable regulations which amend or supplement the content of this Basic Law or make such amendments or supplements possible shall be subject to the provisions of paragraphs (2) and (3) of Article 79.

(2) The Bundestag and, through the Bundesrat, the Länder shall be involved in matters concerning the European Union. The Federal Government shall inform the Bundestag and the Bundesrat comprehensively and as quickly as possible.

(3) The Federal Government shall give the Bundestag the opportunity to state its opinion before participating in the legislative process of the European Union. The Federal Government shall take account of the opinion of the Bundestag in the negotiations. Details shall be the subject of a law.

(4) The Bundesrat shall be involved in the decision-making process of the Federation in so far as it would have to be involved in a corresponding internal measure or in so far as the Länder would be internally responsible.

(5) Where in an area in which the Federation has exclusive legislative jurisdiction the interests of the Länder are affected or where in other respects the Federation has the right to legislate, the Federal Government shall take into account the opinion of the Bundesrat. Where essentially the legislative powers of the Länder, the establishment of their authorities or their administrative procedures are affected, the opinion of the Bundesrat shall in this respect prevail in the decision-making process of the Federation; in this connection the responsibility of the Federation for the country as a whole shall be maintained. In matters which may lead to expenditure increases or revenue cuts for the Federation, the approval of the Federal Government shall be necessary.

(6) Where essentially the exclusive legislative jurisdiction of the Länder is affected the exercise of the rights of the Federal Republic of Germany as a member state of the European Union shall be transferred by the Federation to a representative of the Länder designated by the Bundesrat. Those rights shall be exercised with the

Article 23 is supplemented by the Bund-Länder law (EUZBLG)[4] and the Bund-Länder Agreement (BLV).[5] The BLV goes into considerable detail concerning the practical workings of the cooperation between the federal government (cabinet), the Bundesrat, and the Länder on European Union matters.

The System of Participation in Practice

The Duty of the Federal Government to Provide Information on EU Proposals/Initiatives (Vorhaben)

In order to participate in any serious activity, complete and timely information is essential. Therefore, Article 23 (2) s. 2 obliges the federal government to inform the Bundestag and Bundesrat comprehensively and as quickly as possible.

The government sends the documents to the Bundesrat's Secretariat of the Committee on European Affairs. The Secretariat lists them in a system called KEP[6] and sends four paper copies to the Land missions in Berlin, which distribute them to their respective Land ministries. The Bundesrat receives the documents partly as papers, partly as emails. Every year the Länder receive about four thousand documents. These include documents of the EU Commission and Council; the agendas, reports, and notices of meetings

---

participation of and in agreement with the Federal Government; in this connection the responsibility of the Federation for the country as a whole shall be maintained.

(7) Details regarding paragraphs (4) to (6) shall be the subject of a law which shall require the consent of the Bundesrat.

4. Gesetz über die Zusammenarbeit von Bund und Ländern in Angelegenheiten der Europäischen Union (Law on cooperation between the Federation and the Länder in European Union affairs) of 12 March 1993, *Bundesgesetzblatt* 1993 I, p. 313 (EUZBLG). The EUZBLG is reprinted in *Vertrag von Amsterdam. Texte des EU-Vertrages und des EG-Vertrages mit den deutschen Begleitgesetzen*, ed. Presse- und Informationsamt der Bundesregierung, 2nd ed. (1999): 346–49.

5. Vereinbarung zwischen der Bundesregierung und den Regierungen der Länder über die Zusammenarbeit in Angelegenheiten der Europäischen Union in Ausführung § 9 des Gesetzes über die Zusammenarbeit von Bund und Ländern in Angelegenheiten der Europäischen Union of 29 October 1993, Bundesanzeiger, no. 226 (1993): 10425. The BLV is reprinted in *Vertrag von Amsterdam* (see note 4 above).

6. *Konkordanzliste für Europäische Papiere* without links to the proposals and other documents.

of the Council of Ministers, of the Committee of Permanent Representatives (COREPER),[7] Commission advisory committees, and the Parliament; papers on the decisions of the EU Commission; and documents and information on the formal initiatives, position, and comments of the German government in EU organs. Besides these there are also the materials they receive from the Land missions in various EU negotiations. Last but not least, the Länder missions receive reports on Council of Minister meetings directly by the so-called Observer of the Länder (see below). In practice, the central government informs the Bundesrat very broadly. That means that on some days first my colleagues and afterwards our mail office in the representation of Baden-Württemberg almost break down from the piles of paper to be distributed to the different concerned ministries in Stuttgart. Distribution of the reports we receive by email requires about an hour every working day, because we do not send everything to all ministries (as the Bavarian representation did for a while), but we open the documents and decide who needs which documents.

The Right of the Bundesrat to Participate in the Formation of the German Negotiating Position

Article 23 and the law on cooperation between the federal government and the Länder regulate the decision-making process between the Bundesrat and the federal government.

The Bundesrat meets regularly on Fridays, usually at intervals of three weeks. Like all parliamentary bodies, the Bundesrat has permanent committees that make recommendations for decisions to be taken by the body as a whole. The committee meetings are not public. The relevant ministers or secretaries of the state governments are members of the committees. They may be represented by "commissioners," for example, ministerial experts. Often the committees meet in "civil-servant formation."[8] The last EU committee to make recommendations for the plenary session must act two weeks in advance of the Bundesrat session.

7. The Committee of Permanent Representatives is referred to as COREPER, a contraction of its French title, Comité des représentants permanents.

8. Sometimes there are "political sittings" where the members of the committee meet together with members of the federal government, for example, Joschka Fischer,

As a general rule the Secretariat of the Committee on European Affairs reprints the proposals made by the EU Commission. The Bundesrat gives its opinion on the original draft of the official proposal. To prepare the Bundesrat's decision, the different concerned committees give their recommendations on the subject. The EU Committee is the last one to consider the individual proposals. In the committees every Land has one vote. This is different from the plenary chamber where the number of votes that a state has depends on its population (see table 9.1).[9] All recommendations of the committees are the basis for the plenary decision. If the different committees give different recommendations, the EU Committee tries to establish a common position. The votes of each state in the plenary session must be cast en bloc.

To prepare the voting in the different committees, the EU experts of the Baden-Württemberg ministries meet every three weeks on Mondays, two and a half weeks before the Friday plenary session, when the committee meetings take place in order to coordinate in advance the voting of the Land. We discuss the different propositions already brought up by the other states for the various committees and the propositions for opinions to be introduced by Baden-Württemberg.

In these meetings in Baden-Württemberg, we also inform each other on which issues a ministry has informed the Landtag—the state parliament—in accordance with Baden-Württemberg's constitution, which obligates the state government to inform the Landtag of all important European initiatives.[10] In addition, the state government gives an annual report on European affairs to the Landtag. The state secretary, Willi Stächele, who is also a member of the Landtag, provides information to and meets at various times with the speakers on European affairs of the different parties. Up to now, the Landtag of Baden-Württemberg has not had a Committee on European Affairs, but Herr Stächele brought up the suggestion in his last speech on the annual report of the government.

---

the foreign affairs minister. But the chairman of the EU Committee, Willi Stächele (since June 2001, Minister Christophe-E. Palmer), from Baden-Württemberg, tries to chair the committee meetings as often as he can. Otherwise the "doyen" of the civil servants chairs the session.

9. The votes for Hesse were increased from four to five in 1998.

10. Article 34a, *Verfassung des Landes Baden-Württemberg,* 11 November 1953 (*Gesetzblatt* 173). See Franz Greß, chapter 4, this volume.

Table 9.1 Number of Votes per Land in Bundesrat

Land	Population in Millions	Prime Minister (Spring 2003)	Votes in Bundesrat	Government Parties
Baden-Württemberg	10.65	Teufel	6	CDU/FDP
Bavaria	12.38	Stoiber	6	CSU
Berlin	3.39	Wowereit	4	SPD/PDS
Brandenburg	2.58	Platzeck	4	SPD/CDU
Bremen	0.66	Scherf	3	SPD/CDU
Hamburg	1.73	von Beust	3	CDU/PRO/FDP
Hesse	6.09	Koch	5	CDU
Mecklenburg-Vorpommern	1.75	Ringstorff	3	SPD/PDS
Lower-Saxony	7.98	Wulff	6	CDU/FDP
North Rhine-Westphalia	18.07	Steinbrück	6	SPD/Greens
Rhineland-Palatinate	4.05	Beck	4	SPD/FDP
Saarland	1.07	Müller	3	CDU
Saxony	4.36	Milbradt	4	CDU
Saxony-Anhalt	2.56	Böhmer	4	CDU/FDP
Schleswig-Holstein	2.81	Simonis	4	SPD/Greens
Thuringia	2.4	Althaus	4	CDU
Total votes			69	

Source: http://www.bundesrat.de/aktuell/Stimmen.html.

One hour before the Bundesrat's EU Committee meets, we have two separate coordination meetings: one of the so-called A-Länder (where the European Affairs ministers are all from Social Democratic state governments) and one of the B-Länder (where all of the ministers responsible for European affairs are members of the Christian democratic state governments). Depending on the issue, Land representatives on the EU Committee might on rare occasions end up in a tie vote of 8:8; however, often there is no difference between the A- and B-Länder, which means that the vote in the Bundesrat plenum is unanimous.

Since propositions that could not be prepared in advance are sometimes brought up in the meetings of the individual committees, there is a final coordination in Stuttgart at the beginning of the week during which the Bundesrat's plenary session takes place.

The Bundesrat gives its opinion on about 150 propositions per year. As Udo Diedrichs indicated in the previous chapter in this volume, it is not always possible to identify issues of the Länder as a whole. The issue of employment policy is a good example to show how partisan convictions influence the process. The majority of the A-Länder agreed to a resolution by the Bundesrat calling for a European initiative in this policy field, while the B-Länder assumed the role of the opposition.

Significance of the Bundesrat's Position

Whether the Bundesrat's opinion determines the outcome or is only taken into consideration by the federal government depends on the legislative or executive competence regarding the issue. In areas over which the Federation has exclusive legislative or executive powers under the Basic Law, the opinion of the Bundesrat has only to be taken into account. If the principal focus (*Schwerpunkt*) of the matter falls within the exclusive legislative powers of the Länder or within the sphere of Länder institutional authority or administrative activity, the opinion of the Bundesrat is decisive (*maßgeblich*). The Länder have to designate which parts of the Bundesrat's position are to be considered decisive. If the other committees of the Bundesrat did not clarify this issue, the EU Committee does so.

Procedure in the Event of Differences of Opinion between the Bundesrat and the Federal Government

If the views of the federal government and the Bundesrat differ, a mediation procedure comes into play. If that fails, the view of the Bundesrat will prevail if approved by a two-thirds majority. This procedure was used for the first time in December 1999 concerning the Bundesrat's opinion on the directive, "Effects of Plans and Programs on the Environment."[11] The proposal was first introduced by the EU Commission in 1997. The Bundesrat rejected the proposal and demanded that the federal government oppose it as well. As none of the other EU member states wanted to adopt the directive, it was no longer negotiated in the EU Council of Environmental Ministers. But in 1999 under the German presidency, Jürgen Trittin (the federal minister of the environment from the Green Party) placed the proposal on the agenda of the Council of Environmental Ministers again. The Finns, who followed the German presidency,[12] wanted to reach agreement in the Council in December 1999. The federal government had met with other EU member states and negotiated some concessions. The representatives of the Federal Ministry of the Environment discussed the issue with the Bundesrat representatives. Minister Trittin argued that Germany would have to agree to the proposal after intensive negotiations had achieved concessions. Otherwise, he suggested, next time nobody would make any concessions to German positions, assuming that Germany would still not agree at the end. In this concrete situation at the end of the day the Länder did not form a two-thirds majority, because some of the Länder did not want to stab the federal government in the back.

The Participation of Representatives of the Länder in EU Negotiations

Many important decisions are made in the EU Commission comitology (implementation) committees. Therefore, the Länder send representatives to these committees when they are affected by the issue. The decisions of the Council of Ministers are prepared by working groups. Participation in these meetings is important for influencing negotiations.

---

11. For details on the deliberations of the Bundesrat concerning this directive, see Fischer and Koggel 2000: 1742–51.

12. The presidency of the Council of Ministers changes every six months.

Paragraph 6 of the law on cooperation grants the Länder possibilities of participating at the European level.[13] It provides that at the request of the Bundesrat a representative of the Länder may participate in negotiations in committees of the EU Council and Commission. If the matter under discussion falls within the exclusive legislative authority of the Länder, the negotiations shall be undertaken by the representative of the Länder. The mechanics of Länder participation at the EU level are set out in detail in the BLV.[14] Bundesrat designees are deemed to be members of the German delegation. With the agreement of the federal government, the representatives of the Länder can even issue statements. I am personally a representative in the field of subsidiarity. A short time ago I accompanied my colleague of the Federal Ministry of Financial Affairs, who is the expert on all questions concerning subsidiarity, to a meeting with Commission representatives. I could ask questions and make statements on behalf of the Bundesrat. Afterwards I wrote my report which was distributed to all Länder ministries. In this field it was the first time that Commission representatives met a German delegation to discuss the Commission's communication on "Better Law Making."

Currently, the common list of Länder representatives includes about three hundred (Commission and Council) working groups. There are around one hundred permanent sector-specific working groups within the Council. In addition, ad hoc groups can be assigned to deal with a particular problem within a specified period. To avoid a proliferation of Länder representatives, the members of the Bundesrat EU Committee assess every suggestion for yet another Länder representative to attend a certain meeting, that is, whether it is necessary and whether a consolidation with the representatives in other working groups is possible. Sometimes the federal government

13. In COREPER sessions no Länder representatives are allowed to take part, but in the preparatory meetings of the federal government in Germany two representatives of the Länder are involved. See § 4 EUZBLG. In Council sessions where the exclusive jurisdiction of the Länder is essentially affected, e.g., education and culture, and justice and home affairs, representatives of the Länder on ministerial level take part. The participation of Länder representatives in intergovernmental conferences is regulated in BLV VII. In the IGC in 2000 and the Nice Conference, the Länder were represented by Baden-Württemberg (Secretary of State Willi Stächele) and Rhineland-Palatinate (see chapter 8, this volume).

14. See note 5 above.

colleagues ask the Bundesrat to send a representative of the Länder who is an expert on special issues.

The federal government passes on all documents to the Länder representatives as soon as they are received from the EU Commission or Council. But often the Länder representatives get them (often in English) only the last working day before the particular working group meeting in Brussels. So it is very difficult for the Länder representatives to prepare for the meeting. Even the documents issued by the German ministry are often in English so they can be considered by other country delegations. This results, however, in a practical reduction in the right of the Länder representations to be consulted.[15]

Direct Representation of the Länder at the EU Level

Since the mid-1980s, all German Länder have established missions in Brussels without diplomatic status.[16] Soon after German reunification the "new" Länder also opened missions. In spite of the Foreign Office's request to the contrary, most Länder have changed the name from "information offices" (*Informationsbüro*) to "representation" (*Vertretung*). In the "representation" of Baden-Württemberg, about ten experts and five secretaries are employed. Here various events take place in which the members of the European Parliament (MEPs) from Baden-Württemberg participate. Sometimes members of the state parliament also come to Brussels to meet the MEPs. More often they meet one another in Stuttgart or in Strasbourg.

The Observer of the Länder

There is one more little-known Länder institution: the so-called Observer of the Länder (*Länderbeobachter*) where I had the chance to work for two years in 1996–97. During the negotiations of the Treaty of Rome in 1957, one representative of the Länder took part in the negotiations as a member of the German delegation in order to provide direct information to the Länder and thus to prepare the Bundesrat's

15. The representatives of the German government usually work hard at getting equal recognition of German as a working language in the working groups. In the Council's plenary sessions, all participants can speak in their mother tongue as in European parliament sessions.

16. See note 4 and para. 8, EUZBLG.

Figure 9.1 Duties of the Observer of the Länder

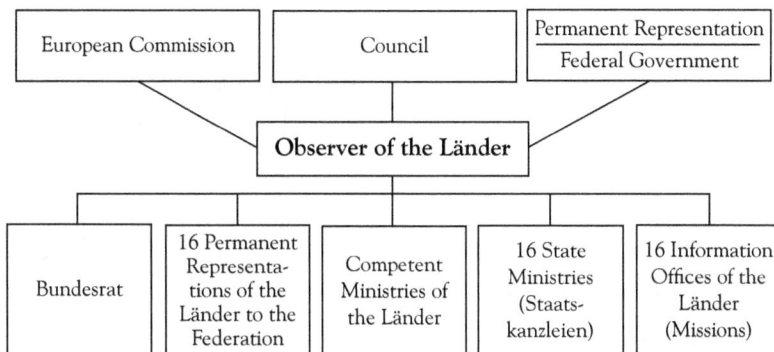

European Commission	Council	Permanent Representation Federal Government

Observer of the Länder

Bundesrat	16 Permanent Representations of the Länder to the Federation	Competent Ministries of the Länder	16 State Ministries (Staatskanzleien)	16 Information Offices of the Länder (Missions)

consent to the treaty. Later, the state ministers for economic affairs asked the federal minister, Ludwig Erhard, to approve one representative of the Länder to observe the Council of Ministers' negotiations.

Today there is still a very small office of two observers (for all 16 states) who take part in Council meetings and report from the general perspective of the Bundesrat. Before the Länder had their own missions, the Observer of the Länder was also responsible for sending paper copies of EU Commission proposals to the Länder.[17] While the missions of the individual Länder generally represent their own interests, the Observer of the Länder works for all Länder (see figure 9.1). The legal basis of the Observer of the Länder is an agreement signed by the governments of all the German states. The *Länderbeobachter* is mentioned in the BLV.[18]

The EU Chamber

The Bundesrat can create an EU Chamber for dealing with European Union affairs. The Chamber's decisions have the same effect as decisions of the Bundesrat itself. The EU Chamber deals with urgent and confidential matters, and it is convened only at the request of the president of the Bundesrat. Each state sends one member of its government

17. Nowadays, the proposals are available via the Internet after their approval by the EU Commission.
18. See BLV VIII 5 and Dette-Koch 1997: 169–71.

to the EU Chamber. The states have the same number of votes in these meetings as they have in the plenary sessions of the Bundesrat. The EU Chamber is a kind of "reduced-format Bundesrat."[19]

In December 1999 the EU Chamber came together after a four-year pause to give the federal government the Bundesrat's decision on the EU directive, "Effects of Plans and Programs on the Environment," which was mentioned above.

Issues Affecting the Länder in 2001 and Beyond

Enlargement of the European Union

The enlargement of the Union—the Reunification of Europe as I prefer to say—is the most important issue for the next ten or even twenty years. Representatives of the Länder take part in EU Council expert group meetings on the accession negotiations. Civil servants of the German Länder are also involved in providing advice regarding the administrative structures in the Central and Eastern European Countries (CEEC).

Debate on the Future of Europe

Before enlargement can proceed, the institutional reforms adopted at the European Council meeting in Nice in December 2000 must be implemented. These reforms are only the minimum changes necessary for dealing with an enlarged EU of up to twenty-seven or twenty-eight member states in the years after 2004. Therefore, the Nice summit got the so-called post-Nice process going, as the heads of the states and governments agreed to debate the distribution of powers between the Union and the member states at the next Intergovernmental Conference (IGC) in 2004. In the convention that was constituted in February 2002 and which drafted a European constitution, Prime Minister Erwin Teufel of Baden-Württemberg represented the Bundesrat.[20]

The EU Commission will launch the debate with a white paper on governance, which is also to be seen in context with Commission

19. This term is taken from the brochure of the Bundesrat, published by the Public Relations Office of the Bundesrat, 3rd edition.

20. See Konferenz der Ministerpräsidenten der Länder 2000; and U. Leonardy, 2001, "Kompetenzabgrenzung in der Europäischen Union," in *Jahrbuch des Föderalismus* (Baden-Baden: Nomos, 454–70).

annual reports on better law making. In the report on Better Law Making 2000, the Commission had placed the stress on how the principle of subsidiarity is applied.[21] New forms of European governance are one of the EU Commission's strategic priorities. The white paper was published on 25 July 2001. In its preparation the Commission also published a document that outlined the motivations, content, and methods applied in the white paper. The Commission introduced this "working paper" with a Chinese proverb: "Tell me and I'll forget, show me and I'll remember, involve me and I'll understand."

Following this motto, the team that was set up to draft the white paper organized wide-ranging informal consultations with the Commission's partners. Interaction was facilitated between the working parties within the Commission and outside actors such as the regional and local correspondents, social partners, and others involved in civil society and the general public. The German Länder are involved in the dialogue. The position of this Conference is prepared by a working group of the minister-presidents. This post-Nice process provides an opportunity to move the civil society on the long way to peace and welfare in the whole European continent.

The Länder positions concerning the post-Nice process will be discussed and adopted by the so-called Europaministerkonferenz— the conference of the ministers and secretaries of state who are responsible in the Länder governments for European affairs. A permanent committee of civil servants meets every month to prepare the European ministers' conference. This conference has to adopt its decisions unanimously. To bring these recommendations under the procedure of Article 23 of the German Basic Law, they have to be approved by the Bundesrat.[22]

The reader may ask why the questions of sharing powers and of subsidiarity are of such importance for the Länder. This can be explained by reference to German history and the Basic Law. The implementation of legislation and its judicial enforcement fall primarily within the domain of the Länder (Rogoff 1999: 415–30).

21. See COM (European Commission), "Better Law Making" (2000: 580). The subsidiarity principle was added in the European treaties at the suggestion of the German Länder. The federal government accepted the suggestion as the German position.

22. As the subject of this essay is Länder participation through the Bundesrat, the procedure within the European Minister Conference cannot be described in detail.

One example of the question of subsidiarity is the communication from the EU Commission on "Services of General Interest in Europe." This concerns questions of competition between services offered by public authorities on the one hand and private organizations on the other hand. In its communication, the Commission leaves the definition of the services of general interest to the member states.

Conclusions and Outlook

The system of cooperation between the federal government and the Länder called for by Article 23 generally works well in practice. In a preliminary discussion of the BLV in 1997, neither Bund nor Länder saw any need for changes. Even if the system is rather complicated, it helps to bring the local view and the view of the regions into account. But in December 2000 the Länder finance ministers discussed a reduction of rights of the representatives of the Länder because of the practical problems described above.

Regionalism is growing in importance in Europe.[23] Many representatives of other European countries come to the Bundesrat or to individual states to hear how the federal system in Germany works. In Great Britain, Italy, and Spain, tendencies exist that would grant regional levels more competences. The European Parliament has also recognized the importance of involving the regions in decision-making. When representatives of the CEEC talk about regions, they often see the regions including parts of different member states, for example, the Upper Rhine Region comprising Baden and Alsace or the region comprising North Rhine-Westphalia and the Netherlands.

Perhaps in the year 2050 we will no longer have national states in Europe, but rather regions and a European government and a European parliament with full parliamentary rights. Of course, by then we will have had our reforms of the Länder, which Uwe Leonardy discusses in chapter 3 in this volume. This is in my opinion a positive vision, and it is one that I support.

---

23. On the European level, the Committee of the Regions (CoR) is also slowly gaining more importance, even if it still has only advisory status. The initiative to establish the CoR came from the German Länder. As the subject of this chapter is Länder participation through the Bundesrat, participation in the CoR is not considered more in depth. For details, see Udo Diedrichs, chapter 8, this volume.

Chapter 10

DIMENSIONS OF CONSTITUTIONAL CHANGE

Germany and the United Kingdom Compared

⌒⊙⌒

Charlie Jeffery

Introduction

Constitutional change has occupied a prominent place in the political agendas of Germany and the United Kingdom over the last decade and more.[1] In Germany there has been a perceived need for constitutional change in the aftermath of unification, along with an apparent inability to move forward and enact substantial change. In the U.K. an intensifying debate about the constitution has culminated in a series of radical constitutional reforms since 1977 under Prime Minister Tony Blair. Here is, apparently, a stark contrast: a U.K. described by Arthur Gunlicks[2] as *"verfassungsreformfreudig"* (enthusiastic about constitutional reform) and a Germany "timorously holding fast to the constitutional status quo ante" (Glaessner and Reutter 2001: 21).

---

1. This chapter builds on my contribution "Verfassungspolitik im Vergleich: Britische Devolution und deutscher Föderalismus" in the book I coedited with Gert-Joachim Glaessner and Werner Reutter, *Verfassungspolitik und Verfassungswandel. Deutschland und Grossbritannien im Vergleich* (Wiesbaden: Westdeutscher Verlag, 2001).

2. In private correspondence.

The argument set out here is that this appearance is misleading and one-dimensional, focused just on the formal enactment of constitutional reform. It uses the U.K. and German examples to make a case that constitutional change is a multidimensional process shaped also by (changing) *practice* in the operation of constitutional provisions and by (changes in) the relationship of the constitutional order to the *society* in which it is embedded. The focus in each case is on territorial politics. Over the last thirty years, territory, in particular the character and powers of subcentral territorial government, has been at the heart of constitutional debates in Western societies: Canada, Spain, Belgium, Italy, Portugal, France. As Banting and Simeon (1985: 11) aptly put it: "The representation and accommodation of the territorial dimensions of politics appears to lend itself to discussion in constitutional terms since what is at stake is the character of the political community itself." In this context it is not surprising that subcentral structures of government—whether and how to "devolve" power to the nations and regions of the U.K. and whether to move toward a new, more "competitive" federalism in Germany—have over the last decade been at the heart of the respective constitutional debates under discussion here.

The chapter starts by setting out the distinctive constitutional frameworks that apply to Germany and the U.K. and moves on to explore how these came under pressure to enact reform in the 1990s. It then sets out three dimensions of constitutional change—formal, informal, and popular—in more detail before examining them against developments in territorial politics in the U.K. and Germany. The concluding comments suggest that in matters of *"Reform(un-)freudigkeit"* initial constitutional appearances might be deceptive.

Constitutions under Pressure

Germany and the U.K. provide interesting but perhaps rather odd bedfellows for exploring constitutional change. Their constitutional orders could hardly be more different. The U.K. is a constitutional law unto itself. In drawing up a typology of worldwide constitutional models in 1985, Daniel Elazar (1985: 237–39) had to reserve one of his five categories—that of "the constitution as a modern adaption of an ancient traditional constitution"—effectively for the U.K. alone (though mentioning in passing the then current situation in Israel and Khomeini's Iran). The U.K. constitution houses a set of incrementally updated seventeenth-century institutions. In the absence of a single, overarching constitutional document, these institutions operate largely on the basis of "conventions," typically unwritten "understandings of what is, or what is not appropriate" (Bogdanor 1997: 12). The result is a "curious compound of custom and precedent, law and convention, rigidity and malleability concealed beneath layers of opacity and mystery" (Hennessey 1995: 3). While all this may conjure up the image of a glorious, unbroken political heritage, the reality is more down-to-earth: any political party capable of maintaining a majority in the House of Commons wields the "sovereignty of the Crown-in-Parliament" and with it, in principle, unbounded political power.

Germany takes up a position at the opposite end of the spectrum. The Basic Law is a "constitution as code," "long, detailed, highly specific and explicit" (Elazar 1985: 234–35). It is meticulous and intricate in meeting what was in 1948 an urgent historical purpose: at last to entrench the rule of law and the separation of powers after the disasters of the Weimar years and the Third Reich. It delineated strictly the relationship between state power and individual freedoms and set out comprehensive rules on the organization and functions of executive, legislature, and judiciary, which separated and balanced their relationships to one another. And the Basic Law has met its purpose extraordinarily well: in no other European state are the rule of law and the separation of powers so firmly entrenched in constitutional law. But it is in the intricacy and detail of German constitutional law that pressures for constitutional change have emerged. There is a thin line between entrenching the rule of law on the one hand and an intrusive, straitjacketing overregulation of political procedure and state-society relations on the other. In many respects that line has been overstepped as the German "love of legalism" (Johnson 1998: 13) has led to more and more questions being regulated in more and more detail by constitutional rather than statute law.

It is, for example, unclear whether Germany really needs roughly the same amount of words to delineate the constitutional right to asylum or the procedure for redrawing Länder boundaries as are devoted to the enumeration of the purpose and powers of the whole judicial branch in the United States. The Basic Law can look like the rule book of a "nanny state," setting out overrigidly what the Germans may or may not do. A symptom of this overconstitutionalization is the *Reformstau* (reform gridlock) continually bemoaned in Germany in recent years; it is, it seems, possible to separate state powers with such refinement that nothing—or at least nothing new or innovative— can be done.

These problems remained largely latent in the old West Germany, but they have become increasingly manifest since German unifica- tion. The extraordinary political demands resulting from unification have overloaded the German government so that it gives in to the potential for gridlock inherent in a checks-and-balances system more than it otherwise might. An unfortunate consequence of this is a ten- dency to agree to disagree, and then ask the Constitutional Court to sort the mess out. This can blemish the reputation of the Court and, by implication, the constitution it polices, as it gets dragged in to solve essentially political rather than legal questions (such as, for example, abortion law, or whether crucifixes can be displayed in schools). It can also result in excessive levels of constitutional regulation. The reform of the constitutional right to asylum in 1993—which bloated a five- word clause into one of 277 words—is a prime example.

It is in this situation that the various German *Verdrossenheiten* (senses of dissatisfaction) with parties, politics, and the state can intensify: "Many are dissatisfied with politics, politicians and the polit- ical system. There was of course never a time when the public would give three cheers for the politicians every day on its own accord. But one cannot ignore the fact that dissatisfaction with the system of gov- ernment and falling trust in political institutions is being expressed right across society" (Patzelt 2000a: 3).

This dissatisfaction naturally has a number of causes, including straightforward distributional conflicts sharpened by intensified global competition, the scandals of the Kohl era, the alienation of many East Germans from the reality of unification—but also the invasive legalism and political gridlock of the post-unification era. The effect of this kind of dissatisfaction for the constitutional order is potentially serious. Constitutions are not "just organizational statutes" (Lhotta 1998: 162f.) but also provide reference points for collective identification in society. A society that identifies with its constitutional order endows that order with legitimacy. Falling trust in political institutions is a signal that collective identification is eroding and, as a result, that constitutional legitimacy is being undermined. It is this scenario that has created a powerful pressure for constitutional change in Germany.

A similar situation emerged in the U.K.—but for more or less the opposite reason. The U.K. is underconstitutionalized. There is too little codification of the rule of law, and there are too few rules on the separation of powers. According to British constitutional doctrine, every newly elected Parliament has absolute sovereignty. The constitution does not represent a higher set of values, and constitutional legislation has no higher status in principle than legislation on, say, garbage collection. It cannot therefore set limits that a government wielding the sovereignty of the "Crown-in-Parliament" may not transgress. It is this lack of limits above all else that has spurred on recent British constitutional debate. There was a first flush of this debate in the mid-1970s. During this period, when economic decline, growing social divisions, and ideological polarization combined with a raft of constitutional issues—direct rule in Northern Ireland, accession to the European Economic Community (EEC), and the growth of Scottish and Welsh nationalism—to pose serious questions about what it was that the British held in common and gave the constitutional order legitimacy (see Johnson 1977). The constitutional debate was, though, truncated by the election of the Conservative Party under Margaret Thatcher in 1979 on a ticket steadfastly committed to radical socioeconomic change but to the constitutional status quo.

The Thatcher years left, however, a potent constitutional legacy. Thatcherite "conviction politics" exploited the possibilities of the constitutional order with a vigor and partisanship that called attention to the lack of limits in the British constitution. Growing consciousness of this lack of limits had a "catalytic effect on British constitutional discussion" (Kastendiek 2001: 37). The subject matter was legion (Foley 1999: 44–102; Barnett 1997: 213–50):

- the danger that a majoritarian electoral system combined with the doctrine of parliamentary sovereignty could allow "elective dictatorship"—as symbolized in the introduction of the so-called poll tax in 1988, which was both technically flawed but more importantly lacked anything like majority public support (Butler et al. 1994);
- the wholesale reform and even abolition of whole tiers of local government, most notably the (Labour-dominated) Greater

London Council and metropolitan councils in the major English conurbations;

- the lack of effective protection of human rights in the British judicial tradition;
- the casual overthrow by government of unwelcome judicial reviews of its actions by simple law or even statutory instrument;
- the progressive delegitimization after 1979 in a left-leaning Scotland and Wales of a U.K. Parliament dominated by English Conservatives; and
- the dwindling acceptance of the hereditary principle on which much of the House of Lords, the U.K.'s second chamber, was constituted.

By the mid-1990s, therefore, both the German and the British constitutions were under strong pressure for reform. In the German case the perceived need was to free up an overrigid and overregulated constitutional order. In the U.K. there was more or less the opposite problem: to tighten up the constitutional framework, add controls and safeguards, and limit the power of government. The constitutional outcomes were equally polarized. In the U.K. there has been what Prime Minister Tony Blair called "the biggest program of democratic reform ever proposed" (Hazell and Cornes 1999: 1) and, indeed, carried out: human rights protection; reform of the House of Lords; the introduction of proportional electoral systems for European, Scottish, Welsh, and London elections; and devolution to Scotland, Northern Ireland, Wales, London and (in a much more restricted sense) the English regions. As a result of this program there is now in the U.K., in embryonic form and for the first time, a set of constitutional statements setting out the rule of law and a form of separation of powers. In comparison to this momentous and unprecedented program of constitutional change, there has remained in Germany an apparent constitutional stagnation.

Dimensions of Constitutional Change

This seemingly clear-cut contrast between successful constitutional reform and continuing immobilism does, though, oversimplify the situation: there have been important underlying changes in constitutional practice in Germany over the last ten years; and, despite the flurry of Blairite reforms, all is not smooth sailing in U.K. constitutional waters. This more nuanced picture can be clarified by conceiving of constitutional change along three dimensions: formal, informal, and popular.

The first, formal dimension, is the most straightforward. Formal constitutional change is about the codified constitution, the acts of constitution making, constitutional amendment, and constitutional reinterpretation by constitutional jurisprudence. In Germany there are detailed and binding rules that regulate the competences and procedures for formal constitutional change. In the U.K., a simple law of the sovereign parliament is sufficient.

The second dimension is informal, rooted in the day-to-day practice of politics and based in the common understandings of the actors involved. It is now routine in the study of constitutional politics to distinguish between the formal constitutional document(s)—constitutional "law"—and "constitutional reality," "between the 'ought' and the 'is' in constitutional relationships" (Johnson 1977: 32; see Glaessner and Reutter 2001: 18). As Bogdanor (1988a: 5) put it: "a working constitution implies reference to certain norms and standards which lie beyond and outside the document itself." This informal, extralegal dimension has the function of "lubricating" the formal constitutional apparatus. British constitutional conventions are such "lubricants," typically lacking in legal force but indispensable to the operation of the system. In Germany there are equally extra-constitutional practices—often complex, sometimes institutionalized[3]—which have emerged as means of setting often cumbersome constitutional structures in motion. In a more general sense such conventions and practices can be understood as manifestations of the political "culture" of a state. The German "search for the rationalist consensus" (Dyson 1982), oriented around technical expertise and fixed legal norms, and the British tradition of "adversary politics" (Finer 1975) are, for example, intimately associated with their respective constitutional orders.

The point is that if constitutions have an informal praxis, then the informal—or "real" (Lane 1996: 11–15)—constitutional praxis, the shared understandings, practices, and cultures of politics, can also

---

3. For example, the "working structures" of German federalism that exist alongside and are intertwined with the formal constitutional structures. See Leonardy 1991.

change. Indeed, the gradual and often imperceptible change of the "is" in constitutional relationships is a vital mechanism in ensuring that the core values expressed in the "ought" of constitutional documents can keep pace with social change: "Thus, although no one would question the validity of the 1814 Norwegian constitution, it remains a fact that the parliamentary principle which replaces Norway's rules about monarchical rule has not been codified" (Lane 1996: 9). Or to return to the U.K. and Germany and a shorter time frame, British politics has arguably become less adversarial since the Thatcher era, while German politics may well have become less consensual since unification. New understandings of the way politics should function can, in other words, displace or modify received understandings and introduce change in informal constitutional practice. Changed practice may coexist with the existing formal constitution (as it seems to do without problem in Norway), or it may create pressure for formal constitutional change "when such constitutional doctrine as there is no longer seems to explain very much of what happens" (Johnson 1977: vii–viii).

The third dimension of constitutional change is the popular one. Constitutions are intended to have an integrative effect by providing points of identification for the people of the state concerned. Indeed, their authority is normally rooted in "the people." As Hofmann (1995: 158) put it: "Since the Resolution of the French National Convention of 1792 the principle has applied in the theory of constitutional democracy that there can be no constitution which has not been accepted by the people." Though this principle might be contested in the U.K., it certainly applies in Germany. This is stated unambiguously in the Preamble of the Basic Law: "Inspired by the determination to promote world peace as an equal partner in a united Europe, *the German people, in the exercise of their constituent power*, have adopted this Basic Law." And a strong argument has been made that the West German people developed a strong sense of shared identity focused on (and therefore legitimizing) that constitution. This "constitutional patriotism" (cf. Glaessner and Reutter 2001: 10) was held to serve as compensation for the absence of *national* reference points for identification that, for reasons of German history, were unavailable.

In the U.K. the relationship between constitution and people stands out from the pattern identified in other constitutional democracies by

Hofmann, because Parliament is sovereign and not the people. But the British constitutional order also, of course, depends on legitimation by the people. British constitutional history, which consists of a gradual conferral of the absolute powers of the medieval monarch onto a Parliament that has progressively acquired a broader popular anchorage, testifies to this need for popular legitimation. Constitutional change in the U.K. in this sense always had a popular dimension. The relationship between the people and the constitution can act as a potent source of constitutional change—not least if that relationship loses its equilibrium. This is arguably what has been happening in Germany amid the social tensions bequeathed by unification. And it is certainly what happened in the relationship between the Scottish people and the U.K. constitution over the last thirty years. Over this period a growing sense that Scottish interests and needs were not well served by the sovereign Westminster Parliament facilitated the emergence of a rival and ostensibly incompatible claim to Scottish *popular* sovereignty (see Wright 1997).

If equilibrium in the relationship between people and constitution is lost in this way it creates a tremendous pressure for the (formal or informal) constitution to change in order for it to reestablish its integrative capacity. In other words, conceiving of constitutional change just in terms of formal amendment processes is only part of the story. A full reading needs also to capture change in informal constitutional practice and pressures for change from the people. How these three dimensions of constitutional change interact is the subject of the following two sections on U.K. devolution and German federalism.

Devolution in the U.K.

Devolution is the core of the constitutional reform program introduced by the post-1997 Labour governments (see Hazell 2000). In rapid-fire tempo a series of asymmetrically empowered devolved authorities were established:

- a Scottish Parliament with extensive exclusive legislative powers and a limited fiscal autonomy;
- a Northern Ireland Assembly also with a range of exclusive legislative powers but embedded in a series of unique cross-border

and interstate bodies linking Ireland, Northern Ireland, and the U.K.;

- a Welsh Assembly with "secondary" legislative powers for adapting and tailoring Westminster-made law to Welsh circumstances and priorities;
- a Greater London Authority comprising a directly elected mayor and a directly elected assembly with administrative powers in transport, the environment, economic development, and policing; and
- business-led Regional Development Agencies monitored by quasi-democratic Regional Chambers focused on the management of the economy in the eight English regions outside London; it seems likely that the Blair government will introduce legislation in its second term to allow some English regions at least to establish directly elected assemblies. These will probably be responsible for administering Westminster legislation with some discretion to reshape general priorities to fit particular regional circumstances (see Sandford and McQuail 2001).[4]

Despite their differences in competence base, all these devolved bodies are in one respect on an equal legal footing: they are all subject to the British constitutional doctrine of parliamentary sovereignty. As was noted above, the competences of the Westminster Parliament know no bounds. It was this that allowed the Blair government in devolution and other matters to carry out far-reaching *formal* constitutional change quickly and more or less nonproblematically. In other words a simple law, with a bare 51 percent majority (though Blair could naturally command more), was all that was needed to restructure the U.K. state as thoroughly as devolution undoubtedly has. But, a future anti-devolution Westminster could just as swiftly abolish the devolution reforms by simple law; no one Parliament may bind its successors. There is in other words no formal possibility of

---

4. The victorious Labour election manifesto for the 2001 election repeated a pledge made in 1997 that regions would move toward elected assemblies where there is "a stronger sense of regional identity and a desire for a regional political voice." Evidently this policy was missing momentum in 1997, as steps were taken after Labour's election victory in 2001 to draft a white paper on the English regional question, which was eventually published in May 2002.

constitutional entrenchment of the devolution laws (or, indeed, other constitutional laws).

For this reason any enduring constitutional reform cannot rely alone on the formal dimension of constitutional change. Referenda were used in the 1970s as a mechanism for circumventing this conundrum, resolving in 1973 that Northern Ireland would remain part of the U.K., in 1975 that the U.K. should remain part of the EEC, and in 1979 that devolution to Scotland and Wales should not proceed. This mechanism was revived by the Blair governments. Devolution for Scotland, Wales, Northern Ireland and London was only enacted after a "yes vote" among the respective electorates confirmed, as it were, that there was sufficient "demand" (see Tindale 1996) for it. It is equally envisaged that any move toward establishing elected assemblies in the English regions will be subject to prior popular endorsement in regional referenda. (And Labour has promised also that constitutional referenda will be held prior to any legislation to change the electoral system for Westminster elections or to joining the European Economic and Monetary Union.)

The referendum serves in this way as "a method of securing de facto [constitutional] entrenchment" in the U.K.; it draws "a distinction between ordinary laws and constitutional laws" (Bogdanor 1988b: 67) not least by qualifying the doctrine of parliamentary sovereignty by establishing a rival notion of popular sovereignty. In other words it introduces a popular dimension to the constitutional reform process. Indeed, in the Scottish case the claim to popular sovereignty had been made explicit in the demands of the Campaign for a Scottish Assembly and the Scottish Constitutional Convention it spawned in 1989—a cross-party organization drawing also on major institutions of Scottish civil society to draw up a plan for devolution to Scotland. The groundswell of wider public opinion that these organizations succeeded in mobilizing had, by 1997, made Scottish devolution a genuinely popular enterprise, as the 74.3 percent vote in favor in the September 1997 referendum confirmed (Denver et al. 2000). But even a wafer-thin yes vote such as in the referendum in Wales a week later (the result was 50.3 percent to 49.7 percent) has created a barrier against the abolition of the Welsh Assembly by a simple law of the "sovereign" Parliament. At the very least, a future "devo-skeptic" Westminster would have to win back its sovereignty to act by securing popular approval for abolition in a counterreferendum before it could move ahead with legislation. It is because constitutional reform has been entrenched in this popular sense that all significant political forces in the U.K.—even the Conservatives, who had been steadfast opponents of devolution from 1979 (see Lansley and Wilson 1997: 164–71)—have now explicitly recognized that devolution is here to stay.

Popular entrenchment, though, does not solve all the problems that the doctrine of parliamentary sovereignty poses for the successful implementation of the devolution reforms. A natural and inevitable feature of genuinely decentralized systems is periodic conflict between the center and the constituent units. The constitutional precedence of the Westminster Parliament has far-reaching implications for conflicts between it and the devolved bodies over the extent of its and their powers. A series of bilateral and multilateral mechanisms has of course been created to help avoid and/or solve such problems (Jeffery and Palmer 2000: 336f.). But, unlike in other decentralized states, and in the absence of a constitutional court, there can be no binding arbitration that can set fixed parameters for approaching subsequent conflicts. The danger in a system where no one parliament may bind its successor is that the rules of the game may constantly be in flux and that the rule maker—the Westminster Parliament—as a result has an inherent advantage.

A solution to this problem may lie in the informal dimension of constitutional change. The understandings, practices, and conventions that "lubricate" the operation of the British constitutional order may change in adaptation to new realities. But such change is not assured. The British adversarial tradition, rooted in the notion of parliamentary sovereignty and entrenched by the nature of the electoral system, has created a "winner-takes-all" mentality. Even Tony Blair, radical decentralizer and confessed "big-tent" politician, is frequently, and not always unfairly, caricatured as a "control freak" committed to running everything from Downing Street. As Andrew Rawnsley (2001: 237) put it with regard to devolution: "That he wanted to have devolution only on his own, tightly managed terms was evident from the beginning." Those terms were illustrated in the controversies that surrounded the selection of the Labour Party's candidates for First Secretary (i.e., Prime Minister) in the Welsh Assembly and for London mayor. In both cases Labour Party electoral colleges were created whose structure favored the Blairite candidates: Alun Michael instead of the locally popular Rhodri Morgan in Wales; and Frank Dobson instead of Ken Livingstone in London (Livingstone, who had been leader of the Greater London Council abolished by the Thatcher government in the mid-1980s, had a resonance and popularity both within and beyond the Labour Party).

Blair's interventions proved to be unproductive. After Dobson (only just) won the battle for the Labour Party mayoral candidacy, Livingstone resigned from the party to stand as an independent and won a resounding victory. In a city with a "guaranteed" Labour majority, Dobson ran in third behind the Conservative candidate Steven Norris. And while Michael indeed became Welsh First Minister, he did so as head of a minority administration after "arguably the worst ever" (Morgan and Mungham 2000: 181) election result for Labour in Wales. Many observers explained the result as a payback for the perception that Michael was "Blair's man in Wales" (Osmond 2000: 1). Michael was unable to cast off this tag and eventually resigned after nine controversial months to be replaced by Rhodri Morgan. Morgan's elevation was greeted by the president of the Welsh Assembly with the acidic comment: "This is the first day of devolution" (Osmond 2000: 1).

There has been evidence of a heavy-handed center in Scotland, too, perhaps most tellingly in the swift snuffing out by Blair of the attempt of the Scottish Executive to style itself as the Scottish "government" (Saren and Brown 2000). This "stranglehold" (Brown 2000) of the center has also been illustrated in the way in which the U.K. government has four times—most recently in October 2002—suspended the operation of the Northern Ireland Assembly in the attempt to gain time to overcome blockages in the Northern Irish peace process. Though the reasons for suspension may generally have been seen as sound ones, there remains a concern that the U.K. government feels it has the power—and the mentality—unilaterally to suspend one of the key provisions of an international treaty between the U.K. and Ireland.

Such issues have fed the feeling among some commentators that the U.K. government is not prepared to "let go" and recognize in practice the autonomy that devolution has formally granted (see Brown 2000; Rawnsley 2001). This may be too pessimistic. After all, both Wales and London ultimately won their conflicts with Blair and the center. Moreover, it remains a possibility that devolution and the wider series of constitutional reforms implemented by the Blair government will bring a change in political mentality in their wake. Both devolution and the empowerment of the judiciary, above all in the field of human rights (see Croft 2000) have brought with them a rudimentary version of a separation of powers. And electoral reform in Scotland, Wales, and London has brought with it new forms of cross-party cooperation, including formal coalitions in Scotland and (after Michael's resignation) Wales.

Informal building blocks for a new constitutional practice based on separation of powers and cooperation are in other words already discernible in outline. But only when these building blocks have broadened out into generally accepted understandings of the need and value of cooperation and power sharing will Blair's constitutional reforms secure the informal underpinnings to complement rapid formal change and popular entrenchment by referendum and guarantee genuine and enduring reform. The formal dimension of British constitutional change is, to conclude, only a first step in the constitutional reform process.

German Federalism from Cooperation to Competition

In the case of German federalism one might suggest that the process has gotten stuck in the formal dimension. If devolution is the core of the constitutional reform process in the U.K., the federal system is for many the heartland of Germany's constitutional stagnation. As Arthur Benz (1999: 69f.) has put it: "It seems as if the federal system in united Germany is caught in the 'joint-decision trap' ... where the beneficiaries of the status quo block all attempts at reform, or at the very least extract an exorbitant price for them." This image of a "blocked" federalism reflects the fact that the structures of the German federal system are anachronistic. These structures were used after 1949 as instruments for implementing often strictly defined uniform national standards of public policy—or, as the Basic Law put it, *Lebensverhältnisse*, or living conditions—in the old West Germany. The emphasis on "uniformity of living conditions" needed to be understood initially in the context of overcoming the territorial imbalances left by World II and the division of Germany and later in terms of implementing the policies of "big" government in the era of

Keynesian interventionism from the mid-1960s (see Jeffery 1999b). In 1969 it received additional constitutional sanction in the reforms to the Basic Law introduced by the CDU/CSU-SPD Grand Coalition: the introduction of Joint Tasks, mixed financing of investment projects, and shared tax revenues, each designed to facilitate cooperation between Federation and Länder in achieving uniform national standards.

This kind of *cooperative federalism* was entirely consistent with a situation in which the ten West German Länder (eleven with West Berlin) were in social and economic terms relatively homogeneous. But the structures of cooperative federalism, essentially still unchanged, are inadequate to the task of delivering effective public policies across a socially and economically much more differentiated united Germany. Achieving "uniform" living conditions has not been a realistic goal since 1990, but German federalism is still set up as if it were.[5] In this situation the federal system has come under significant pressure to change, with a veritable academic industry growing up to propose solutions. This industry is full of ideas about what should be done, but it typically comes to the conclusion that nothing can be done. And, ostensibly, a series of examples of failed reform initiatives confirm the latter view: the "non-reform" (Jeffery 1995) of federalism in the post-unity Joint Constitutional Commission of Bundestag and Bundesrat; the equally negligible reform of the system of financial equalization in the 1993 Solidarity Pact (Jeffery and Mackenstein 1999); and the failed merger of Berlin and Brandenburg in 1996 (Stolorz 1997). Failed reform breeds pessimism about the possibility of reform. For Stolorz (1997) in the mid-1990s the perspectives were "depressing," and for Leonardy (1999) a little later the federal system was running the danger of becoming *de*formed if it were not reformed soon. Most

---

5. Before 1994 the Basic Law in two clauses (Article 72/2, dealing with competence allocations between federation and Länder, and Article 106/3, dealing with tax allocation between federation and Länder) referred to the aim of maintaining "uniformity" of living conditions. In a series of constitutional changes introduced in 1994, "uniformity" was changed to the more flexible term "equivalence" in Article 72/2. It was left unchanged in Article 106/3, however, because of the mistaken assumption that the finance section of the Basic Law would be changed (see Leonardy, chapter 3 this volume, note 7). For the sake of simplicity, this contribution stays with the terminology of uniformity.

pessimistic of all was Heidrun Abromeit (1996: 36) in an article about the seeming "alternativelessness" of cooperative federalism: "Let me put forward a heretical thesis: German federalism is unreformable. It is capable only of minor adaptation. This is problematic given that in the 1990s the objective need for reform has grown starkly—i.e., the cleft between need for reform and ability to reform has opened up massively."

Such pessimism is exaggerated and misplaced, not least because it has a narrowly formalistic notion of change focused on the (im)possibility of formal constitutional amendment. It is, indeed, highly unlikely that there will be much formal constitutional change to the federal system in the coming years; the hurdles posed by the need to marshal two-thirds majorities in Bundestag and Bundesrat in support of reform—that is, stretching across federal government and opposition *and* across a good range of the Länder—are too high (Sturm 1999: 81). But, as has been noted, constitutional change does not have to be initiated by formal constitutional procedure. New forms of political practice based on new understandings of politics may just emerge, perhaps in reaction to changes in society. The proposition explored in the rest of this section is that precisely such change is under way in German federalism, with new practices of federalism emerging that are rooted and justified in the social consequences of unification.

Taking the informal dimension first, authors such as Arthur Benz have persistently noted (1985; here 1999: 56) that "cooperative federalism is much more flexible and much more open to institutional adaptation and political change than is often assumed." This inherent flexibility implies that the practice of federalism may depart from what is prescribed in the constitutional text, but may nonetheless still work effectively. In fact this is precisely what happened during the 1950s and 1960s as a practice of intensive policy coordination and financial and operational interdependence between Federation and Länder emerged that bore less and less relation to the initial vision of federalism set out in 1949 in the Basic Law. The constitutional reforms of 1969 only formalized and systematized what was already happening (cf. Lehmbruch 1985: 34; Benz 1999: 63).

There is plenty of evidence to suggest that since unification the practice of German federalism has again moved away from the cooperative imperative of the 1969 constitutional text. For example, two of the key practices underlying cooperative federalism have been the maintenance of solidarity across the Länder and coordination in setting policy standards. Both have eroded. Old understandings of solidarity have been challenged by disputes over the financial equalization process. The complaint brought to the Federal Constitutional Court by Baden-Württemberg, Bavaria, and Hesse which led to the Court's November 1999 judgment, has set the tone. The "richer" Länder—including Hamburg and North Rhine-Westphalia—are no longer inclined to transfer their surpluses to their "poorer" counterparts now that the sums flowing through the system have burgeoned since unification. The issue has "spilt over" into other areas, too, not least in discussions also led from southern Germany about the possibility of regionalizing social insurance funds and thus ending cross-regional subsidization (Blumenwitz 1998; Münch 1998).

Alongside financial desolidarization, a growing tendency to accept greater policy differentiation among the Länder has emerged. This is logical enough following unification. Germany has become more heterogeneous, and distinctive policy packages tailored to different Länder circumstances have begun to outweigh older practices of seeking coordinated, nationwide policy solutions. At the same time, policy differentiation has become politicized, with Länder profiling and legitimizing their own solutions in the regional economy, in education, in policing and so on by contrasting it with alternatives undertaken elsewhere (see Jeffery 1999a).

In other words, alongside the vestiges of cooperative federalism (which has, of course, certainly not been wholly supplanted), a new political practice has emerged focused on territorial self-interest. The pioneer of this practice has been Bavaria, which has over the last five or so years propagated a vision of "competitive" rather than cooperative federalism. Much more overtly than any other Land, Bavaria has pointed to the disjunction of cooperative structures and the greater differentiation of Länder interests since unification, and argued that the old cooperation imperative needs as a result to be downgraded in favor of promoting "competition, self-responsibility and difference" (Männle 1997: 10). Bavaria's success in "selling" this competitive vision has been striking: Baden-Württemberg has been on board from the outset; Hesse has also joined force, both under the SPD before 1999, but in particular since the election of a

CDU government in January 1999 completed a Christian Democratic *Südschiene* (southern "track") for reform; Social Democratic and relatively affluent Hamburg and North Rhine-Westphalia also share an interest in reforming financial equalization in the direction of more "self-responsibility" and, for them, reduced payments into the equalization process; and even Saxony and Thuringia in the east, despite their very different economic and financial circumstances, have come to advocate more flexibility and differentiation in Länder politics (see Jeffery 2001a).

This new understanding of federalism coexists alongside older commitments to cooperation, coordination and solidarity. And the Länder that adhere to these older commitments—Berlin, Brandenburg, Bremen, Lower Saxony, Mecklenburg-Vorpommern, Rhineland-Palatinate, the Saarland, Saxony-Anhalt, and Schleswig-Holstein—are still a big enough grouping to block significant formal constitutional reform. But it is clear which grouping is setting the agenda and establishing a new modus operandi of federalism based on differentiated, territory-specific rather than coordinated, federation-wide interests. This new practice of federalism in Germany is increasingly reflected in politics within the Länder. Voting behavior in Land elections has increasingly detached itself from the rhythms of federal party politics (Jeffery and Hough 2001). Land electorates are increasingly—and increasingly unpredictably—concentrated on Land-specific issues, with the result that party-political alignments in government and opposition in the Länder have grown incongruent with those at the federal level. The unusual election results and coalition alignments that have resulted (Jeffery 1999b) reflect—to redeploy a term from the British devolution debate—a popular "demand" for differentiated political outcomes in Germany. The *informal* shift away from cooperative federalism that was noted above is in this sense also socially anchored in changed *popular* preferences. The result—a closer "correlation between the preferences of Länder electorates and the actions of Länder governments" (Jeffery 19991: 161)— shows that while the formal dimension of constitutional change in Germany has run into the sand, the reality of the constitution has nonetheless changed substantially as the informal and popular dimensions have moved on.

Conclusions

Constitutional change is a multidimensional process. The two examples addressed here—the U.K. devolution process and the debate on reforming German federalism—confirm that prospects for implementing significant constitutional change depend on an interaction of formal, informal and popular dimensions of change. Table 10.1 summarizes the findings of this contribution by showing whether in the U.K. and Germany constitutional change has occurred along these different dimensions.

Table 10.1 shows in the German case that a one-dimensional emphasis on the formal dimension of change—as in the "pessimists'" analysis of the apparent incapacity of the German federal system for reform—is inadequate. A whole series of formal reform initiatives has indeed foundered in the federal joint-decision trap; but at the same time the informal practice and popular expectations of German federalism have become detached from that which is codified in the Basic Law. The formal constitutional structures, aimed at equivalent living conditions, solidarity, and cooperation, are no longer in accordance with informal practices and popular preferences that stress diversity, self-responsibility, and competition. A significant constitutional reform has in other words happened, irrespective of what the constitution says. Perhaps, as in 1969, the formal constitution will one day catch up.

In the U.K., formal constitutional change was enacted rapidly by ordinary statutes of the sovereign parliament. In order to prevent a simple abolition of post-1997 changes by ordinary statute, popular endorsement for change was secured through referenda that documented the level of popular "demand" for change and qualified the formal constitutional doctrine of parliamentary sovereignty. But as long as traditional understandings and practices of U.K. politics persist—as embodied in the caricature of Tony Blair as a "control

Table 10.1 Dimensions of Constitutional Change in the U.K. and Germany

Dimension	U.K.	Germany
Formal	Yes	No
Informal	?	Yes
Popular	Yes	Yes

freak"—formal constitutional change, even with popular endorsement, remains fragile and conditional. The key question for the
future of British politics is, therefore, whether and how quickly U.K.
politics can think itself into a new kind of informal constitutional
practice that is consistent with both popular expectations and the
overhauled formal constitution. Only when this has happened will
the epithet of *Verfassungsreformfreudigkeit* genuinely be deserved.

Conclusion

TOWARD AN UNDERSTANDING OF GERMAN POLITICS AT THE TURN OF A NEW CENTURY

Arthur B. Gunlicks

The contributions in this book describe and analyze a number of issues that have been, are now, and will continue to be important for an understanding of German politics. Some of these, such as fiscal federalism, are issues that affect other federations as well; however, Germany has a system of public finance that is very different from that of most other federations and dramatically different from American practices. In comparison to the United States, the German system is far more complex, in large part because of its efforts to bring about "uniform" or, since 1994, "equivalent" living conditions. This statement does not mean equal living standards throughout the country, but it does mean more or less equal public facilities and infrastructure throughout the nation. This goes far beyond the American grant-in-aid system that provides some states with more funds than their inhabitants pay in federal taxes. The German system also provides for federal grants, but in addition it requires richer regions to transfer funds to poorer ones and even richer municipalities to transfer funds to poorer municipalities within the counties that make up the Länder territories. This degree of communitarian sharing stands in sharp contrast to the "fend for yourself" federalism of the United States.

The question of consolidation of regional units has arisen in other federations, including the United States, but nowhere does there appear to be the focus of attention on reducing the number of units that one finds in Germany. In other federations there are also complaints about the imbalance of power between the central government and the regional units, and/or among the regional units, but such complaints seem to have abated in the United States in recent years, perhaps because of a conservative Supreme Court that has decided a number of cases in the last decade or more in favor of the states. In Germany the current focus on "competitive federalism" has helped to revive the debate on territorial reforms, but whether there is sufficient political, or even public, support for such reforms is doubtful.

Part of the current discussion concerning "competitive federalism" is also directed at the decline over the past decades of the powers of the Land parliaments in favor of the Land executives and the federal government. This decline is due not only to the constitutional requirement to provide "uniform" or "equivalent" living conditions, which has led to a greater reliance on federal policymaking powers, but also to developments in the European Community/Union that in many cases have had the effect of limiting not only federal but also Land powers, whether legislative or executive. Nevertheless, the Bundesrat continues to protect the interests of the Länder in a federal system that was never designed to foster strongly autonomous territorial units.

The apparent misunderstanding by much of the German public of the proper functioning of the German parliamentary system is probably matched in varying degrees by misunderstandings that exist in other countries, but given the high educational standards of the German public, decades of political education in the schools and elsewhere, and the large amounts of public money spent on this endeavor, the findings regarding public attitudes are surprising and even somewhat worrisome. In all democratic systems, even the oldest, there is a good deal of evidence that much of the public is disenchanted with political parties and politics. In Germany this is called *Politikverdrossenheit*, which is undoubtedly related to the findings in chapter 5 on widespread public misunderstanding about the German political system. It is not surprising, then, to learn that some of the traditional ideological positions are weakening, party membership is declining, and voting turnout has decreased. This is hardly unique to Germany, but probably in no other country have these developments led to so much discussion regarding the introduction of direct democracy through the initiative and referendum. This has been resisted at the national level, as in the United States, but all of the Länder and local governments now have plebiscitary features. Whether direct democracy is an antidote to *Politikverdrossenheit*, or, as some observers would argue when they look at California, a procedure that enhances public frustration and disillusionment, is certainly a controversial question that will not be resolved any time soon.

Political parties are undergoing significant change in several European countries today, but there is an interesting example of continuity and change in Germany. Stability is reflected in the continued dominance of the Social Democrats (SPD) and Christian Democrats (CDU/CSU) and in the continued relevance of the Free Democratic Party (FDP). However, even before unification the Greens emerged as a significant force that attracted the better-educated youth vote, in particular, and challenged the FDP for third place in the party rankings. Since unification the former communists, the PDS, have become a virtual equal to the SPD and CDU in eastern Germany and a coalition partner or supporter of a minority government in two of the eastern Länder and Berlin. In spite of the growth in numbers of parties since unification, party membership has declined and dissatisfaction with the "party state" has increased. Whether the difficulties the parties face today can be overcome by a limited resort to direct democracy in internal party procedures and operations or in the political system overall remains to be seen.

The topic of direct democracy has become a major point of discussion in Germany since unification, and it has led to two- and three-stage procedures for direct legislation in all of the Länder and their local governments. The direct election of mayors is now common, whereas until the 1990s it was found in southern Germany only. What is especially interesting from an American perspective are the differences between the procedures and conditions for direct legislation in the American and German states. Examples are the very different requirements for signatures to get proposals on the ballot and the requirement in some Länder that petitions generally must be signed in a public office rather than on the street; different requirements for majority approval, that is, a simple majority in the United States but a simple majority that constitutes a certain percentage of the population in most German Länder; important limitations on the subject matter of initiatives in Germany; and no television commercials but public financing of initiative proposals in some Länder. Referenda have been rejected at the federal level (most recently in the summer of 2002), but they have become firmly established at the regional and local levels. This does not mean that direct legislation has become a common occurrence (there is no "California" in Germany), but a number of interesting and important referenda have been held in recent years.

The role of the German Bundesrat in the domestic public policy process is unique among federations, and its growing influence in European decision-making has become the subject of a veritable academic growth industry in Germany. Since the Single European Act (SEA) of 1987 and the Treaty on European Union (TEU) in 1993, the Bundesrat has become a key player in the relations between the EU and Germany. One obvious question that has arisen in the course of this development is how and to what extent German policymaking regarding the EU is centralized and coherent or fragmented by the necessity of involving the Land governments in what can be a very complicated process of decision-making in the context of regional and cross-national regional interest representation. The two contributions concerning the Bundesrat and the EU provide a number of interesting and informative conclusions regarding this process.

In the final chapter, the thesis is presented that there are three dimensions of constitutional change—formal, informal, and popular. In the British case a good deal of formal change has occurred during the Blair years, for example, devolution in Scotland and Wales, whereas many Germans are frustrated by the apparent impossibility of amending the Basic Law to any significant degree in bringing about reforms of the federal system. The alleged decline of the Länder has led to numerous calls in past decades and especially in recent years for a strengthening of their autonomy by granting them more fiscal independence and policy authority through constitutional change. But how much change occurs in a political system because of formal constitutional amendment in contrast to subtle, incremental change based on attitudes and practices is an intriguing question.

The durability of changes in Great Britain may well depend on the popular mood, because majority votes in the House of Commons can reverse formal changes, whereas informal changes and popular opinion in Germany may be bringing about a less visible but more permanent change. The change from the "cooperative federalism" in the Basic Law to a more "competitive federalism" in political practice today is a major finding in this chapter. But this thesis is not, or not yet, the "conventional wisdom" in most German discussions of the subject. Indeed, the rather modest changes in the financing of the federal system that will take place from 2004 to 2020, the resistance of at least ten of the sixteen Länder to significant changes in the system of public finances, the apparent lack of public enthusiasm for territorial consolidation, the apparent lack of enthusiasm by many politicians in the Länder for increased tax authority, partisan politics, and many other factors would seem to suggest that the thesis that German federalism has changed to any measurable extent in recent years is not immune from challenge.

It is clear that the issues presented in this anthology are important to a current understanding of German politics, just as it is also clear that there are many other issues that have not been featured. The issues that were covered will be a focus of attention for a long time, because they are not going to be resolved to anyone's satisfaction in the coming years, and they will not simply go away.

BIBLIOGRAPHY

Abromeit, H. 1996. "Zwischen Reformbedarf und Reformunfähigkeit – Die Alterna-
    tivlosigkeit des kooperativen Föderalismus." In *Leistungen und Grenzen föderaler
    Ordnungsmodelle. Ettersburger Gespräche.* Weimar: Thüringer Ministerin für Bun-
    desangelegenheiten in der Staatskanzlei.
Allied Museum, ed. 2000. *The International Agreement on German Unity.* Berlin: Publica-
    tions of the Allied Museum.
Allswang, J. M. 2000. *The Initiative and Referendum in California, 1898–1998.* Stanford:
    Stanford University Press.
Anschütz, G. 1929. *Die Verfassung des Deutschen Reiches vom 11. August 1919. Ein Kom-
    mentar für Wissenschaft und Praxis.* Berlin: Stilke.
Aretin, K. O. 1985. *Vom deutschen Reich zum deutshen Bund.* Vol. 2. Göttingen: Vanden-
    hoeck und Ruprecht
Arnim, H. H. v. 1991. *Die Partei, der Abgeordnete und das Geld.* Mainz: Hase und
    Koehler.
———. 1995. *Staat ohne Diener.* Munich: Knaur.
———. 2000. *Vom schönen Schein der Demokratie: Politik ohne Verantwortung – am Volk
    vorbei.* Munich: Droemer.
———. 2001. *Das System: Die Machenschaften der Macht.* Munich: Droemer.
Auswärtiges Amt. 2000. *Mitwirkung der Länder in Angelegenheiten der EU.* Retrieved 26
    January 2001 from http://www.auswärtiges-amt.de/www/de/eu_politik/
    deutschland/länder-mitwirkung_html.
Bachmann, U. 1999. "Warum enthält das Grundgesetz weder Volksbegehren noch
    Volksentscheid?" In *Mehr direkte Demokratie wagen. Volksbegehren und Volksentscheid:
    Geschichte – Praxis – Vorschläge,* ed. H. K. Heußner and O. Jung, 75–86. Munich:
    Olzog.
Bagehot, W. 1891. *The English Constitution.* 6th ed. London: Paul Trench.
Banting, K. G., and R. Simeon. 1985. "Introduction: The Politics of Constitutional
    Change." In *The Politics of Constitutional Change in Industrial Nations,* ed. K. G. Bant-
    ing and R. Simeon. London: Macmillan.
Barnett, A. 1997. *This Time: Our Constitutional Revolution.* London: Vintage.
Bayerischer Landtag, ed. 1987. *Beiträge zum Parlamentarismus.* Vol. 1. Munich.
Bayerisches Hauptstaatsarchiv München, Staatskanzlei 10 095ff. (BHStAM StK)
    (Neugliederung des Bundesgebietes nach Art. 29[2] GG; similar files can be found in
    the state archives of all other member states of the FRG).
Bayerisches Hauptstaatsarchiv München, Staatskanzlei 10 010 – Bayerische
    Leitgedanken für die Schaffung eines Grundgesetzes.
Bayerisches Hauptstaatsarchiv München, Staatskanzlei 10 012 – Entwurf eines
    "Grundgesetzes des deutschen Volkes."

Bibliography

BayVerfGE (Decision of Bavarian Constitutional Court). 1999. Entscheidung vom 17.9.1999: *Die Öffentliche Verwaltung*: 28–32.
———. 2000. Entscheidung vom 31.3.2000: *Die Öffentliche Verwaltung*: 911–15.
Benz, A. 1985. *Föderalismus als dynamisches System*. Opladen: Leske und Budrich.
———. 1999. "From Unitary to Asymmetric Federalism in Germany: Taking Stock after 50 Years." *Publius: The Journal of Federalism* 29, no. 4: 55–78.
Bernard, V. 1973–81. *Histoire de l'idée fédéraliste*. 3 vols. Paris and Nice: Presse d'Europe.
Bertelsmann Commission. 2000. "Governance and Constitutional Policy." *Disentanglement 2005*. Gütersloh: Bertelsmann Foundation.
Beyme, K. V. 1998. "Niedergang der Parlamente. Internationale Politik und nationale Entscheidungshoheit." *Internationale Politik* 53, no. 4 (April): 21–30.
Birsl, U., and P. Lösche. 1998. "Parteien in West- und Ostdeutschland: Der gar nicht so feine Unterschied." *Zeitschrift für Parlamentsfragen* 29, no. 1: 7–24.
Blair, T. 2000. "Europe's Political Future." Speech at the Polish Stock Exchange, Warsaw. Retrieved from http://www.fco.gov.uk.
Blume, G., and A. Graf von Rex. 1998. "Weiterentwicklung der inhaltlichen und personellen Mitwirkung der Länder in Angelegenheiten der EU nach Maastricht, Die Regierungskonferenz 1996 als Bewährungsprobe für die Ländermitwirkungsrechte." In *Europapolitik der deutschen Länder, Bilanz und Perspektiven nach dem Gipfel von Amsterdam*, ed. F. H. U. Borkenhagen, 29–49. Opladen: Leske und Budrich.
Blumenwitz, D. 1998. "Konsens und Konkurrenz beim Aufbau föderaler Strukturen – Anmerkungen zum Länderfinanzausgleich und zur Föderalisierung der Sozialversicherung." In *Föderalismus zwischen Konsens und Konkurrenz*, ed. U. Männle. Baden-Baden: Nomos.
Bocklet, R. 1999. *Rede im Bundesrat*. Bundesrat 743. Sitzung, Stenographisches: 375–76. 15 October.
Bogdanor, V. 1988a. "Introduction." In *Constitutions in Democratic Politics*, ed. V. Bogdanor. Aldershot: Gower.
———. 1988b. "Britain: The Political Constitution." In *Constitutions in Democratic Politics*, ed. V. Bogdanor. Aldershot: Gower.
———. 1997. *Power and the People: A Guide to Constitutional Reform*. London: Victor Gollancz.
Boldt, H. 1980. "Parlamentarismustheorie. Bemerkungen zu ihrer Geschichte in Deutschland." *Der Staat* 19: 385–412.
Boogman, J. C., ed. 1980. *Federalism: History and Significance*. The Hague: Nijhoff.
Borkenhagen, F. H. U., ed. 1998. *Europapolitik der deutschen Länder, Bilanz und Perspektiven nach dem Gipfel von Amsterdam*. Opladen: Leske und Budrich.
Bracher, K. D. 1999. "Der erste deutsche Demokratieversuch und seine Folgen." *Die Politische Meinung* 358: 5–19.
Brecht, A. 1945. *Federalism and Regionalism in Germany: The Division of Prussia*. London, New York, and Toronto: Oxford University Press.
Broder, D. S. 2000. *Democracy Derailed: Initiative Campaigns and the Power of Money*. New York: Harcourt.
Brugmans, H. 1969. *La pensée politique du fédéralisme*. Leiden: Sijdhoff.
Brunet, R. 1922. *The New German Constitution*. Translated from the French by J. Gollomb. Foreword by C. A. Beard. New York: Alfred A. Knopf.
Bulletin of the Press and Information Office. 1957. Declaration of the Federal Government (Hallstein) to the BT, 22 March, no. 56 22473–80.
Bulmer, S. 1993. "Germany and European Integration: Toward Economic and Political Dominance?" In *Germany and the European Community: Beyond Hegemony and Containment?* ed. C. F. Lankowski, 73–99. New York: St. Martin's Press.

Bulmer, S., C. Jeffrey, and W. Patterson. 1998. "Deutschlands europäische Diplomatie: Die Entwicklung des regionalen Milieus." In *Deutsche Europapolitik, Optionen wirksamer Interessenvertretung*, ed. Werner Weidenfeld, 11–102. Bonn: Europa Union Verlag.

Bundesgesetzblatt. 1949, 1969, 1976, 1994. Bundesministerium der Justiz.

Bundesminister des Innern. 1955. *Gutachten: Die Neugliederung des Bundesgebietes*. Bonn: Heymanns.

———. 1973. *Bericht: Sachverständigen-Kommission für die Neugliederung des Bundesgebiets, Vorschläge zur Neugliederung des Bundesgebiets*. Bonn: Universität Buchdruckerei.

———. 1999. *Bewährung und Herausforderung. Die Verfassung vor der Zukunft*. Opladen: Leske und Budrich.

Bundesrat. 1993. 800/93. 5 November.

———, ed. 1989. *Vierzig Jahre Bundesrat*. Bonn: Bonn Aktuell.

Bundesrat Sekretariat, ed. 1988. *Bundesrat und Europäische Gemeinschaften. Dokumente*. Bonn: Bonn Aktuell.

Bundestags-Drucksache. 1976. No. 7/5924. 12 September.

———. 1993. 12/6000. 5 November.

Burgess, M. 1990. *Federalism and European Union: Political Ideas, Influences and Strategies in the European Community, 1972–1987*. London and New York: Routledge.

———. 2000. *Federalism and European Union: The Building of Europe, 1950–2000*. London and New York: Routledge.

Butler, D., A. Adonis, and T. Travers. 1994. *Failure in British Government: The Politics of the Poll Tax*. Oxford: Oxford University Press.

BVerfGE (Decisions of the Federal Constitutional Court). 1958. Vol. 8. Pp. 104–22. Tübingen: J. C. B. Mohr.

———. Vol. 96. J. C. B. Mohr. Pp. 139–52.

———. Beschluss vom 25.11.1999 – 2 BvR 1958/99. Retrieved from http://www.bverfg.de.

———. Beschluss vom 3.7.2000 – 2 BvK 3/98. Retrieved from http://www.bverfg.de.

CEUA (Secretariat of the Committee on the Affairs of the European Union). 1998. *The Committee on the Affairs of the European Union of the German Bundestag*. Bonn: Printing Service of the German Bundestag.

Chatzimarkakis, G. 1996. *Europäischer Grundvertrag 2002. Für ein Europa der Freiheit*. Bonn: Bouvier.

Chirac, J. 2000. "Our Europe." Speech to the German Bundestag, Berlin. Retrieved from http://www.ambafrance.org.uk.

Ciuffoleti, Z. 1994. *Federalismo e regionalismo. Da Cattaneo alla Lega*. Bologna: Editori Laterza.

Croft, J. 2000. *Whitehall and the Human Rights Act 1998*. London: Constitution Unit.

Cronin, T. E. 1989. *Direct Democracy: The Politics of Initiative, Referendum, and Recall*. Cambridge and London: Harvard University Press.

Currie, D. P. 1998. "Neuere Entwicklungen im amerikanischen Verfassungsrecht." *Jahrbuch des öffentlichen Rechts der Gegenwart* 46 (Neue Folge): 511–25.

Dann, O., ed. 1994. *Die deutsche Nation. Geschichte – Probleme – Perspektiven*. Vierow: S. H. Verlag.

Degen, M. 1998. "Der Ausschuss der Regionen – Bilanz und Perspektiven." In *Europapolitik der deutschen Länder, Bilanz und Perspektiven nach dem Gipfel von Amsterdam*, ed. F. H. U. Borkenhagen, 103–25. Opladen: Leske und Budrich.

Degenhart, C. 1999. "Volksgesetzgebungsverfahren auf Verfassungsänderung nach der Verfassung des Landes Nordrhein-Westfalen." In *Die verfassungsrechtliche Ausgestaltung der Volksgesetzgebung*, ed. P. Neumann and S. Von Raumer, 57–108. 1st ed. Baden-Baden: Nomos.

Denver, D., et al. 2000. *Scotland Decides: The Devolution Issue and the Scottish Referendum*. London: Frank Cass.

Derlien, H. U., and S. Lock. 1994. "Eine neue politische Elite? Rekrutierung und Karrieren der Abgeordneten in den fünf neuen Landtagen." *Zeitschrift für Parlamentsfragen 25*, no. 1: 61–94.

Dette-Koch, E. 1997. "Die Rolle des 'Länderbeobachters' im Rahmen der Mitwirkung der Länder an der Europäischen Integration." *Thüringische Verwaltungsblätter*: 169–75.

Detterbeck, K., and W. Renzsch. 2002. "Politischer Wettbewerb im deutschen Föderalimus." In *Jahrbuch des Föderalismus*, 69–81. Baden-Baden: Nomos.

Deuerlein, E. 1972. *Föderalismus*. Munich and Bonn: List.

Deutscher Bundestag. 1977. *Zur Sache 2/77: Beratungen und Empfehlungen zur Verfassungsreform, Teil II Bund und Länder.* Bonn: Presse- und Informationszentrum.

———. 1993. *Zur Sache 5/93: Bericht der Gemeinsamen Verfassungskommission.* Bonn: Presse- und Informationszentrum.

———, ed. 1996. *Materialien zur Verfassungsdiskussion und zur Grundgesetzänderung in der Folge der deutschen Einheit.* 3 vols. Bonn: Presse- und Informationszentrum.

Diamond, R., P. R. di Donato, P. J. Marley, and P. V. Tubert. 1975. "California's Political Reform Act: Greater Access to the Initiative Process." *Southwestern University Law Review* 7: 453–595.

Dippel, H., ed. 1991. *Die Anfänge des Konstitutionalismus in Deutschland. Texte deutscher Verfassungsentwürfe am Ende des 19. Jahrhunderts.* Frankfurt am Main: Keip Verlag.

Doberer, K. K. 1947. *Die Vereinigten Staaten von Deutschland.* Munich. Willi Weimann Verlag. [Original 1944: *The United States of Germany.* London: Lindsey Drummond.]

Dorondo, D. R. 1992. *Bavaria and German Federalism: Reich to Republic, 1918–33, 1945–49.* New York: St. Martin's Press.

Dörrlamim, R., et al. 1995. "Letzte Chance für AKK-Rückkehr." *Mainz-Vierteljahreshefte* 2: 16–42.

Dubois, P. L., and F. Feeney. 1998. *Lawmaking by Initiative.* New York: Agathon Press.

Dyson, K. 1982. "West Germany: The Search for a Rationalist Consensus." In *Policy Styles in Western Europe*, ed. J. Richardson. London: Routledge.

Efler, M. 1999. "Der Kampf um Mehr Demokratie in Hamburg." In *Mehr direkte Demokratie wagen. Volksbegehren und Volksentscheid: Geschichte – Praxis – Vorschläge*, ed. H. K. Heußner and O. Jung, 205–22. Munich: Olzog.

Eicher, H. 1988. *Der Machtverlust der Landesparlamente: Historischer Rückblick, Bestandsaufnahme, Reformansätze.* Berlin: Duncker & Humblot.

Elazar, D. J. 1985. "Constitution-Making: The Preeminently Political Act." In *The Politics of Constitutional Change in Industrial Nations*, ed. K. G. Banting and R. Simeon. London: Macmillan.

Eschenburg, E. 1956. *Herrschaft der Verbände?* 2nd ed. Stuttgart: Deutsche Verlags-Anstalt.

Europa-Parlament. 1994. Ausführliche Sitzungsberichte, Debatte, 28 September.

Europäische Kommission, Mission in der Bundesrepublik Deutschland, ed. 1994. *Die künftige Verfassungsordnung der Europäischen Union. Eine Dokumentation* (Europäische Gespräche 2/94).

European Union. Web site: http://europa.eu.int.

Färber, G. 1999. "Finanzverfassung. Unbestrittener Reformbedarf – divergierende Reformvorstellungen." In *50 Jahre Herrenchiemseer Verfassungskonvent – Zur Struktur des deutschen Föderalismus*, 89–131. Bonn: C. H. Beck'sche Buchdruckerei.

———. 2001. "Efficiency Problems of Administrative Federalism." Paper presented at the Annual Conference of the IPSA Research Committee on Comparative Federalism and Federation Research, 4–7 October 2001, Javéa, Spain. In *Speyer Diskussionsbeiträge*, no. 1, Forschungsinstitut für öffentliche Verwaltung. Speyer.

Farell, M., S. Fella, and M. Newman, eds. 2002. *European Integration in the 21st Century: Unity in Diversity?* London: Sage Publications.

Feldkamp, M. F., ed. 1999. *Die Entstehung des Grundgesetzes für die Bundesrepublik Deutschland 1949. Eine Dokumentation.* Stuttgart: Reclam.

Finer, S. E., ed. 1975. *Adversary Politics and Electoral Reform.* London: Anthony Wigram.

Fischer, J. 2000. "From Confederacy to Federation: Thoughts on the Finality of European Integration." Speech at the Humboldt University, Berlin.

Fischer, K., and C. Koggel. 2000. "Die Europakammer des Bundesrates." *Deutsche Verwaltungsblätter*, vol. 115:1742–51.

Fischer, K. H., ed. 2001. *Der Vertag von Nizza. Text und Kommentar einschliesslich der konsolidierten Fassung des EUV und EGV sowie des Textes der EU-Charta der Grundrechte.* Baden-Baden: Nomos.

Fischer, W. 1998. "Forderungen der Länder zur Regierungskonferenz 1996/97." In *Europapolitik der deutschen Länder, Bilanz und Perspektiven nach dem Gipfel von Amsterdam*, ed. F. H. U. Borkenhagen, 9–27. Opladen: Leske und Budrich.

Foley, M. 1999. *The Politics of the British Constitution.* Manchester: Manchester University Press.

Fraenkel, E. 1979. *Deutschland und die westlichen Demokratien.* 7th ed. Stuttgart: Kohlhammer.

Friedrich-Naumann-Stiftung. 2002. "Für einen reformfähigen Bundesstaat: Die Landtage Stärken, den Bundesrat erneuern." Retrieved from http://www3.fnst.de/ lbinst/ publikeralismus.

Gaiser, W., M. Gille, W. Krüger, and J. de Rijke. 2000. "Politikverdrossenheit in Ost und West? Einstellungen von Jugendlichen und jungen Erwachsenen." *Aus Politik und Zeitgeschichte*, B 19–20: 12–23.

Gaolanska, A. 1999. *Landesparteiensysteme im Föderalismus: Rheinland – Pfalz und Hessen, 1945–1966.* Wiesbaden: Deutscher Universitäts Verlag.

Gebhardt, C. 2001. *Direkte Demokratie im parlamentarischen System.* Würzburg: Ergon.Geitmann, R. 1999. "Der Siegeszug der kommunalen Direktdemokratie." In *Mehr direkte Demokratie wagen. Volksbegehren und Volksentscheid: Geschichte – Praxis – Vorschläge*, ed. H. K. Heußner and O. Jung, 237–254. Munich: Olzog.

Gesetz- und Verordnungsblatt für das Land Nordheim-Westfalen, Nr. 8 vom 5. April 2002.

Glaessner, G.-J., and W. Reutter. 2001. "Verfassung, Politik und Politikwissenschaft." In *Verfassungspolitkk und Verfassungswandel. Deutschland und Grossbritannien im Vergleich*, ed. G. J. Glaessner, W. Reutter, and C. Jeffery. Stuttgart: Westdeutscher Verlag.

Goetz, K. H. 1996. "Integration Policy in a Europeanized State: Germany and the Intergovernmental Conference." *Journal of European Public Policy* 1: 23–44.

Grabbe, H. J. 1978. "Die deutsch-alliierten Kontroversen um den Grundgesetzentwurf im Frühjahr 1949." *Vierteljahrschrift für Zeitgeschichte* 26: 393–418.

Grebner, F. 1999. *Heute 16 Länder – Vorschlag 7 Länder.* Mainz: published by author.

Greß, F., ed. 1990. *Landesparlamente und Föderalismus: Hat das parlamentarische System in den Bundesländern eine Zukunft?* Wiesbaden: Hessischer Landtag.

Greß, F., and R. Huth. 1998. *Die Landesparlamente: Gesetzgebungsorgane in den deutschen Ländern.* Heidelberg: Hüthig.

Greß, F., and R. Lehne. 1999. "Länder Governance in a Global Era: The Case of Hesse." *Publius: The Journal of Federalism* 29, no. 4 (fall): 79–98.

Greß, F., and J. Janes, eds. 2001. *Reforming Governance: Lessons from the United States of America and the Federal Republic of Germany.* Frankfurt am Main and New York: Campus/Palgrave.

Grimm, D. 1988. *Deutsche Verfassungsgeschichte 1766–1866.* Frankfurt am Main: Suhrkamp.

Gross, A. 1999. "Die schweizerische direkte Demokratie." In *Mehr direkte Demokratie wagen. Volksbegehren und Volksentscheid: Geschichte – Praxis – Vorschläge*, ed. H. K. Heußner and O. Jung. Munich: Olzog.

Große Hüttmann, M., and M. Knodt. 2000. "Die Europäisierung des deutschen Föderalismus." *Aus Politik und Zeitgeschichte* 52/53: 31–37.

Große-Sender, H. A., ed. 1990. *Kommission "Erhaltung und Fortentwicklung der bundesstaatlichen Ordnung innerhalb der Bundesrepublik Deutschland – auch in einem Vereinten Europa."* 2 vols. Düsseldorf: Landtag Nordrhein-Westfalen.

Grotewohl, O. 1947. *Deutsche Verfassungspläne*. Berlin: Dietz.

Gruner, W. D. 1992. *Deutschland mitten in Europa*. Hamburg: Krämer.

———. 1993. *Die deutsche Frage in Europa, 1800 bis 1990*. Munich, Zürich: Piper.

———. 1995. "Deutschlandpolitische Grundpositionen und Zielvorstellungen in den westdeutschen Besatzungszonen 1945–1949," ed. Deutscher Bundestag, 1404–88. *Materialien der Enquetekommission "Aufarbeitung von Geschichte und Folgen der SED-Diktatur in Deutschland."* Vol. V/2: *Deutschlandpolitik, innerdeutsche Beziehungen und internationale Rahmenbedingungen*. Baden-Baden, Frankfurt am Main: Nomos.

———. 1998. "Der Föderalismus als Gestaltungsprinzip: Historische, philosophische und aktuelle Deutungen an deutschen Beispielen seit dem 18. Jahrhundert." In *Subsidiarität und Föderalismus in der Europäischen Union*, ed. H. Timmermann, 51–76. Berlin.

———. 1999a. "1849–1919–1949: Deutsche Verfassungstraditionen zwischen der Paulskirchenverfassung und dem Bonner Grundgesetz." In *Jubiläumsjahre – Historische Erinnerung – Historische Forschungen*, ed. W. D. Gruner, 271–340. Rostock.

———. 1999b. "Der Europarat wird fünfzig – 'Vater' der europäischen Integration. Gründungsvorstellungen, Wirkungen, Leistungen und Perspektiven nach 50 Jahren." In *Jubiläumsjahre – Historische Erinnerung – Historische Forschungen*, ed. W. D. Gruner, 117–234. Rostock.

———. 2001. "Les Länder Allemands et la création de la CECA." In *Le Couple France-Allemagne et les institutions européennes. Une postérité pour le Plan Schuman*, ed. M. T. Bitsch, 35–61. Brussels: Établissements Émile Bruylant.

Gunlicks, A. B. 1999. "Fifty Years of German Federalism: An Overview and Some Current Developments." In *The Federal Republic of Germany at Fifty: The End of a Century of Turmoil*, ed. P. H. Merkl, 186–202. London: Macmillan.

———. 2000. Financing the German Federal System: Problems and Prospects." *German Studies Review* 23, no. 3 (October): 533–55.

Hahn, R. 1987. *Macht und Ohnmacht des Landtags von Baden-Württemberg: Die Rolle des Landtags von Baden-Württemberg im politischen Prozeß 1972–1981*. Kehl, Strasbourg, and Arlington: N. P. Engel Verlag.

Hahnzog, K. 1998. "Auch in Bayerns Kommunen: Weg von der Zuschauerdemokratie – hin zur lebendigen Mitmachdemokratie." In *Bürgerbegehren und Bürgerentscheid*, ed. Akademie für politische Bildung, Tutzing, and Landeszentrale für politische Bildungsarbeit. Munich: Tutzing.

———. 1999. "Bayern als Motor für unmittelbare Demokratie." In *Mehr direkte Demokratie wagen. Volksbegehren und Volksentscheid: Geschichte – Praxis – Vorschläge*, ed. H. K. Heußner and O. Jung. Munich: Olzog.

Hanstein, W. v. 1947. *Deutschland oder deutsche Länder: Eine geschichtliche Betrachtung*. Dresden: Voco Republikanische Bibliothek.

Hartmann, B. J. 2001. "Volksgesetzgebung in Ländern und Kommunen." *Deutsche Verwaltungsblätter*: 776–85.

Hazell, R., ed. 2000. *The State of the Nations: The First Year of Devolution in the United Kingdom*. Thorverton: Imprint Academic.

Hazell, R., and R. Cornes. 1999. "Introduction." *Constitutional Futures: A History of the Next Ten Years*, ed. R. Hazell. Oxford: Oxford University Press.

Hennessey, P. 1995. *The Hidden Wiring: Unearthing the British Constitution*. London: Indigo.

Hernekamp, K. 1979. *Formen und Verfahren direkter Demokratie*. Frankfurt am Main: Metzner Verlag.

Herzog, R. 1996. "Festvortrag." In *50 Jahre Landtag Nordrhein-Westfalen, Festakt am 2. Oktober 1996*, ed. Der Präsident des Landtags Nordrhein-Westfalen, 21–36. Düsseldorf: Landtag Nordrhein-Westfalen.

———. 1998. *Lessons from the Past, Visions for the Future* (German Issues 18). American Institute for Contemporary German Studies. Baltimore: The Johns Hopkins University Press.

Hesse, A. 1999. *Rundfunkrecht*. 2nd ed. Munich: Vahlen.

Hesse, K. 1962. *Der unitarische Bundesstaat*. Karlsruhe: Müller.

Hessischer Landtag, ed. 1990. *Hessische Schriften zum Föderalismus und Landesparlamentarismus*. Wiesbaden.

Heußner, H. K. 1994. *Volksgesetzgebung in den USA und in Deutschland*. Cologne: Heymanns.

———. 1999a. "Ein Jahrhundert Volksgesetzgebung in den USA." In *Mehr direkte Demokratie wagen. Volksbegehren und Volksentscheid: Geschichte – Praxis – Vorschläge*, ed. H. K. Heußner and O. Jung, 101–22. Munich: Olzog.

———. 1999b. "Volksgesetzgebung und Todesstrafe." *Recht und Politik* 34, no. 1: 92–100.

———. 2001. "Größe des Gemeinwesens und gesellschaftliche Struktur." In *Demokratie lebendiger gestalten*, ed. Thüringer Landtag, 79–92. Erfurt.

Heußner, H. K., and O. Jung. 1999a. "Einleitung." In *Mehr direkte Demokratie wagen. Volksbegehren und Volksentscheid: Geschichte – Praxis – Vorschläge*, ed. H. K. Heußner and O. Jung, 11–21. Munich: Olzog.

———, eds. 1999b. *Mehr direkte Demokratie wagen. Volksbegehren und Volksentscheid: Geschichte – Praxis – Vorschläge*. Munich: Olzog.

Hofmann, G., and W. A. Perger, eds. 1992. *Die Kontroverse: Weizsäckers Parteienkritik in der Diskussion*. Frankfurt am Main: Eichborn.

Hofmann, H. 1995. "Zur Verfassungentwicklung in der Bundesrepublik Deutschland." *Staatswissenschaften und Staatspraxis*, vol. 6:155–81.

Hölscheidt, S. 2001. "The German Bundestag: From Benevolent 'Weakness' Towards Supportive Scrutiny." In *National Parliaments on Their Way to Europe: Losers or Latecomers?* ed. A. Maurer and W. Wessels, 117–46. Baden-Baden: Nomos.

Holtmann, E. 2001a. "'Rousseau' auf der Zeitreise durch Deutschland im Jahr 2001." *Gegenwartskunde* 50: 153–59.

———. 2001b. "Wandel der politischen Kultur? Verständnis und Mißverständnis des Parlamentarismus in der Öffentlichkeit." In *Aufbau und Leistung des Parlamentarismus in den neuen Bundesländern*, ed. C. Lieberknecht and H. Oberreuter, 77–98. Rheinbreitbach: Neue Darmstaedter Verlags-Anstalt.

Hrbek, R., ed. 2000. *Europapolitik und Bundesstaatspolitik. Die "Europafähigkeit" Deutschlands und seiner Länder im Vergleich mit anderen Föderalstaaten*. Baden-Baden: Nomos.

———. 2001. "Die deutschen Länder und das Vertragswerk von Nizza" *Integration* 1: 102–13.

———. 2002. *Federalism and Party Politics: An International Comparison*. Baden-Baden: Nomos.

Hübner, E., and H.-H. Rohlfs. 1988. *Jahrbuch der Bundesrepublik Deutschland 1988/89*. Munich: Deutscher Taschenbuch Verlag.

Huelshoff, M. G. 1999. "Germany and European Integration: Bonn between Berlin and Brussels." In *Between Bonn and Berlin: German Politics Adrift*, ed. M. N. Hampton and C. Søe, 217–35. New York: Rowman and Littlefield.

Hufschlag, H.-P. 1999. *Einfügung plebiszitärer Komponenten in das Grundgesetz?* Baden-Baden: Nomos.

Hüppauf, B., ed. 1993. "United Germany and Europe towards 1990 and Beyond." *European Studies Journal* 1 (special issue).

Huth, R. 1988. *Die Konferenz der Präsidenten der deutschen Landesparlamente: Eine Studie über ihre Geschichte und Funktion unter besonderer Berücksichtigung ihres Beitrages zur Stärkung landesparlamentarischer Kompetenzen.* Wiesbaden: Verlag Wirtschafts- und Sozialpolitik.

Institut für Zeitgeschichte München (IfZGM), ed. 1945. *120/20 Nachlass Hoegner, Züricher Erklärung vom 24.4.1945.* Zurich.

Janssen, A. 2000. "Wege aus der Krise des deutschen Bundesstaates – Anmerkungen zu einem notwendigen Vorschlag zur Reform des Grundgesetzes." *Zeitschrift für Gesetzgebung* 15, Sonderheft Stärkung des Föderalismus: 41–63.

Jeffery, C. 1995. "The Non-reform of the German Federal System after Unification." *West European Politics* 18, no. 2: 252–72.

———. 1999a. "From Cooperative Federalism to a 'Sinatra-Doctrine' of the Länder?" In *Recasting German Federalism: The Legacies of Unification*, ed. C. Jeffery. London: Pinter.

———. 1999b. "Party Politics and Territorial Representation in the Federal Republic of Germany." *West European Politics* 22, no. 2: 130–66.

———. 2001a. "German Federalism from Cooperation to Competition." In *German Federalism Past, Present and Future*, ed. M. Umbach. Oxford: Oxford University Press.

———. 2001b. "Verfassungspolitik im Vergleich: Britische Devolution und deutscher Föderalismus." In *Verfassungspolitik und Verfassungswandel. Deutschland und Grossbritannien im Vergleich*, ed. G. J. Glaessner, W. Reutter, and C. Jeffery. Stuttgart: Westdeutscher Verlag.

Jeffery, C., and D. E. Hough. 2001. "The Electoral Cycle and Multi-Level Voting in Germany." *German Politics* 10, no. 2: 73–98.

Jeffery, C., and H. Mackenstein. 1999. "On the Road Back to Karlsruhe: Financial Equalisation in the 1990s." In *Recasting German Federalism: The Legacies of Unification*, ed. C. Jeffery. London: Pinter.

Jeffery, C., and R. Palmer. 2000. "Vereinigtes Königreich – Devolution und Verfassungsreform." Ed. Europäisches Zentrum für Föderalsimus-Forschung Tübingen. In *Jahrbuch des Föderalismus 2000*. Baden-Baden: Nomos.

Joerges, C., Y. Mény, and J. H. H. Weiller, eds. 2000. *What Kind of Constitution for What Kind of Polity? Responses to Joschka Fischer.* Badia Fiesolana: European University Institute and Harvard Law School.

Johne, R. 2000a. *Die deutschen Landtage im Entscheidungsprozeß der Europäischen Union: Parlamentarische Mitwirkung im europäischen Mehrebenensystem.* Baden-Baden: Nomos.

———. 2000b. "Vertretung der Landtage im Ausschuß der Regionen: Zur parlamentarischen Komponente unmittelbarer Interessenvertretung der deutschen Bundesländer in der Europäischen Union." *Zeitschrift für Parlamentsfragen* 31, no. 1: 103–15.

Johnson, N. 1977. *In Search of the Constitution: Reflections on State and Society in Britain.* Oxford: Pergamon.

———. 1998. "From 'Modell Deutschland' to 'Reformstau': The Political Problems of Contemporary Germany." *University of Birmingham Discussion Papers in German Studies*, no. IGS98/10.

Jung, O. 1989. *Direkte Demokratie in der Weimarer Republik.* Frankfurt am Main: Campus.

———. 1993. "Jüngste plebiszitäre Entwicklungstendenzen in Deutschland auf Landesebene." *Jahrbuch des öffentlichen Rechts der Gegenwart* 41 (Neue Folge): 32–67.

———. 1994. *Grundgesetz und Volksentscheid*. Opladen: Westdeutscher Verlag.

———. 1999a. "Das Quorenproblem beim Volksentscheid." *Zeitschrift für Politikwissenschaft* 3: 863–98.

———. 1999b. "Siegeszug direktdemokratischer Institutionen als Ergänzung des repräsentativen Systems?" In *Demokratie vor neuen Herausforderungen*, ed. H. H. von Arnim, 103–37. Berlin: Duncker und Humblot.

———. 2000a. "Abschluß und Bilanz der jüngsten plebiszitären Entwicklung in Deutschland auf Landesebene." *Jahrbuch des öffentlichen Rechts der Gegenwart* 48 (Neue Folge): 39–85.

———. 2000b. "Aktuelle Probleme der direkten Demokratie in Deutschland." *Zeitschrift für Rechtspolitik* 33: 440–47.

———. 2001a. "Eckpunkte nicht überzeugend gesetzt: Wie die SPD die Beteiligungsrechte der Bürger auf Bundesebene ausbauen will." *Recht und Politik* 37: 61–75.

———. 2001b. "Historische Erfahrungen mit direkt-demokratischen Elementen in der deutschen (Verfassungs-)Geschichte." In *Demokratie lebendiger gestalten*, ed. Thüringer Landtag, 11–39. Erfurt.

———. 2001c. "Die rebellierende Vertretung." In *Demokratie und Selbstverwaltung in Europa*, ed. A. Bovenschulte, H. Grub, F. A. Löhr, M. von Schwanenflügel, and W. Wietschel, 145–68. Baden-Baden: Nomos.

Jürgens, G. 1993. *Direkte Demokratie in den Bundesländern*. Stuttgart: Boorberg.

———. 1999. "Die anderen Bundesländer." In *Mehr direkte Demokratie wagen. Volksbegehren und Volksentscheid: Geschichte – Praxis – Vorschläge*, ed. H. K. Heussner and O. Jung, 223–36. Munich: Olzog.

Kalke, J. 2001. *Innovative Landtage: Eine empirische Untersuchung am Beispiel der Drogenpolitik*. Wiesbaden: Westdeutscher Verlag.

Kampwirth, R. 1999. "Die Angst der Parteien vor dem 'entfesselten' Volk." In *Mehr direkte Demokratie wagen. Volksbegehren und Volksentscheid: Geschichte – Praxis – Vorschläge*, ed. H. K. Heußner and O. Jung, 177–88. Munich: Olzog.

Kastendiek, Hans. 2001. "Traditionelles und neues Verfassungsdenken in Grossbritannien." In *Verfassungspolitik und Verfassungswandel. Deutschland und Grossbritannien im Vergleich*, ed. G. J. Glaessner, W. Reutter, and C. Jeffery. Stuttgart: Westdeutscher Verlag.

Katzenstein, P. J., ed. 1997a. *Tamed Power: Germany in Europe*. Ithaca, N.Y., and London: Cornell University Press.

———. 1997b. "United Germany in an Integrating Europe." In *Tamed Power, Germany in Europe*, ed. P. Katzenstein, 1–48. Ithaca, N.Y., and London: Cornell University Press.

Kempf, U., and H-G. Merz, eds. 2001. *Kanzler und Minister 1949–1998. Biographisches Lexikon der deutschen Bundesregierungen*. Wiesbaden: Westdeutscher Verlag.

Kirsch, M. 1999. *Monarch und Parlament im 19. Jahrhundert. Der monarchische Konstitutionalismus als europäischer Verfassungstyp – Frankreich im Vergleich*. Göttingen: Vandenhoeck und Ruprecht.

Klatt, H. 1999. "Centralizing Trends in Western German Federalism, 1949–89." In *Recasting German Federalism: The Legacies of Unification*, ed. C. Jeffery, 40–57. London: Pinter.

Kliegis, B., and U. G. Kliegis. 1999. "Der Volksentscheid über die Rechtschreibreform in Schleswig-Holstein 1998." In *Mehr direkte Demokratie wagen. Volksbegehren und Volksentscheid: Geschichte – Praxis – Vorschläge*, ed. H. K. Heußner and O. Jung, 287–306. Munich: Olzog

Knipping, F., ed. 1994. *Federal Conceptions in EU Member States: Traditions and Perspectives*. Baden-Baden: Nomos.

Knodt, M., and B. Kohler-Koch, eds. 2000. *Deutschland zwischen Europäisierung und Selbstbehauptung*. Baden-Baden: Nomos.

Konferenz der Ministerpräsidenten der Länder. 2000. *Vorläufiges Ergebnisprotokoll*. 14 December. Berlin.

Konferenz der Präsidenten der deutschen Landesparlamente. 1983. "Standortbestimmung und Perspektiven der Landesparlamente." *Zeitschrift für Parlamentsfragen* 14, no. 3: 357–61.

Kropp, S. 2001. *Regieren in Koalitionen: Handlungsmuster und Entscheidungsbildung in deutschen Länderregierungen*. Wiesbaden: Westdeutscher Verlag.

Kropp, S., and R. Sturm. 1998. *Koalitionen und Koalitionsvereinbarungen: Theorie, Analyse und Dokumentation*. Opladen: Leske und Budrich.

Kubel, A. 1981. "Bewährungen und Versäumnisse im Bundesstaat." In *Miterlebt-Mitgestaltet, Der Bundesrat im Rückblick*, ed. R. Hrbek, 50–64. Stuttgart: Bonn Aktuell.

Kühne, J.-D. 1989. "Volksvertretungen im monarchischen Konstitutionalismus (1814–1918)." In *Parlamentsrecht und Parlamentspraxis in der Bundesrepublik Deutschland. Ein Handbuch*, ed. H.-P. Schneider and W. Zeh, 49–100. Berlin: De Gruyter.

Kühnhardt, L. 1991. "Foderalismus und Subsidiarität." *Aus Politik und Zeitgeschichte* B: 37–45.

Kühnhardt, L., and H. G. Pöttering. 1998. *Kontinent Europa: Kern, Übergänge, Grenzen*. Zürich: Edition Interfromm.

Kurz, B. 1999. "Ein Vorschlag für die Bundesebene: Der Gesetzentwurf von Mehr Demokratie e.V. zur Einführung einer bundesweiten Volksgesetzgebung." In *Mehr direkte Demokratie wagen. Volksbegehren und Volksentscheid: Geschichte – Praxis – Vorschläge*, ed. H. K. Heußner and O. Jung, 363–76. Munich: Olzog.

Laband, P. 1907. "Die geschichtliche Entwicklung der Reichsverfassung seit der Reichsgründung." *Jahrbuch des öffentlichen Rechts der Gegenwart* 1.

———, ed. 1998 [1911–14]. *Das Staatsrecht des Deutschen Reiches*. 4 vols. Berlin: Mohr [Reprint Keip Verlag].

Landtag Nordrhein-Westfalen, ed. 1986. *Schriften des Landtags Nordrhein-Westfalen*. Vol. 1. Düsseldorf.

Landtag Rheinland-Pfalz, ed. 1998. *Parlamentsreform: Bericht der Enquete-Kommission des Landtages Rheinland-Pfalz*. Mainz: Landtagsdruckerei.

———. 2001. *Haushaltsreform und parlamentarisches Budgetrecht in Rheinland-Pfalz*. Mainz: Landtagsdruckerei.

Lane, J. E. 1996. *Constitutions and Political Theory*. Manchester: Manchester University Press.

Langewiesche, D., and G. Schmidt, eds. 2000. *Die föderative Nation*. Munich: Oldenbourg.

Lansley, A., and R. Wilson. 1997. *Conservatives and the Constitution*. London: The Conservative 2000 Foundation.

Larsen, C. 1999. "States Federal, Financial, Sovereign and Social: A Critical Inquiry into an Alternative to American Financial Federalism." *The American Journal of Comparative Law* 47 (summer): 429–88.

Läufer, T., ed. 1998. *Der Vertrag von Amsterdam. Text des EU-Vertrages und des EG-Vertrages*. Bonn: Bundeszentrale für Politische Bildung.

Lehmbruch, G. 1985. "Constitution-Making in Young and Aging Federal Systems." In *The Politics of Constitutional Change in Industrial Nations*, ed. K. G. Banting and R. Simeon. London: Macmillan.

———. 2002. "Der unitarische Bundesstaat in Deutschland." *Politische Vierteljahresschrift* 42, no. 32: 53–110.

Leitantrag des Vorstandes der SPD. 2001. "Verantwortung für Europa." Berlin: SPD.
Leonardy, U. 1973a. "Entscheidungszwänge zur Neugliederung des Bundesgebietes." *Zeitschrift für Parlamentsfragen*: 175–82.
———. 1973b. "Praxisorientierte Weiterentwicklung des Bund/Länder-Verhältnisses." *Die neue Gesellschaft*: 469–73.
———. 1973c. "Die Reform der Staatsorganisation im Bund/Länder-Verhältnis – Zu Verbundplanung und Länderneugliederung." In *Langzeitprogramm 4, Kommentare*, ed. H. Heidermann, 100–111. Bonn: Neue Gesellschaft.
———. 1973d. "Verfassungsreform und Vergassungsauftrag im Bund/Länder-Verhältnis." *Die neue Gesellschaft*: 166–71.
———. 1978. "Halten wir den Staat für perfekt?" *Die neue Gesellschaft*: 100–111.
———. 1989. "Plebiszit ins Grundgesetz – Ergänzung oder Irrweg?" *Zeitschrift für Parlamentsfragen*: 442–50.
———. 1993a. "Thesen zur Entwicklung des Föderalismus an den Kreuzwegen der deutschen und der europäischen Entwicklung." In *Regierung in der Bundesprepublik*, ed. H. H. Hartwich and G. Werner, 211–16. Opladen: Leske und Budrich.
———. 1993b. "Demarcation of Regions: International Perspectives." In *Regionalism: Problems and Prospects*, ed. B. de Villiers and J. Sindane, 1–31. Pretoria: Human Sciences Research Council.
———. 1999a. "Deutscher Föderalismus jenseits 2000: Reformiert oder deformiert?" *Zeitschrift für Parlamentsfragen*: 135–62.
———. 1999b. "German Federalism towards 2000: To Be Reformed or Deformed?" In *Recasting German Federalism*, ed. C. Jeffery, 285–311. London: Pinter.
———. 2001. "Die Neugliederung des Bundesgebietes: Auftrag des Grundgesetzes." In *Föderalismus in Deutschland*, ed. K. Eckert and H. Jenkis, 9–35. Berlin: Duncker & Humblot.
Levi, L. 1978. *Federalismo e integrazione europea*. Palermo: Palumbo Editore.
Leyendecker, H. 2000. "Helmut Kohl, die CDU und die Spenden: Eine Fortsetzungsgeschichte." In *Helmut Kohl, die Macht und das Geld*, ed. H. Leyendecker, H. Prantl, and M. Stiller, 13–244. Göttingen: Steidl.
Lhotta, R. 1998. "Verfassungsreform und Verfassungstheorie: Ein Diskurs unter Abwesenden?" *Zeitschrift für Parlamentsfragen* 29: 159–79.
Limbach, J., R. Herzog, and D. Grimm, eds. 1999. *Die deutschen Verfassungen. Reproduktion der Verfassungsoriginale von 1849, 1871, 1919 sowie des Grundgesetzes von 1949*. Munich: C. H. Beck.
Linder, W. 1999. *Schweizerische Demokratie*. Bern, Stuttgart, and Vienna: Haupt.
Lipgens, W., ed. 1968. *Europa-Föderationspläne der Widerstandsbewegungen 1940–1945*. Munich: Oldenbourg.
Linder, W., and W. Loth, eds. 1985. *Documents on the History of European Integration*. Berlin and New York: De Gruyter.
Loewenstein, D. H., and R. M. Stern. 1989. "The First Amendment and Paid Initiative Petition Circulators: A Dissenting View and a Proposal." *Hastings Constitutional Law Quarterly* 17: 175–223.
Luthhardt, W. 1999. "Abschied vom deutschen Konsensmodell zur Reform des Föderalismus." *Aus Politik und Zeitgeschichte* B 13: 12–33.
Magiera, S. 1999. "Kompetenzverteilung in Europa – Möglichkeiten und Grenzen der Beachtung der dritten Ebene." In *Arbeitsteilung in der Europäischen Union – die Rolle der Regionen*, ed. F. H. U. Borkenhagen et al., 19–29. Gütersloh: Verlag Bertelsmann Stiftung.
Magleby, D. B. 1984. *Direct Legislation: Voting on Ballot Propositions in the United States*. Baltimore: The Johns Hopkins University Press.

Mahrenholz, E.-G. 1986. "Teilhabe, Entscheidungslegitimation und Minderheitenrechte in der repräsentativen Demokratie, sieben Thesen zu Fragen der direkten Demokratie." In *Menschengerecht*, ed. H. Däubler-Gmelin and W. Adlerstein, 371–91. Heidelberg: Juristischer Verlag Müller.

Maier, J. 2000. *Politikverdrossenheit in der Bundesrepublik Deutschland: Dimensionen, Determinanten, Konsequenzen*. Opladen: Leske und Budrich.

Madison, J. 1910. *The Writings of James Madison*. Ed. Gaillard Hunt. New York: G. P. Putnam.

Mangoldt, H. v. 1953. *Das Bonner Grundgesetz*. Berlin and Frankfurt am Main: Franz Vahlen.

Männle, U. 1997. "Grundlagen und Gestaltungsmöglichkeiten des Föderalismus in Deutschland." *Aus Politik und Zeitgeschichte* B24/97.

———. 2001. "The Revival of German Federalism: Two Examples." In *Reforming Governance: Lessons from the United States of America and the Federal Republic of Germany*, ed. F. Greß and J. Janes, 161–71. Frankfurt and New York: Campus/Palgrave.

———, ed. 1999. *Föderalismus zwischen Konsens und Konkurrenz*. Baden-Baden: Nomos.

Maunz, T., R. Herzog, and R. Scholz. *Grundgesetz (Kommentar)*. Munich: C. H. Beck. [Loose-leaf edition, last update: October 1999—Art. 29 commented by Maunz and Herzog up to 1977 and by Scholz up to 1996.]

Maurer, A. 2002. "Germany: Fragmented Structures in a Complex System." In *Fifteen into One*, ed. W. Wessels, J. Mittag, and A. Maurer. Manchester: Manchester University Press.

Maurer, A., and W. Wessels. 2000. "Die Ständige Vertretung Deutschlands bei der EU – Scharnier im administrativen Mehrebenensystem." In *Deutschland zwischen Europäisierung und Selbstbehauptung*, ed. M. Knodt and B. Kohler-Koch, 293–324. Frankfurt and New York: Campus Verlag.

Mehr Demokratie e.V., ed. 2000. *Volksbegehrens-Bericht 2000*. Retrieved from http://www.mehr-demokratie.de/volksbegehren2000.html.

Minister für Bundes- und Europaangelegenheiten des Landes Nordrhein-Westfalen 2000. *Bericht und Stellungnahme zu den Ergebnissen des Europäischen Rates von Nizza*. 18 December. Düsseldorf.

Möckli, S. 1994. *Direkte Demokratie*. Bern, Stuttgart, and Vienna: Haupt.

Möllers, M. H. W., and R. C. van Ooyen. 2000. "Parlamentsbeschluß gegen Volksentscheid: Die demokratische Legitimation der Rechtschreibreform in Schleswig-Holstein." *Zeitschrift für Politik* 47: 458–67.

Morgan, K., and G. Mungham. 2000. *Redesigning Democracy: The Making of the Welsh Assembly*. Bridgend: Seren.

Muckel, S. 1999. "Ist ein Volksgesetzgebungsverfahren, das auf die Änderung der Landesverfassung gerichtet ist, nach der Verfassung des Landes Nordrhein-Westfalen zulässig?" In *Die verfassungsrechtliche Ausgestaltung der Volksgesetzgebung*, ed. P. Neumann and S. von Raumer, 57–108. Baden-Baden: Nomos.

Müller, W. 1999. "Vom Volksrat zur Volkskammer: Der Weg zur ersten Verfassung der DDR 1948/49." In *Jubiläumsjahre – Historische Erinnerung – Historische Forschungen*, ed. W. D. Gruner. Rostock.

Müller-Hilmer, R. 1999. "Die niedersächsische Landtagswahl vom 1. März 1998: Die Kür des Kanzlerkandidaten." *Zeitschrift für Parlamentsfragen* 30, no. 1: 41–55.

Münch, U. 1998. "Entflechtungsmöglichkeiten im Bereich der Sozialpolitik. Zur Diskussion um eine Föderalisierung der Sozialversicherung." In *Föderalismus zwischen Konsens und Konkurrenz*, ed. U. Männle. Baden-Baden: Nomos.

Münch, U., and T. Zinterer. 2000. "Reform der Aufgabenverteilung zwischen Bund und Ländern: Eine Synopse verschiedener Reformansätze zur Stärkung der Länder 1985–2000." *Zeitschrift für Parlamentsfragen* 31, no. 3: 657–79.

Bibliography

Neumann, P. 1999. "Die zunehmende Bedeutung der Volksgesetzgebung im Verfassungs-
recht das Beispiel Nordrhein-Westfalen." In *Die verfassungsrechtliche Ausgestaltung der
Volksgesetzgebung*, ed. P. Neumann and S. von Raumer, 17–56. Baden-Baden: Nomos.
———. 2001. "CDU in NRW auf Mehr Demokratie-Kurs." *Zeitschrift für direkte
Demokratie* 50, no. 1: 35.
Nipperdey, T. 1983. *Deutsche Geschichte 1800–1866*. Munich: C. H. Beck.
Oberländer, S. 2000. *Aufgabenwahrnehmung im Rahmen der EU durch Vertreter der Länder*.
Baden-Baden: Nomos.
Oberreuter, H. 1985. "Funktion und Bedeutung politischer Institutionen." In *Die poli-
tische Grundordnung der Bundesrepublik Deutschland in Politik- und Geschichtsbüchern*,
ed. M. Hättich, 185–258. Melle Knoth.
Office for Official Publications of the European Communities, ed. 1997. *European Union:
Consolidated Treaties*. Luxembourg: Europa Komisjon.
Ogg, F. A. 1924. *The Governments of Europe*. New York: Macmillan.
Oschatz, G.-B., and H. Risse. 1995. "Die Bundesregierung an der Kette der Länder?" *Die
öffentliche Verwaltung*: 427–28.
Osmond, J. 2000. *Devolution Relaunched: Monitoring the National Assembly, December
1999 to March 2000*. Retrieved from http:www.ucl.ac.uk/constitution-unit/research/
devol.htm.
Ottnad, A. 1999. "Neugliederung der Bundesländer?" In *Verflochten und verschuldet: Zum
finanz-politischen Reformbedarf des deutschen Föderalismus in Europa*, ed. C. Hüttig and
F. Nägele, 214–39. Loccum: Loccumer Protokolle.
Ottnad, A., and E. Linnartz. 1998. "Sieben sind mehr als sechzehn – Ein Vorschlag zur
Neugliederung der Bundesländer." *Informationen zur Raumentwicklung*: 647–59.
Parlamentarischer Rat. 1948–49. *Verhandlungen des Hauptausschusses*. Bonn.
Patzelt, W. J. 1994. "Das Verhältnis von Bürgern und Parlament – Aufgaben der politischen Bildungsarbeit." In *Die schwierigen Bürger*, ed. G. Hepp and S. Schiele,
216–39. Schwalbach am Taunus: Wochenschau-Verlag.
———. 1996. "Deutschlands Abgeordnete: Profil eines Berufsstandes, der weit besser ist
als sein Ruf." *Zeitschrift für Parlamentsfragen* 27: 462–502.
———. 1997. "German MPs and Their Roles." In *Members of Parliament in Western
Europe: Roles and Behavior*, ed. W. C. Müller and T. Saalfeld, 55–78. London: Ilford.
———. 1998a. "Ein latenter Verfassungskonflikt? Die Deutschen und ihr parlamentarisches Regierungssystem." *Politische Vierteljahresschrift* 39: 725–57.
———. 1998b. "Wider das Gerede vom 'Fraktionszwang'! Funktionslogische Zusam-
menhänge, populäre Vermutungen und die Sicht der Abgeordneten." *Zeitschrift für
Parlamentsfragen* 29: 323–47.
———. 1999a. "The Very Federal House: The German Bundesrat." In *Senates: Bicamer-
alism in the Contemporary World*, ed. S. C. Patterson and A. Mughan, 59–92. Colum-
bus: Ohio State University Press.
———. 1999b. "What Can an Individual MP Do in German Parliamentary Politics?"
Journal of Legislative Studies 5: 23–52. [Special Issue: "The Uneasy Relationship
between Parliamentary Members and Leaders"]
———. 2000a. "Reformwünsche in Deutschlands latentem Verfassungskonflikt." *Aus
Politik und Zeitgeschichte* 28: 3–4.
———. 2000b. "'Seiteneinsteiger, Neulinge Ossis. Die Integration ostdeutscher Abge-
ordneter in gesamtdeutsche Parlamente.'" *Zeitschrift für Parlamentsfragen* 31, no. 3:
542–68.
———, ed. 2001. *Die Volkskammer der DDR. Sozialistischer Parlamentarismus in Theorie
und Praxis*. Wiesbaden: Westdeutscher Verlag.
Patzelt, W. J., and R. Schirmer. 1996. "Parlamentarismusgründung in den neuen Bundesländern." *Aus Politik und Zeitgeschichte* 46, no. 27: 20–28.

Poguntke, T. 1997. "Politische Parteien." In *Handbuch Politisches System der Bundesrepublik Deutschland*, ed. O. W. Gabriel and E. Holtmann, 501–23. Munich and Vienna: Oldenbourg.

Political Declaration by the Constitutional Regions of Bavaria, Catalonia, North Rhine-Westphalia, Salzburg, Scotland, Wallonia and Flanders. 28 May 2001. Retrieved from http://www.europa.eu.int/futurum/documents/contrib/dec280501_en.htm.

Prantl, H. 2000. "Herrschaft und Barschaft von der Veralltäglichung des Ungesetzlichen: Ein Skandal und seine Folgen." In *Helmut Kohl, die Macht und das Geld*, ed. H. Leyendecker, H. Prantl, and M. Stiller, 475–595. Göttingen: Steidl.

Präsident des Landtags Rheinland-Pfalz, ed. 2000. *Verfassungsreform: Der Weg zur neuen Landesverfassung vom 18. Mai 2000.* Mainz.

Präsidenten der deutschen Landesparlamente. 1983. Konferenz, "Standortbestimmung und Perspektiven der Landesparlamente." *Zeitschrift für Parlamentsfragen* 14, no. 3: 367–61.

Preuss, H. 1923. *Deutschlands republikanische Reichsverfassung.* Berlin: Neuer Staat.

Przygode, S. 1995. *Die deutsche Rechtsprechung zur unmittelbaren Demokratie.* Baden-Baden: Nomos.

Public Record Office (PRO) London. 1919. Cabinet 24/75: Memorandum, "The German Constitution." Confidential. 7 February.

———. 1943. Foreign Office 371/944460: Research Department, "A Confederal or Federal Germany?" 1 October.

———. 1944. Foreign Office 371/39080: Memorandum, "Confederation, Federation and Decentralization of the German State, and the Dismemberment of Prussia." 27 January.

Rauh, M. 1977. *Die Parlamentarisierung des Deutschen Reiches.* Düsseldorf: Droste Verlag.

Rawnsley, A. 2001. *Servants of the People: The Inside Story of New Labour.* Rev. ed. London: Penguin.

Redslob, R. 1918. *Die parlamentarische Regierung in ihrer wahren und ihrer unechten Form. Eine vergleichende Studie über die Verfassungen von England, Belgien, Ungarn, Schweden und Frankreich.* Tübingen: Mohr.

Redwood, J. 1999. *The Death of Britain?* London: Macmillan.

Renzsch, W. 1998. "Parteien im Bundesstaat, Sand oder Öl im Getriebe?" In *Föderalismus zwischen Konsens und Konkurrenz*, ed. U. Männle, 93–100. Baden-Baden: Nomos.

Ritter, G. A. 1962. *Deutscher und britischer Parlamentarismus. Ein verfassungsgeschichtlicher Vergleich.* Tübingen: Mohr.

Rogoff, M. A. 1999. "The European Union, Germany, and the Länder." *Columbia Journal of European Law* 5 (fall): 415–30.

Rometsch, D. 1996. "The Federal Republic of Germany." In *The European Union and Member States: Towards Institutional Fusion?* ed. D. Rometsch and W. Wessels, 61–104. Manchester: Manchester University Press.

Rosenthal, A. 1998. *The Decline of Representative Democracy: Process, Participation, and Power in State Legislatures.* Washington, D.C.: Congressional Quarterly Press.

Sandford, M., and P. McQuail. 2001. *Unexplored Territory: Elected Regional Assemblies in England.* London: Constitution Unit.

Saren, J., and J. Brown. 2001. "Government." In *Scotland Report*: Retrieved from http:www.ucl.ac.uk/constitution-unit/research/devol.htm. February.

Sbragia, A. M. 1992. "Thinking about the European Future: The Uses of Comparison." In *Euro-Politics*, ed. A. M. Sbragia, 288. Washington, D.C.: The Brookings Institution.

Scharpf, F. W. 1985. "Die Politikverflechtungsfalle: Europäische Integration und deutscher Föderalismus im Vergleich." *Politische Vierteljahresschrift* 26: 323–56.

————. 1994. *Optionen des Föderalismus in Deutschland und Europa*. Frankfurt am Main and New York: Campus.

Schiffers, R. 1971. *Elemente Direkter Demokratie im Weimarer Regierungssystem*. Düsseldorf: Leinen.

Schiller, T. 2000. "Die Praxis der direkten Demokratie auf kommunaler Ebene." In *Direkte Demokratie*, ed. H. H. von Arnim, 83–111. Berlin: Duncker und Humblot.

Schimmer, A. 1999. "Ihre Stimme für den Bußtag, weil Feiertage unbezahlbar sind." In *Mehr direkte Demokratie wagen. Volksbegehren und Volksentscheid: Geschichte – Praxis – Vorschläge*, ed. H. K. Heußner and O. Jung, 269–86. Munich: Olzog.

Schmitt-Beck, R. 2000. "Die hessische Landtagswahl vom 7. Februar 1999: Der Wechsel nach dem Wechsel." *Zeitschrift für Parlamentsfragen* 31, no. 1: 3–17.

Schmuck, O. 1996. *Die Reform der Europäischen Union. Aufgaben der Regierungskonferenz 1996*. Bonn: Friedrich-Ebert-Stiftung.

Schneider, H. 1979. *Länderparlamentarismus in der Bundesrepublik*. Opladen: Leske und Budrich.

Schönberger, C. 1997. *Das Parlament im Anstaltsstaat. Zur Theorie parlamentarischer Repräsentation in der Staatsrechtslehre des Kaiserreichs (1871–1918)*. Frankfurt am Main: Klostermann.

————. 2001. "Die überholte Parlamentarisierung. Einflußgewinn und fehlende Herrschaftsfähigkeit des Reichstags im sich demokratisierenden Kaiserreich." *Historische Zeitschrift* 272: 623–65.

Schöne, H. 2000. "Vereinheitlichung und Diversität: Elitenintegration im Abgeordnetenhaus von Berlin." *Zeitschrift für Parlamentsfragen* 31, no. 3: 569–83.

Schröder, G. 2001a. *Leitantrag zum Nürnberger Parteitag 19.21.11*. Berlin: SPD.

————. 2001b. "Do We Need Less Europe or More Europe?" Speech of Chancellor Schröder to the German Bundestag. Retrieved from http://www.bundesregierung.de.

Schultze, R. O. 1999. "Föderalismusreform in Deutschland: Widersprüche – Ansätze – Hoffnungen." *Zeitschrift für Politik*: 173–94.

————. 2000. "Indirekte Entflechtung: Eine Strategie für die Föderalismusreform?" *Zeitschrift für Parlamentsfragen* 31: 681–98.

Schüttemeyer, S. S. 1986. *Der Bundestag im Urteil der Bürger. Eine Sekundäranalyse zur Parlamentarismusperzeption in der Bundesrepublik Deutschland*. Opladen: Leske und Budrich.

Schüttemeyer, S. S., and M. Lübker. 2000. "Der Brandenburgische Landtag nach zehn Jahren – ein Parlament wie jedes andere? " *Zeitschrift für Parlamentsfragen* 31, no. 3: 585–98.

Schütt-Wetschky, E. 1984. *Grundtypen parlamentarischer Demokratie. Klassisch-altliberaler Typ und Gruppentyp. Unter besonderer Berücksichtigung der Kritik am 'Fraktionszwang.'* Freiburg: Alber.

————. 2001. "Gewaltenteilung zwischen Bundestag und Bundesregierung? Nach dem Scheitern des Gewaltenteilungskonzeptes des Parlamentarischen Rates: Gemeinwohl durch Parteien statt durch Staatsorgane?" In *Der demokratische Verfassungsstaat in Deutschland. 80 Jahre Weimarer Reichsverfassung, 50 Jahre Grundgesetz, 10 Jahre Fall der Mauer*, ed. K. Dicke, 67–117. Baden-Baden: Nomos.

Schwartz, J., ed. 1980. *Der Aufbau Europas*. Bonn: Studienverlag.

Seipel, M., and M. Mayer. 1997. *Triumph der Bürger*. Munich: Mehr Demokratie e.V.

Sheehan, J. J. 1981. "What Is German History?" *Journal of Modern History* 53: 1–23.

Sidjanski, D. 1992. *L'avenir fédéraliste de l'Europe. La Communauté europenne des origines au traité de Maastricht*. Paris: Presses Universitaires de France.

Skierka, V. 1992. "Die Affaire Barschel." In *Die Skandale der Republik*, ed. G. M. Hafner and E. Jacoby, 332–45. Reinbek bei Hamburg: Rowohlt.

Sontheimer, K., and W. Bleek. 1997. *Grundzüge des politischen Systems der Bundesrepublik Deutschland*. 9th ed. Munich: Piper.

Spahn, P. B., and W. Föttinger. 1997. "Germany." In *Fiscal Federalism in Theory and Practice*, ed. T. Ter-Minassian. Washington, D.C.: IMF.

SPD, ed. 1947. *Protokolle der Verhandlungen des Parteitages der Sozialdemokratischen Partei Deutschlands*. Hamburg.

Stolorz, C. 1997. "Bedrückende Perspektiven des Föderalismus im vereinigten Deutschland." *Zeitschrift für Parlamentsfragen* 28, no. 2: 311–34.

Streinz, R., and M. Pechstein. 1995. "The Case of Germany." In *National Administrative Procedures for the Preparation and Implementation of Community Decisions*, ed. S. A. Pappas, 133–59. Maastricht: European Institute of Public Administration.

Sturm, R. 1999. "Der Föderalismus im Wandel. Kontinuitätslinien und Reformbedarf." In *50 Jahre Bundesrepublik Deutschland*, ed. E. Jesse and K. Löw. Berlin: Duncker & Humblot.

———. 2001. *Föderalismus in Deutschland*. Berlin: Landeszentrale für politische Bildungsarbeit.

Tindale, S. 1996. "Devolution on Demand: Options for the English Regions and London." In *The State and the Nations: The Politics of Devolution*, ed. S. Tindale. London: Institute for Public Policy Research.

von Dewitz, L. 1998. "Der Bundesrat – Bilanz der Arbeit im EU-Ausschuss seit 1992." In *Europapolitik der deutschen Länder, Bilanz und Perspektiven nach dem Gipfel von Amsterdam*, ed. F. H. U. Borkenhagen, 69–83. Opladen: Leske und Budrich.

Vorländer, H. 1999. *Die Verfassung. Idee und Geschichte*. Munich: C. H. Beck.

Weber, M. 1919. *Deutschlands künftige Staatsform*. Frankfurt am Main: Verlag der Frankfurter Societaets-Druckerei.

Weber, T. 2001a. "Initiative zur Einführung der Direkten Demokratie auf Bundesebene Menschen für Volksabstimmung." *Zeitschrift für direkte Demokratie* 51: 31–32.

———. 2001b. "Repräsentative Demokratie in Deutschland: Die Notwendigkeit, sich zu ändern." *Zeitschrift für direkte Demokratie* 13, no. 51: 7.

Weidenfeld, W., ed. 1998. *Deutsche Europapolitik, Optionen wirksamer Interessenvertretung*. Bonn: Europa Union Verlag.

———. 2002. *Europa-Handbuch*. Gütersloh: Verlag der Bertelsmannstiftung.

Wessels, W. 2000. *Die Öffnung des Staates, Modelle und Wirklichkeit grenzüberschreitender Verwaltungspraxis 1960–1995*. Opladen: Leske und Budrich.

Wettach, U. 1994. *Ländergesetzgebung in der Bundesrepublik Deutschland: Eine rechtstatsächliche Untersuchung am Beispiel ausgewählter Regelungsbereiche*. Frankfurt am Main: Peter Lang.

Wheare, K. C. 1953. *Federal Government*. London: Oxford University Press.

Wright, H. F., ed. 1919. *The Constitutions of the States at War, 1914–1918*. Washington, D.C.: Government Printing Office.

Wright, K. 1997. *The People Say Yes: The Making of Scotland's Parliament*. Glendaruel: Argyll.

Zeh, W. 1999. "Bundestag und Bundesrat bei der Umsetzung von EU-Recht." In *Der Politikzyklus zwischen Bonn und Brüssel*, ed. H.-U. Derlien and A. Murswieck, 39–51. Opladen: Leske und Budrich.

Zeitschrift für Gesetzgebung. 2000. *Stärkung des Föderalismus: Text und Kommentierung des am 23. Mai 2000 von den Präsidenten der deutschen Landesparlamente beschlossenen Diskussionspapieres*, Sonderheft 15.

Zumschlinge, K. 1999. "Die Europakompetenzen der Landesregierungen und die Rolle der Landesvertretungen in Brüssel. " In *Der Politikzyklus zwischen Bonn und Brüssel*, ed. H.-U. Derlien and A. Murswieck, 53–64. Opladen: Leske und Budrich.

NEWSPAPERS

Allgemeine Zeitung. 1999. "AKK-Rückkehr." 14 October.
Berliner Zeitung. 2000. "Eine neue Kommission soll die Länderfusion vorantreiben."
   2 February.
Bulletin Quotidien Europe. 1999. 3 and 7 September.
Frankfurter Allgemeine Zeitung [FAZ]. 1975. "Volksabstimmung über die Neugliederung-
   Vorschlag des Stuttgarter Landtagsvizepräsidenten Krause." 5 February.
———. 1998. "Döring will mit Neugliederung die innere Einheit gewinnen." 13 July.
———. 2000a. "Sorgfalt geht vor Terminplanung – Berlin und Brandenburg fassen
   einen neuen Fusionsversuch ins Auge." 9 March.
———. 2000b. "Den Speck gerecht Verteilen." 15 March.
———. 2001. "Kleine Länder für den Bund attraktiver." 26 June.
Frankfurter Rundschau. 2000. "Brandenburg und Berlin wollen bis 2010 fusionieren."
   9 March.
Frankfurter Zeitung. 1919. Interview with Friedrich Ebert. 2nd morning edition.
General-Anzeiger. 1999. "Mainz bläst zum letzten Gerecht." 30–31 October.
———. 2000. "Länder einig: Grundsätze zum neuen Finanzausgleich – Föderalismus:
   Keine Neugliederung des Bundesgebietes." 27 March.
Hamburgisches Gesetz – und Verordnungsblatt. 2001. Part I, no. 18. 21 May.
Handelsblatt. 2001. 17 July.
Hannoversche Allgemeine Zeitung. 2000. "Bremen möchte sich auf Kosten Niedersachsens
   etwas ausdehnen." 7 March.
Independent, The. 2000. "Now Mr. Blair Has Every Reason to Be Terrified." 14 February.
Mainzer Rhein-Zeitung. 1999. AKK-Gemeinden: Neue Initiative zur Rückführung."
   11 October.
Neue Juristische Wochenschrift. 2000. 1097–1104, 2 BvF 2 + 3/98 and 1 + 2/99.
Das Parlament. 2000a. "Föderalismus soll weiter gestärkt werden." 31 March–7 April.
———. 2000b. "Speckgürtel Einverleibung." 31 March–7 April.
Rheinische Post. 2001. 21 February.
Süddeutsche Zeitung. 1998. "Auftrag zur Neugliederung Deutschlands." 21 August.
———. 2000. 2–3 and 5 September 2000.
———. 2001. 16, 19, and 21–22 July.
———. 2001. 5–6 September.
Der Tagesspiegel. 1998. "Reform auf gesamtdeutscher Ebene." 11 August.

JOURNALS

Zeitschrift für direkte Demoktratie [ZfDD]. 1998. Vol. 41.
———. 2000. Vol. 47.
———. 2001. Vols. 50 and 53.
Zeitschrift für Rechtspolitik. 1998. Vol. 31.

INDEX